THE CONSISTENCY CONTROVERSY

THE CONSISTENCY CONTROVERSY

Readings on The Impact of Attitude on Behavior

Allen E. Liska

A SCHENKMAN PUBLICATION

HALSTED PRESS DIVISION
JOHN WILEY & SONS
New York—London—Sydney—Toronto

3 Mount Auburn Place, Cambridge, Mass. 02138

Distributed by Halsted Press Division, John Wiley & Sons, Inc.

Library of Congress Cataloging in Publication Data

Liska, Allen E. comp.
The consistency controversy.

"A Schenkman publication."
"A Halsted Press book."
Bibliography: p.
1. Attitude (Psychology)—Addresses, essays, lectures. 2. Human behavior—Addresses, essays, lectures. I. Title.
BF323.C5L57 152.4'52 73-22151
ISBN 0-470-54122-9
ISBN 0-470-54123-7 (pbk.)

Printed in the U.S.A.

CONTENTS

PREFACE

The general subject matter of this book deals with the extent to which attitude has an impact on behavior. In common parlance the question is frequently phrased as the study of the relationship between what people preach and what they practice, between what they say and what they do, between words and deeds. The fact that people do not always act consistently with their attitudes has long been recognized in Western culture and is reflected in such common sense sayings as "Talk is cheap," "Practice what you preach," "Put up or shut up," and "Put your money where your mouth is." While social scientists point to the central role of attitude in explaining behavior, they have been exceedingly slow to study this phenomenon systematically and have frequently assumed a consistent relationship between attitude and behavior. Yet, a discrepancy between attitude and behavior has been consistently "rediscovered" with each new generation of social scientists, and this generation is no exception. For since the sixties the topic has become a major issue in the social sciences, particularly within the disciplines of sociology, political science, and psychology. For example, in voting research, the issue has been expressed as the impact of political attitudes on voting and participation in political campaigns; in the Human Relations tradition it has been expressed in terms of the impact of work attitudes on work performance; in racial research it has been posed in terms of the impact of prejudice on discrimination; and in persuasive communication research it has been phrased in terms of the impact of attitude change on behavior change.

In editing this collection of readings my aim is threefold: One, I wish to emphasize the historical origins of the controversy, and how it has been reformulated over the years. Two, I wish to bring together papers from various intellectual and research traditions which deal with the attitude-behavior problem. Although the problem in general form is common to various traditions, social scientists confronting the problem seldom look for direction beyond the boundaries of their own intellectual and research tradition. This is particularly true if the tradition is centered within one academic discipline. And three, I wish to emphasize diversity in contemporary approaches to the problem.

In attempting to accomplish these goals I have organized the book into five sections: 1) Historical Origins of the Controversy, 2) "Discovery" of Attitude-Behavior Inconsistency, 3) Methodological Reexamination, 4) Theoretical Reexamination, and 5) Attitude and Behavior Change as a Special Case of the Problem. While the sections have been ordered to emphasize the historical development of the problem, within this general order the emphasis of the book is on contemporary approaches. This is reflected in the fact that only four of the fifteen papers are located in sections one and two. Generally, the first two sections are meant to provide the reader with a historical review of the problem in terms of which the various contemporary approaches (sections three, four and five) can be considered and appreciated.

In particular I feel that the organization of the book will make it useful to both undergraduates and professional social scientists. For the undergraduate this book will nicely function as a supplementary textbook in a variety of courses. It will allow the student to partially break away from the textbook and get involved in one of the contemporary controversies in social science. Also, in bringing together a diverse set of viewpoints and approaches from various intellectual and research traditions, the book may broaden and sharpen the professional reader's conceptualization of the controversy.

INTRODUCTION

The aim of this introductory section is to structure the collection of papers in the volume. In coordination with the five section topics I will discuss various major themes of the controversy and each of the 15 papers as it relates to those themes.

HISTORICAL ORIGINS OF THE CONTROVERSY

Historically (Allport, 1935), the attitude concept derives from three intellectual and research traditions: experimental psychology of consciousness, psychoanalysis, and sociology. During the late 19th and early 20th centuries experimental psychologists discovered that such phenomena as reaction time, perception, recall, judgment, etc. are affected by a readiness or preparedness to respond. Lange (1888 in Allport, 1935) reported that a subject who is prepared to respond upon a signal, reacts quicker than one whose consciousness is not focused on the expected reaction. Various terms (set, intention, purpose, etc.) emerged to describe states of consciousness which influence responses under experimental conditions. Psychoanalysts were also interested in internal determinants of behavior. However, rather than emphasizing consciousness in explaining socially insignificant experimental behavior, they emphasized unconsciousness in explaining man's passions and emotional life. In sociology the term attitude was first systematically used by Thomas and Znaniecki (1918) to explain differential responses to the social structure. Specifically, they defined attitude as a process of individual consciousness which determines individual activity in the social world. As examples, they included tendencies, feelings, ideas, needs, fears, interests and thoughts.

Looking backward, it appears that experimental psychologists invented a concept to explain differences in individual behavior which emerged in traditional experimental problems; psychoanalysts invented a concept to explain differences in individual emotional behavior; and sociologists invented a concept to explain differences in individual reactions to the social structure. For the most part only sociologists systematically used the term attitude to refer to this concept. Yet, the data from the other research traditions seemed to require a concept with similar properties.

Abstracting from various usages and terms, Allport (1935, p. 810) attempted to capture the general meaning or properties of the concept in this definition: "An attitude is a mental and neural state of readiness, organized throughout experience, exercising a directive or dynamic influence upon the individual's response to all objects and situations with which it is related."

Note this definition does not clearly define the attitude concept by content other than defining it as a mental and neural state of readiness. Rather the defining properties are relational, that is, the concept is defined as some internal state which is organized through experience (it is not innate) and which affects behavior. This does not exclude much. Yet, if the commonalities between diverse research traditions are to be captured, such generality is required. The exact content of the concept depends on the exact content of the research problems to be solved. Set may be useful, if reaction time is the problem (experimental psychology). Repressed sexual motivation may be useful, if mental illness is the problem (psychoanalysis). And party preference may be useful, if voting behavior is the problem (social science).

Avoiding the problem of establishing an exact contentual theoretical definition of attitude, in the 1920's, 1930's and 1940's a considerable amount of work focused on attitude measurement (Bogardus, 1925; Thurstone and Chave, 1929; Likert, 1932; and Guttman, 1944), culminating in Lazerfeld's (1950) effort to synthesize an underlying theory of measurement. This era of about 20-30 years did much to empirically identify the attitude concept and perhaps legitimate its use in empirical research. However, the properties which at the time seemed to maximize a reliable and quantitative operational definition diverged considerably from the conceptual properties which the original formulators seemed to require in a concept to explain individual behavioral differences. With the operationalization of the concept, for example, the notion of a readiness to respond became disassociated with subjective meanings and became identified with a set of latent responses which under certain conditions become activated. Moreover, rather than measuring a representative sample of such responses, the demands of the era for reliability resulted in the measurement of a very select sample of verbal responses to symbolic objects which seemed most applicable to standardization. Quantification demands further limited the sample of responses to those that could be ordered unidimensionally. For the most part this restricted the measurement to emotional or affective responses which could be ordered on a positive-negative dimension. In general, then, while in textbook theory attitude was defined in terms which refer to internal states generally reflecting Allport's definition, in actual research practice attitude referred to affective responses (verbal or written) elicited by symbolic objects in interview or questionnaire situations.

Perhaps as an attempt to overcome the limitations of measurement, an implicit postulate seemed to develop that the attitude response universe is homogeneous (Green, 1954). Therefore, even an unrepresentative limited set of responses measured in a limited number of situations should be able to predict other responses in other situations. However, while certainly controversial, this assumption was never really a stimulus to research. For during the era the attitude research problem changed. Whereas the conceptual properties of the concept were originally formulated to solve research problems of individual behavior differences, by the post World War II period the concept had become a convenient (measureable) unit of analysis by which to study problems in social influence (see Sherif and Cantril, 1945, 1946). Such required a reliably measured concept by which the degree of social influence could be systematically compared across various hypothesized causal variables.

THE "DISCOVERY" OF ATTITUDE-BEHAVIOR INCONSISTENCY

The operational properties of the attitude concept which seemed to facilitate the task of studying social influence processes were not capable, however, of predicting differences in individual behavior. The inability of the attitude concept as it emerged from the operational era to predict behavior was well documented in the 1950's and during the early and middle 1960's, although studies showing attitude-behavior inconsistency can be traced over the last four decades. The classic and perhaps most frequently cited study was reported by LaPiere in 1934 (chapter 2). It showed a very low relationship between hotel-restaurant managers' willingness to accommodate a Chinese couple as expressed on a questionnaire and their actual behavior when confronting a Chinese couple in a face-to-face situation. Specifically, LaPiere reported that out of 251 encounters across the West Coast only one establishment refused them accommodations; however, six months later in response to a questionnaire only one manager replied that he would accept members of the Chinese race in his establishment.

While unequivocal in its conclusions, this study had little immediate effect on attitude research or theory. In fact, another two decades passed before any attempt at a similar study or quasi-replication was reported. In 1949 an issue of the *Journal of Social Issues* was devoted to detailing this state of affairs. Although the results of the 1949 issue were quite slim, the 1950's did produce a greater awareness of the problem. Research in the 1950's seemed designed to document the extent and breadth of the problem. A number of studies were reported (Kutner, et. al., 1952; Lohman and Reitzes, 1954; and Minard, 1952) which confirmed and extended LaPiere's findings. Kutner et. al. (1952) in a quasi-replication of LaPiere's study showed that while restaurant owners frequently refuse to take reservations for racially mixed groups, upon presenting themselves in the restaurant all racially mixed groups are served with courtesy. Both Lohman (1954) and Minard (1952) reported that the degree of discrimination toward Negroes depends on the social situation, with discrimination occurring in social roles (neighborhood, social life) and relatively little discrimination occurring in occupational roles. Generally, inconsistency between attitude and behavior was documented in a variety of topical areas including prejudice and discrimination, attitude toward cheating and cheating behavior, attitude and behavior of classroom teachers, what people say and do about their health practices, attitude and behavior concerning alcohol, preaching and practicing patriotism, attitude toward the handicapped and hiring the handicapped, and attitude toward child rearing and actual child rearing practices (Deutscher, 1966, chapter 4).

Although this type of anomalous data continued to accumulate, with some exceptions (notably Brayfield and Crockett, 1955; and Blumer, 1955) it was not until the middle sixties that social scientists began to question some of the basic assumptions of attitude theory and research.

Festinger, in his presidential address to the Division of Personality and Social Psychology at the annual meeting of the American Psychological Association in 1963 (published 1964, chapter 3), stated that he was at first sceptical upon reading that there was a dearth of studies relating attitude change to behavior change (p. 405) but, "after prolonged search with the help of others I succeeded in locating three relevant studies, one of which is of dubious relevance and one of which required reanalysis of the data. The absence of research and of theoretical thinking about the effect of attitude change on subsequent behavior is indeed astonishing." In analyzing the three studies, Festinger concluded that they, too, provide no evidence that such a relationship exists.

In a somewhat different style, the same position was taken by Deutscher in his presidential address to the Society for the Study of Social Problems in 1965 (published 1966, chapter 4). Whereas Festinger dealt with the relationship between attitude change and behavior change, Deutscher dealt with the general relationship between attitude and behavior. Upon an extensive review of the literature, Deutscher concluded that there is simply no evidence to suggest that attitude is a good predictor of behavior.

Vroom (1964) working within the Human Relations tradition reviewed studies on the relationship between work attitude (satisfaction with work) and work behavior (job turnover, absenteeism, performance). Generally, he concluded that the relationship between work satisfaction and performance remains unproven.

By the middle of the 1960's there emerged a general consensus across various research traditions (survey sociology, persuasive communication, Human Relations) that the relationship between attitude and behavior is problematic and a fitting topic for research.

METHODOLOGICAL REEXAMINATION

As a response to this anomalous state of affairs, various social scientists have recently begun to reexamine the validity of attitude, behavior, and attitude-behavior consistency measures. Although it essentially maintains the properties of the operational definition of attitude, their work can be viewed as an attempt to correct the abuses and perhaps to balance the demands of measurement reliability with those of measurement validity.

Concerning attitude-behavior consistency measures, Ehrlich (1969, chapter 8) has argued that frequently the attitude object may be differentially constructed by the researcher and respondents, although both use the same term. Consequently, the behavior which the researcher views as attitudinally consistent may not be so construed by the respondents. For example, various researchers have reported that attitude toward college cheating is not a good predictor of cheating behavior. Yet, the definition of cheating may differ considerably between the researchers (generally college professors) and the respondents (college students). My own observations suggest that the definition of college cheating employed by college professors includes a much larger assortment of acts than that employed by students. Hence, college students' attitudes toward cheating may not predict various acts defined as cheating by researchers simply because they are not so defined by students. A related area of concern is the extent to which behavior defined by the researcher as attitudinally consistent is not so defined by the respondents. Although both the researcher and the respondents may be referring to the same attitude object, for many respondents the behavior patterns which the researcher views as attitudinally inconsistent may be viewed as attitudinally consistent and vice versa (Ehrlich, 1969, chapter 8). Hence, much observed attitude-behavior inconsistency may therefore be the result of a discrepancy between the researcher's and respondent's definitions of both the attitude object and attitudinally consistent behavior.

Focusing on another methodological problem, various researchers have identified differences between the measurement of attitude and the measurement of behavior, which may obscure the observation of attitude-behavior consistency. For example, approximately twenty-five years ago Hyman (1949) argued that much attitude-behavior inconsistency may be a result of differences between the attitude and behavior measurement situations. The typical attitude measurement situation (interview or questionnaire) is constructed to make the respondent feel anonymous, that is, not responsible for his verbal or written behavior. Hyman argues that this procedure seems perfectly reasonable if private attitude is the object of measurement, but then there is no reason to believe that verbal behavior observed under these situations and conceptualized as an index of private attitude will predict behavior in everyday situations where people are subject to social pressure and demands. Rather, Hyman (1949, p. 40) states, "If our aim is to predict a given kind of behavior in a given social setting, we should design our tests so that they incorporate the fundamental aspects of the setting into the test."

Eighteen years later Fendrich (1967, chapter 5) reported an empirical test of Hyman's hypothesis. Comparable to Hyman, Fendrich argues that the typical attitude test situation is probably constructed by respondents as socially fun, unreal, or play-like. If the behavior observed in the test situation is to predict behavior in everyday life, the test situation must be similar to everyday situations in which people are sanctioned for their behavior. To decrease the play-like atmosphere of the attitude test situation, Fendrich asked the respondents to commit themselves verbally to certain forms of attitudinally relevant behavior prior to the attitude measurement. Fendrich argues that asking respondents to commit themselves to behavior with consequences outside of the measurement situation functions to destroy the play-like definition of test situations. Generally, the reported data seem to confirm the hypothesis; for in predicting various other behavior patterns outside of the laboratory, the attitude-behavior relationship is much stronger when the attitude measurement is preceded by commitment statements.

Tittle and Hill (1967, chapter 6) working generally on a comparable problem have emphasized the "abnormality" of behavior measures. They point out that behavior is typically measured as a singular response to a constructed set of circumstances unlikely to recur with any degree of regularity in the subjects' everyday lives. For example, in a number of studies behavior discrimination is measured in terms of white respondents' willingness to have their picture taken with a Negro. Tittle and Hill argue that attitudes toward non regular behavior patterns may not be well formed or well organized, thus, reducing their impact on behavior. In such cases behavior may be more affected by situational contingencies, while attitude may be more predictive of behavior which occurs in situations which are common, patterned, or part of a social role. In a reanalysis of 15 studies, Tittle and Hill report that attitude-behavior consistency is much higher for studies where the behavior measured represents a repetitive patterned configuration; and in their own study where behavior is measured as general political participation (a repetitive patterned behavior) they report a moderate attitude-behavior relationship.

Another methodological approach focuses on the relationship between the measurements of attitude and behavior objects. To quote Fishbein: "We have often measured attitude toward an inappropriate stimulus object—thus for example, we have often measured attitude toward a class of people or objects when we should have been measuring attitude toward a particular member of the class." (1966, p.214). Fishbein seems to be saying that if we wish to predict behavior toward a specific attitude object, then we should measure attitude toward that specific object. This directive is apparently based on the implicit assumption that members of a general class of people or objects are seldom completely homogeneous. Given some degree of heterogeneity between members of a general class and between situations in which these members are encountered, although a general attitude may well predict commonalities in behavior (a general behavioral orientation) toward most members of the general class across situations, it may not be a good predictor of various specific behavior patterns toward a particular member of the class encountered in a particular situation. For example, a person's general level of prejudice toward a particular minority group may predict to some extent a person's general level of discrimination across situations (such as marital, social, residential, economic, and political) toward most members of the minority group. It may not be a good predictor, however, of a person's discriminatory behavior toward any particular member of the minority group in any particular situation, which may be best predicted by attitude toward the specific member in the specific situation. Generally, Fishbein seems to be arguing that a strong relationship between attitude and behavior depends on the extent to which attitude and behavior are measured at an equivalent level of generality. In support of this hypothesis, Wicker and Pomazal (1971, chapter 7) report the emergence of a much stronger relationship between an attitude toward participation as a subject in a psychological experiment (specific attitude) and actually participating in a psychological experiment, than between an attitude toward general psychological or scientific research (general attitudes) and actually participating in a psychological experiment.

To summarize, the anomalous research showing attitude-behavior inconsistency has stimulated various researchers to reexamine measurement technology, particularly measurement validity. To some extent this general concern may be viewed as an attempt to correct some of the abuses of the operational era where reliability was emphasized. Specifically, the studies reprinted in this section have attempted to show that the relationship between attitude and behavior can be depressed by the play-like atmosphere of attitude test situations (Fendrich, 1967), the "social abnormality" of behavior measures (Tittle and Hill, 1967) and the lack of generality equivalence between attitude and behavior measures (Wicker and Pomazal, 1971).

THEORETICAL REEXAMINATION

While acknowledging the significance of methodological problems, various social scientists have stressed the necessity of underlying theoretical revision. Most of the approaches can be classified into one of two types, which to some extent tend to reflect two different conceptualizations of attitude (DeFleur and Westie, 1963; chapter 1). The predominant approach has been to emphasize that attitude is only one among many causes of behavior and that the relationship between attitude and behavior cannot be examined in isolation of such other variables. If such variables, for example, affect behavior in a direction opposite to that of the attitude measured, attitude and behavior may appear as inconsistent. This is not to suggest that attitude does not have an impact on behavior, but only that the impact of other variables frequently counterbalances and obscures the impact of attitude on behavior. In these terms attitude-behavior inconsistency is conceptualized not as an anomaly, but as a focal point of research. The research task is simply to identify such other variables.

I do not mean to suggest that in past work attitude had been conceptualized as the only variable affecting behavior. Clearly, this was not the case. Yet, research seemed to proceed as if the impact of attitude on behavior could be analyzed in isolation from other variables. Quite simply, the focal point of reconceptualization has been to transform the study of the relationship between attitude and behavior from a bivariate to a multivariate research problem.

On the other hand, other social scientists (e.g., Leventhal, et al., 1967; chapter 14; and Bryan, 1970a) have responded to reports of attitude-behavior inconsistency by conceptualizing attitude and behavior as correlates, not necessarily causally related. They have simply argued that attitude and behavior are affected by different causal variables; thus attitude-behavior inconsistency is frequently to be expected. Although it is noted that under certain conditions the correlation will be stronger than others, in terms of this conceptualization attitude-behavior inconsistency is no longer viewed as an anomaly. The size of the correlation and identifying the conditions which affect the size are not conceived as significant research problems. To some extent this distinction between attitude as a cause and attitude as a correlate of behavior is similar to the distinction between the intervening and probability conceptualizations of attitude made by DeFleur and Westie (1963, chapter 1).

The reader should note that whether attitude is conceptualized as one among many causes of behavior or as just a correlate of behavior, attitude-behavior inconsistency is no longer conceived as a theoretical anomaly. In terms of the former it is conceptualized as a focal point of research, and in terms of the latter it is conceptualized as an insignificant datum. Hence, both approaches can be conceived as conceptual solutions to the problem.

As the correlate reconceptualization has not generated much research, which is consistent with the logic of the formulation, I will restrict this discussion to the alternative reconceptualization. In the final section dealing with attitude and behavior change I will discuss some of the research which supports the correlate formulation.

Interactive Effects

In discussing attitude as one among many causes of behavior, I will distinguish between additive and interactive variables. Let us consider first interactive variables, variables which affect the impact of attitude on behavior, although they have no independent effect on behavior. Researchers have suggested various factors which may affect the impact of attitude on behavior, but most efforts have generally been restricted to post factum attempts to explain a lack of attitude-behavior consistency. Few studies have been specifically designed to establish the extent to which a factor or set of factors affects the impact of attitude on behavior.

Ehrlich (1969, chapter 8) in his general review points to various potential areas of research. He notes, for example, that attitudes may not be well formed unless the three components (affect, cognition, and conation) are strongly interrelated or balanced and that unbalanced or ill formed attitudes may have a low impact on behavior. As many attitude studies measure no more than one dimension (e.g., LaPiere, 1934, chapter 2), they do distinguish between well and ill formed attitudes. Hence much of the reported attitude-behavior inconsistency may be a consequence of trying to predict behavior from ill formed attitudes.

Another condition which seems necessary for the emergence of attitude-behavior consistency is the opportunity and competence to behave in an attitudinally consistent manner. "Opportunity" refers to the extent to which interaction with the attitude object is possible. For example, Negro prejudice and nonprejudice cannot be easily expressed in behavior in Northern rural U.S. because of the low Negro population. "Competence" refers to an individual's capacity to behave in an attitudinally consistent manner. In various situations people may simply lack the skills and resources necessary to perform various attitudinally consistent acts. The anti-semitism manifested in Nazi Germany required a certain amount of technological competence. Indeed, few societies could have so "effectively" manifested racial prejudice. Differences between people in terms of attitude-behavior consistency may well reflect differences in opportunity and competence (Ehrlich, 1969, chapter 8).

The concept "attitude neutralization" has also been used to explain the lack of attitude-behavior consistency. The concept of "neutralization" has been extensively used in the area of juvenile delinquency to explain delinquent behavior on the part of those adolescents who seem to hold middle class attitudes. Matza and Sykes (1957) have argued that frequently delinquents hold verbalizations (such as believing that the victim "had it coming," that the act really did not hurt anybody, or that they are victims of circumstances and are not really responsible for their behavior) which function to justify certain acts of delinquency under certain circumstances. The verbalizations serve to free the adolescent to engage in acts of delinquency while maintaining middle-class attitudes.

Recently, Schwartz (1968, chapter 9) has systematically applied the concept to the attitude-behavior inconsistency problem. He focuses on two conditions: one, the extent to which people are aware of the consequences of their actions and, two, the extent to which they assume responsibility for these consequences. He argues that unless these two conditions are met the behavior situation is not defined in morally relevant terms. As such, moral attitudes remain irrelevant to behavior. Measuring these two conditions as personality variables, Schwartz reports a low relationship between attitude and behavior for people with low awareness of action consequences and low ascription of responsibility, and a strong relationship for people with high awareness of action consequences and high ascription of responsibility. In other papers where awareness of action consequences and ascription of responsibility are treated as situational variables, Schwartz (e.g., 1970) reports similar findings.

It is important to note here that the variables thus far discussed (ill defined attitudes, opportunity to behave toward the attitude object, capacity to actualize attitudinally consistent behavior, and neutralizations) are not conceived as having independent effects on the direction of behavior. That is, Ehrlich is not arguing that well defined attitudes, the opportunity to interact with the attitude object and the skill to perform attitudinally consistent acts have an independent effect on the direction of behavior (although they may have); rather he is arguing that each of these affects the impact of attitude on behavior. The same is the case for Schwartz. He is not arguing that the awareness of behavior consequences and the ascription of responsibility have an independent effect on the direction of behavior, but that each of these affects the impact of attitude on behavior.

Additive Effects

As previously indicated, most studies which examine the effect of other variables focus on those variables which possess an independent effect on behavior and thereby obscure the effect of attitude. Attention has been particularly directed toward the role of social support and to some extent toward the role of multiple attitudes.

Research reveals that people hold attitudes toward numerous social characteristics, such as race, social class, religion, ethnicity, sex, etc. Consequently, a person's behavior toward any other is probably affected by the totality of the other's social characteristics. This problem has been briefly considered in the area of political behavior, where voting is frequently conceptualized as an expression of, not one attitude but a multitude of attitudes. For example, in the American Voter study (Campbell, et.al., 1960) attitudes were measured during the 1952 and 1956 presidential elections toward the following political objects: the personal attributes of Eisenhower, the personal attributes of Stevenson, groups involved in politics, domestic politics, foreign policy, and the comparative record of the two parties in managing affairs of government. On the basis of attitudes toward Eisenhower, 75% of the electorate's behavior was correctly predicted. On the basis of attitudes toward Eisenhower, and domestic issues, 79% of the electorate's voting behavior was correctly predicted and on the basis of all six attitudes, 86% of the electorate's voting behavior was correctly predicted. Through the use of multiple attitudes, the percentage of attitude-behavior inconsistents was reduced from 25% to 14%.

More recently Jeffries and Ransford (1972, chapter 10) have examined the Yorty-Bradley mayoralty election in Los Angeles. The election is of particular interest as Bradley's race (Black) was a major campaign issue. They investigated the independent, joint, and interactive effects of attitudes toward five specific campaign issues, general prejudice and a general attitude termed "troubled American beliefs" (TAB). The term includes concern over declining law and order, threat from the extreme left, and declining patriotism. While revealing some interaction effects, the study shows that each of the attitudes toward the five specific issues and each of the two general attitudes has an independent effect on voting. Consequently, the joint effect of two or more attitudes considerably improves the voting prediction. E.g., 39% of the low-prejudiced voted for Yorty, while 87% of the highly prejudiced voted for Yorty, a difference of 48%; and 26% of those low on TAB voted for Yorty, while 86% of those high on TAB voted for him, a difference of 60%. However, of those low on both, only 10% voted for Yorty; and of those high on both, 90% voted for him.

It seems that one approach to the problem of attitude-behavior inconsistency is simply to increase the number of relevant attitudes as independent variables in the predictive equation.

Consider now the effect of social support, by which I mean simply the extent to which attitudes are congruent with social norms. Given the extensive degree of social mobility and pluralism in American society it is not at all unusual for people to be in situations where their attitudes are incongruent with the social norms. If we assume that both attitudes and social norms possess independent effects on behavior, in situations where attitudes and social norms are incongruent, the degree of attitude-behavior consistency will probably be weak, as the effect of social norms counterbalances the effect of attitudes on behavior. In situations where attitudes and social norms are congruent the degree of attitude-behavior consistency will probably be strong, as the effect of social norms reinforces the effect of attitudes on behavior.

Given the plausibility of this hypothesis introducing the concept social norms as an explanatory concept has been the predominant approach to the attitude-behavior consistency problem. For example, in a recent study DeFleur and Warner (1969, chapter 11) have focused on the extent to which the relationship between prejudice and integrationist or segregationist behavior is affected by whether or not the behavior is observable to a segregationist community. The results show that both high prejudice and public exposure increase segregationist behavior. High prejudice is more consistent with segregationist behavior when the behavior is observable to a segregationist community, and low prejudice is more consistent with integrationist behavior when the behavior is not observable. For example, of the low prejudiced 21% more showed integrationist behavior than those who did not when behavior was not observable to a segregationist community, while only 9% more showed integrationist behavior than those who did not when the behavior was observable to a segregationist community.

Using a sample of 5,422 students from 99 different colleges and universities, Bowers (1968, chapter 12) has examined the effects of personal attitudes and social norms toward 9 different patterns of college deviance (such as shoplifting from the school store, stealing books from the library, etc.) on the actual engagement in such acts. The results also suggest an independent and significant relationship between personal disapproval and deviant behavior, and between social normative disapproval and deviant behavior. Both personal and social normative disapproval reduce deviance. Consequently, personal disapproval is more consistent with behavior at a congruent level of social support. For example, for those who strongly disapprove of the deviant pattern in question, only 2% engaged in the deviant pattern when 80-100% of the college also disapprove, but 11% engaged in the pattern when only 20-30% of the college disapprove.

In general, the conclusions of Warner and DeFleur (1969) in terms of racial discrimination and Bowers (1968) in terms of college deviance are quite similar: both attitude and social support possess an independent effect on behavior; attitude, therefore, is more consistent with behavior at a congruent level of social support. This relationship has been demonstrated in numerous recent studies. The reader's attention is particularly directed toward Ajzen and Fishbein, 1969, 1970, 1971, 1972; Wicker, 1969; De Friese and Ford, 1969; and Evens and Ehrlich, 1973. Note, that this does not mean that attitude has more impact on behavior at a congruent level of social support, but only that the additive effects of social support and attitude are greater than the independent effects of attitude alone. Consequently, the attitude-behavior relationship appears more consistent at a congruent level of social support.

Emergent Research Issues

As previously stated, reconceptualizing the relationship between attitude and behavior from a bivariate to a multivariate research problem "solves" the attitude-behavior inconsistency problem in the sense that it transforms the theoretical anomaly into a focal point for research; but, perhaps, more importantly it also generates various new research issues—issues which simply would not be generated by a bivariate conceptualization. To illustrate, I will briefly note two issues involving social support.

1. Relative Attitude and Social Support Weights: While the data reported in some studies can be utilized to roughly estimate the relative effects of attitude and social support on behavior, few studies focus on the conditions which affect these weights. One such study has been reported by Warner and DeFleur (1969, chapter 11). Briefly, they show that the effect of social support depends on the visibility of behavior, that is, as behavior becomes less socially visible, the effect of social support on behavior decreases. Consequently, while effect of attitude does not absolutely increase (although it might), the effect of attitude relative to social support increases. More recently (Friders, et.al., 1971) these results have been extended. Also, as part of a rather interesting set of experiments dealing with the impact of attitude and social support on behavior, Ajzen and Fishbein (1969, chapter 13) have come to grips with this question. They report that in an experimental game situation, attitude has a greater impact than social support on behavior for players who are told by the experimenter to be competitive, and the perceived norm of the other players (social support) has more impact than attitude on behavior for players who are told to be cooperative. In explaining these effects, they argue that the actor's motivational orientation, which in the study depends on the experimenter's instructions, functions to activate or make salient either attitude or social norms. In more general terms they seem to be suggesting that the differential effect of attitude and social support depends on social cues which activate either attitude, social support, or both.

2. Interaction vs. Additive Effects of Social Support: Bowers (1968, chapter 12) reported that attitude and social support show an interactive effect, that is, the impact of attitude on behavior is accentuated at certain levels of social support. Generally, Bowers' research poses the

problem of partitioning the joint attitude—social support effect on behavior into the independent effects of social support, the independent effects of attitude and the interaction effects of attitude and social support. It also raises further questions, such as, under what conditions will the interactive effect be maximized and why? Why should a certain level of social support accentuate the impact of attitude or why should certain attitudes accentuate the impact of certain levels of social support? At this time, while a few researchers have casually reported interactive effects, none have systematically explored the above issue. Yet, for those interested in understanding the impact of attitude on behavior, this would seem to be a critical issue.

Although the concept of social support partially clarifies the relationship between attitude and behavior, it also generates other significant research problems, such as the weighting of attitude and social support and the examination of attitude-social support interactive effects. A critical examination of the other variables previously mentioned in conjunction with attitude and behavior also reveals various such multivariate research problems.

In concluding this section, the question of temporal order should be noted. For the most part, researchers concerned with the impact of attitude on behavior assume that upon controlling for other variables, any residual attitude-behavior relationship reflects the impact of attitude. However, other research traditions suggest other causal models as equally plausible. For example, dissonance research clearly suggests that under certain conditions attitudes function to rationalize behavior, and, thus, can be conceived as a consequence of behavior (Aronson, 1966).

A recent study by Bellin and Kriesberg (1967) accentuates the importance of differentiating between attitude as a cause and as a consequence of behavior. Bellin and Kriesberg focus on the extent to which attitude toward public housing is related to applying for public housing. They report a moderate relationship. The relationship is accentuated for those who had already applied at the time of the attitude measurement. For those who had not already applied at the time of the attitude measurement over the next three years the rate of application is not significantly affected by attitude toward public housing. This suggests that attitudes predominantly tend to adjust to behavior, rather than affect behavior.

In terms of the attitude-behavior relationship reported in static or cross-sectional studies, Bellin and Kriesberg's research and dissonance research strongly suggest that only some portion of the relationship between attitude and behavior (controlling for other relevant variables) can be attributed to the impact of attitude on behavior. Future research may well focus on establishing what portion of the attitude-behavior relationship is attributable to which of the two processes and the conditions which foster one process rather than the other.

To summarize, recent research clearly suggests that attitude-behavior consistency should be viewed as a multivariate problem. Other variables have been shown to influence the effect of attitude on behavior and to influence behavior directly, thus, obscuring the effect of attitude. When such variables are controlled and introduced systematically recent research shows a significant relationship between attitude and behavior. What proportion of this relationship can be attributed to the effect of attitude on behavior rather than the effect of behavior on attitude still remains vague.

ATTITUDE CHANGE AND BEHAVIOR CHANGE

For the most part the above conclusion is based on research in which the attitude-behavior relationship has been treated as a static research problem. In attitude change research, various social scientists from different research traditions have questioned whether attitude change has any impact on behavior change. Some have suggested that it may be more profitable to view attitude change and behavior change as correlates.

Leventhal et. al., (1967, chapter 14) in a series of experiments dealing with dental hygiene, tetanus innoculations and smoking have addressed themselves to this question. Specifically, they have focused on the relationship between the level of fear and the elaboration of behavior recommendations in a persuasive communication, and the extent of attitude and behavior change. "Fear" refers to the extent to which the subjects are exposed to a message which associates continued past behavior (e.g., poor dental hygiene, or smoking) with negative consequences (e.g., gum disease, or cancer). The "elaboration of behavior recommendations" refers to the extent to which the message includes a specific concrete plan of action detailing how the subjects may go about changing their behavior. The results of this line of experiments seem to suggest that although level of fear seems to be the major cause of attitude change, the level of recommendations seems to be the major cause of behavior change. The fact that attitude change and behavior change appear to be affected by different components of the message led Leventhal et. al. to suggest that the relationship between attitude and behavior may be spurious or partly spurious. That is, attitude-behavior consistency will occur under the conditions of either high fear and specific recommendations or low fear and non-specific recommendations; and attitude-behavior inconsistency will occur under the conditions of either low fear and specific recommendations or high fear and non-specific recommendations.

Comparable findings have been reported in Human Relations research. Reviews of the literature (Brayfield and Crockett, 1954; and Vroom, 1964) suggest that the frequently held assumption that work satisfaction has an impact on work performance is not empirically supported. Such findings have stimulated a theoretical reexamination of the relationship. For example, Porter and Lawler (1968) have presented data suggesting that work satisfaction should be viewed as an effect rather than a cause of work performance; and Cherrington et al. (1971, chapter 15), have argued that the relationship between work satisfaction and performance is not causal but contingent on other factors. They have reported data showing that work performance and work satisfaction are both related to reinforcement. People increase their performance when rewarded and decrease it when not rewarded. People are satisfied with their performance when they are rewarded and dissatisfied when they are not rewarded. If people are rewarded for high work performance, then work satisfaction will be directly related to high work performance; if people are rewarded for low work performance, then work satisfaction will be inversely related to work performance; and if people are rewarded independently of work performance, then work satisfaction will not be related to work performance. In an experimental laboratory situation using college students, Cherrington et. al. (1971) have established these conditions and reported results which support their hypothesis.

In a series of experiments dealing with the effects of behavior models Bryan and Walbek (1970a) seem to have reached a similar conclusion. Children from the 2-4 grades are asked to participate in a game which allows them to win numerous penny gift certificates. The experiment is structured so that all of the children are first exposed to a model who plays the same game plus one of the following four conditions: 1) a model who practices and preaches charity, 2) a model who practices greed but preaches charity, 3) a model who practices and preaches greed, or 4) a model who practices charity and preaches greed. "Practice" refers to the extent to which the model shares his winnings with others; and "preaching" refers to the extent to which the model verbally advocates the virtues of sharing the winnings. In terms of the model's effect on the children, Bryan and Walbek report that the preaching of the model influences what the children preach to other children, but not what they actually practice, and that the practices of the model influence what the children actually practice but not what they preach. Hence, when the preaching and practices of children are consistent, it is not because they are causally related, but because the children have been exposed to models who practice what they preach.

From three research traditions (persuasive communication, Human Relations, and behavior modeling) a very similar conclusion can be drawn: attitude change (or formation) and behavior change (or formation) are not necessarily causally related. Each is affected by different causal variables. Consequently, attitude change and behavior change are directly related when the causes of both are directly related, that is, when behavior models happen to practice what they preach, when people happen to be rewarded for high performance, and when people are exposed to messages of change which happen to include both elements of high fear and elaborate recommendations. As these conditions are frequently not met, attitude change is frequently not related to behavior change.

The conclusion that the relationship between attitude change and behavior change may be spurious is quite contradictory to the survey-field studies which tend to suggest that upon controlling for other variables (for example, social norms) attitude has a significant impact on behavior. Although clearly a matter requiring careful and extended consideration, I will briefly note certain differences between the laboratory-experimental change studies and the survey cross-sectional or static studies which may account for the different findings.

One, the variables which have been found to affect attitude-behavior consistency in the static studies have not been controlled in the attitude-behavior change research. For example, for the three studies discussed here many other attitudes other than the attitude measured may have affected the behavior under consideration. Controlling for such other attitudes and other such variables may considerably clarify the relationship between attitude change and behavior change.

Two, there is a distinct possibility that newly formed attitudes may not have much impact on behavior compared to the more stable enduring attitudes measured in survey field studies. Such may be the case because it simply takes time to consider and cognitively explore the behavior implications of newly formed attitudes. Cook et. al. (1970) have discussed this issue in another context, pointing out that many subjects change their attitudes in response to a persuasive communication because they are not aware of the behavior implications. When such implications are brought to their attention, much less attitude change occurs.

Finally, consider the implications of the fact that for the most part attitudes studied in laboratory experiments are less ego-involving than attitudes studied in survey field research. In the papers discussed here attitudes toward work done in a laboratory experiment (Cherrington, et. al., 1971), toward forms of dental hygiene (Leventhal, et.al., 1967), and toward giving experimental tokens to others (Bryan and Walbek, 1970a), appear to be far less ego-involving than, for example, racial attitudes (Warner and DeFleur, 1969) and political attitudes (Jeffries and Ransford, 1972) as measured in the survey studies. This point was originally made by Hovland (1959; and reemphasized recently by Sherif, 1965) who, in comparing laboratory and survey persuasive communication attitude research, reported, that while laboratory studies tend to show significant attitude change, survey studies do not. In reconciling these differences Hovland noted that relative to the survey studies, experimental-laboratory studies focus on less ego-involving attitudes, which are probably more susceptible to change. On the basis of this conclusion, it also seems reasonable to hypothesize that such attitudes may not have a significant impact on behavior.

Generally, I am suggesting that the experimental-laboratory studies of attitude change tend to be constructed in a way which maximizes attitude change, while minimizing the impact of newly formed attitudes on behavior. Of course, these hypotheses are somewhat speculative and certainly not meant to be exhaustive, but are set forth quite modestly in an exploratory tone.

SUMMARY

Historically, attitude emerged as a concept formulated to explain individual behavioral differences—a problem common to the history of psychology, psychoanalysis, and sociology. The specific problem of attitude-behavior inconsistency may be attributed to the rise of operationalism. The operations which seemed to maximize reliability and quantification were not also capable of solving the traditional problem of predicting differences in individual behavior. However, during the operational era this fact drew only isolated attention (e.g., LaPiere, 1934) as the major research role of attitude had shifted from predicting individual differences to functioning as a unit of analysis for the study of social influence. Hence, considered as a unit of analysis for the study of other substantive problems, emphasis on reliability rather than validity seems justifiable.

In the 1950's and particularly in the 1960's a renewed interest in predicting individual action differences emerged, highlighting the incapacity of the operationally defined attitude concept. Consequently, some researchers severely questioned its usefulness and the practicality of much social influence research where attitude served as the unit of analysis (Deutscher, 1965, chapter 4). However, the general reaction of social scientists to this anomalous state of affairs has not been to abandon the operational properties of the concept, which have since proved to be so useful in dealing with other research questions, but to supplement them with other methodological and explanatory concepts. In some cases these concepts seemed to include properties once implicitly part of the traditional attitude concept but abandoned to satisfy certain demands of operationalism. Of the various concepts employed predominant concern has focused on the concept of social norms, which either counterbalance or reinforce the effects of attitude.

In terms of the formal organization of this book, these themes are developed in the following five sections: Section 1 includes two papers pertaining to the historical origins of the controversy. DeFleur and Westie (1963) provide a historical review of the problem, and LaPiere (1934) represents one of the first empirical studies of the problem. Section 2 includes two papers appearing in the mid-sixties which review the extent of attitude-behavior inconsistency reported in the literature. Festinger (1964) focuses on the relationship between attitude change and behavior change and Deutscher (1965) focuses on the general relationship between attitude and behavior. Section 3 includes three papers which examine the effect of measurement validity. Fendrich (1967) examines the effect of play-like attitude measurement situations; Tittle and Hill (1967) examine the effect of measures of isolated segments of behavior; and Wicker and Pomazal (1971) examine the effect of unequivalent measures of attitude and behavior. Section 4 includes six papers which emphasize the role of explanatory variables. Ehrlich (1969) presents a general discussion of conditions which may affect the extent of attitude-behavior consistency; Schwartz (1968) examines the effect of attitude neutralizations; Jeffries and Ransford (1972) examine the effect of multiple attitudes; and Warner and DeFleur (1969), Bowers (1968) and Ajzen and Fishbein (1970) examine the effect of social support. Section 5 includes two papers which focus on the relationship between attitude change and behavior change as a special case of the general problem. Leventhal's et. al. (1967) study falls within the persuasive communication tradition and Cherrington's et. al. study falls within the Human Relations literature.

In conclusion, the research seems to suggest that a substantial relationship between attitude and behavior exists, but that the relationship is frequently masked or altered by the effect of other methodological or explanatory variables. Upon the control of such other variables, studies are reasonably consistent in reporting a substantial relationship; e.g., correlation coefficients range from .20 - .50. While sometimes small in terms of absolute magnitude, the relationship is generally substantial in terms of its proportion to the total explained variance. Exactly how this relationship translates into the relationship between attitude change and behavior change, and exactly what portion of the relationship can be attributable to the impact of attitude rather than the impact of behavior remain problems for future research.

Looking backward over the last four decades, social scientists have shifted from assuming the attitude-behavior relationship to measuring the attitude-behavior relationship to recently researching the conditions which affect the attitude-behavior relationship. If the incipient contemporary trend continues to develop, attitude-behavior research in the 1970's should be multivariate and more complex in nature. For example, the simultaneous consideration of a set of independent variables introduces such problems as 1) determining the relative weights of the different variables and the conditions which affect these weights, and 2) establishing interaction effects and the conditions which affect the capacity of various combinations of variables to generate such effects. Perhaps, however, the most pressing problem of the 1970's is the need to formulate a unitary conceptual and methodological framework in terms of which the work in various research traditions can be integrated.

I

HISTORICAL ORIGINS OF THE CONTROVERSY

1

ATTITUDE AS A SCIENTIFIC CONCEPT

Melvin L. DeFleur
And
Frank R. Westie

Behavioral scientists frequently urge that the major concepts of our several disciplines be subjected to continuous efforts towards clarification and rigor. While such clarification is often advocated, it has, with notable exceptions, been less frequently demonstrated by the preparation of articles or monographs devoted to the task of bringing together the issues, controversies, and consensuses with respect to a principal concept.

Perhaps no other concept from the behavioral sciences has been used so widely by theorists and researchers as the term *attitude*. Since its introduction into our thinking a number of decades ago, this concept has become basic to the investigation of a tremendous variety of social behaviors. Untold numbers of articles, monographs, and textbooks have accumulated with attitude as the central research variable. Not only is the concept widely employed within the behavioral sciences themselves, but related disciplines with new-found empirical interests are now making extensive use of the term. A concept so widely employed merits the closest possible attention as long as there remain disagreements, debates, and controversies concerning definition, measurement, theoretical utility, and its behavioral referents.

The present paper has as its goal a summary of the scope of this disagreement, both past and present, and an examination of the unresolved issues which constitute the basis of the controversies. By this reexamination it is hoped that the current status of attitude as a scientific concept can be clarified. In addition, a set of specific proposals is suggested as a means for establishing this conceptual tool on a more rigorous basis for future research.

Reprinted from *Social Forces* (Vol. 42, October, 1963, pp. 17-31) by permission of the authors, *Social Forces*, and the University of North Carolina Press.

HISTORICAL PERSPECTIVE

As an ordinary non-scientific word, attitude referred in the 17th Century to the physical positioning of an artist's subject with respect to a background. An extension of meanings took place during the subsequent centuries and the term acquired such interpretations as the mental positioning of an individual on a political issue; modes of thought characteristic of groups or classes; or even a person's general motivational predispositions toward his world.[1] Needless to say, a concept which denoted such a wide variety of referents was more useful for the task of the poet or novelist than for the scientific analysis of human social conduct.

The incorporation of the term attitude into the scientific study of man's social and psychological nature may be described as involving a series of rather clear stages or eras. A transitional stage occurred during the mid-nineteenth century, when scattered usages of the term first began to appear in the writings of those philosophers who were to be the fathers of some of the modern behavioral sciences. During this time, a major focus of interest and speculation was on the "mental processes" of the individual. Writing an "Exposition of Mind," Alexander Bain used the term "attitude" when analyzing the "power of the Will over trains of thought," and he noted that the "forces of the mind may have got into a set track or attitude."[2] Herbert Spencer used the term in much the same way to describe an aspect of the mental process.[3]

Following these scattered beginnings, the second stage in the use of the term parallels the rise of more systematic and scientific attempts to explore man's mental life. The pioneers of modern experimental psychology were probing the "elements of consciousness" in the late decades of the 1800's. With the aid of newly invented "brass instruments" for the precise measurement of time, one of the tasks posed by Wilhelm Wundt and his followers was the exploration of reaction time.[4] Experiments involving "mental chronometry" led to the formation of a series of new concepts which were in a sense varieties of attitudes and which gave the term a respectable place within experimental psychology. As these experiments progressed, it became clear that an individual who was alert and ready to perform a task at a given signal could act much more quickly by concentrating his attention on the task, rather than on the anticipated signal. Thus, there was less delay between a signal and, for example, the pressing of a telegraph key by a subject if he were "set" in a state of readiness to make the response.[5] This mode of subject-orientation led the experimentalists to speak on the "task-attitude" or *Aufgabe.* Other analogous states of readiness or mental preparedness were discovered which materially altered perception, reaction time, recall and various other of the "mental processes." These "sets" were labelled by the experimenters according to the kind of disposition, readiness, or anticipation which they involved:

> In addition to the *Aufgabe,* there was the *Absicht* (conscious purpose), the *Zielvorstellung* (idea of the relation between the self and the object to which the self is responding), the *Richtungsvorstellung* (or idea of direction), the *determinierende Tendenz* (any disposition which brings in its train the spontaneous appearance of a determined idea), the *Einstellung,* a more general term (roughly equivalent to "set"), the *Haltung* (with a more behavioral connotation), and the *Bewusstseinslage* (the "posture or lay of consciousness").[6]

With the growth of the behaviorism movement within psychology, the search for elements of consciousness and the study of mental processes fell into dispute. The method of introspection or self-examination upon which many of these studies depended no longer was accepted with unquestioned validity. Psychologists turned to studies of learning, perception, and motivation, based largely upon experiments with animal subjects. Consequently, many of these early concepts have little importance in modern experimental psychology. However, the term attitude itself survived this change in intellectual fashion, and became a permanent part of psychological terminology.

The third stage in the evolution of the attitude concept accompanied the development of social psychology, a new discipline that was emerging from both sociology and psychology. Two sociologists, W. I. Thomas and Florian Znaniecki, are generally regarded as the first to use attitude as a key concept in an extensive and systematic way.[7] Following the publication of their *Polish Peasant in Europe and America,* at the end of the first world war, the concept as we know it today (as a term indicating a relationship between an individual and a socially significant object) became widely adopted in the behavioral sciences. A considerable body of writings developed during the 1920's as social psychologists and others began to make more extensive use of the term, and as attempts were made to clarify its meaning.

The beginnings of the fourth important stage in the development of the attitude concept are found in the growth or concern with the measurement of attitudes in the 1920's. As the behavioral sciences began to mature, and as behaviorism and operationism became more significant intellectual thoughtways in these sciences, increasing pressures were exerted for the development of quantitative techniques to aid in the objective observation of behavior.

A widely known monograph by Thurstone and Chave, and the earlier "social distance" studies of Bogardus are two important milestones which mark the rise of interest in "attitude scales."[8] Contributions to this problem have since been made by thousands of researchers. An attempt to summarize adequately the various scaling procedures and empirical attitude studies would fill volumes.[9]

With the increased acceptance of operationism, the view was widely held that fussing about verbally formulated definitions was no longer necessary. Some operationists stated with intriguing simplicity that "attitudes are what the attitude scales measure." This side-stepping of the problem of independent definition did little to increase clarity of thinking about attitudes. Nor did great clarification of the concept necessarily come with the invention of mathematical scaling models. In fact, along with the development of measurement techniques there came decreased consensus, if anything, concerning the definition of attitude. This is not to say that the invention of scales themselves created the confusion. Rather, this confusion came about when an increasing number of researchers conducted studies of attitudes from different viewpoints. As they discussed their conclusions and findings, the behavioral sciences found themselves embarrassed by a growing number of different meanings for the term.

Relatively few researchers, even among the operationists, were content to let attitudes be defined simply by their measuring devices. Most researchers and writers continued to formulate verbal definitions of this increasingly important concept. To give some idea of the many ways in which the term was being used in the 1930's, we can examine an encyclopedic summary of attitude studies published by Erland Nelson in 1939.[10] In his survey of 183 books and articles dealing with attitudes, he found 30 contemporary writers attempting to clarify the definition of the concept. After considering the various definitions and discussions of attitude advanced by these writers, Nelson attempted to list the meanings assigned to the term. Although possibly some of these are very similar, in spite of the differences in language, it is instructive to consider the list of meanings compiled by Nelson. Reduced to simple terms, attitudes were variously defined as:

1. Organic drives
2. Purposes
3. Motives
4. A "core of affect"
5. The emotional concomitants of action
6. Permanently felt dispositions
7. A special case of disposition
8. Generalized conduct
9. A neural set, or a neuromuscular set
10. A stabilized set
11. A state of readiness
12. A disposition modifying rising experience
13. Verbal responses for or against a psychological object
14. Socially compelled behavior of an enduring type

15. A response which is more obviously a function of disposition than of the immediate stimulus
16. The result of organization of experience
17. A directive or dynamic influence on the response to which related
18. A determiner of the direction of an activity
19. A guide for conduct. A point of reference for new experience
20. A trial response—substitute behavior
21. A way of conceiving an object. A posture of consciousness
22. A "sum total of inclinations, feelings, notions, ideas, fears, prejudices, threats, and convictions about any specific topic"
23. An integration of the specific responses into a general set

Thus, the scientific meanings of the term attitude ranged from the simple insistence that attitudes are tendencies toward overt action (from Bogardus) to the complex "sum total of inclinations, feelings, prejudices, threats, and convictions about any specific topic" (the 22nd above, an early definition from Thurstone).

THE CONCEPT ATTITUDE IN MODERN BEHAVIORAL SCIENCE

From the chaos of conflicting and diverse definitions of attitude characterizing social psychology in the 1930's, there has emerged a much narrower set of views as to the meaning of this concept. Though some arguments persist, they are now carried on with less intensity, and concern a much more restricted range of possibilities.

There are basically but two major or general conceptions of attitude current in the literature. Though there are as many specific definitions of attitude as there are writers on the subject, most fit into one or the other of the two basic categories. While both of these conceptions of attitudes have certain elements in common (e.g., both assume a stimulus-response framework), they differ in the kinds of *inferences* their proponents would derive from the behavior referent (observable attitudinal responses). These two types of conceptions may be called (1) *probability conceptions* and (2) *latent process conceptions.*[11]

The primary inference implied in probability conceptions is that attitudinal responses are more or less consistent. That is, a series of responses toward a given attitudinal stimulus is likely to show some degree of organization, structure, or predictability. Responses of a specified type, say verbal rejection behavior, may be more likely to occur than, say, acceptance or indifference responses for a given individual when he is confronted repeatedly with a defined attitude stimulus. If this is the case, such a response organization can be termed a negative attitude. The attitude, then, is an inferred property of the responses, namely their consistency. Stated in another way, attitude is equated with the *probability of recurrence of behavior forms of a given type or direction.*

The second type of attitude conception, the latent process view, begins with the fact of response consistency, but goes a step beyond this and postulates the operation of some hidden or hypothetical variable, functioning within the behaving individual, which shapes, acts upon, or "mediates" the observable behavior. That is, the observable organization of behavior is said to be "due to" or can be "explained by" the action of some mediating *latent variable.* The attitude, then, is not the manifest responses themselves, or their probability, but an intervening variable operating between stimulus and response and inferred from the overt behavior. This inner process is seen as giving both direction and consistency to the person's responses. Let us examine these two conceptions in greater depth.

BEHAVIORAL CONSISTENCY OR "PROBABILITY" DEFINITIONS

To illustrate the probability conception of attitude we can examine three typical examples from the writings of contemporary behavioral scientists:

(Campell) "An individual's social attitude is an enduring syndrome of response consistency with regard to a set of social objects."[12]

(Kretch and Crutchfield) "An enduring organization of motivational, perceptual and cognitive processes with respect to some aspects of the individual's world."[13]

(Fuson) "The probability of occurrence of a defined behavior in a defined situation."[14]

The following points are clear: first, the conceptual framework of these definitions is a stimulus-response framework. Second, they stress *consistency* of response to stimulus objects or situations of one variety or another. Various terms are used to call attention to these essential features of the individual's attitudinal responses. Such words as "enduring organizations" and "response consistency," are employed as different ways of denoting that responses of some *particular* type are *more likely,* or have a higher probability, than other forms of response from the individual confronted with the attitude stimulus. For example, individuals who qualify as having a "prejudicial attitude toward Mexicans" may be found to have a relatively high probability of (1) using epithets such as "spic," "greaser," or "Mex" or of saying other uncomplimentary things about Americans of Mexican ancestry, and/or (2) behaving overtly in such a way that rejection of such persons is clearly implied, and/or (3) feeling uncomfortable in the presence of such persons. The fact that he has demonstrated such consistency of response toward this particular attitude-stimulus would be an adequate basis for classifying him as an individual with a "negative attitude" toward this group, using the probability type definition.

In terms of their logical structure, such definitions imply that there are definable sets of behaviors which an individual can perform as responses toward the stimulus in question; that there is a determinable probability of such responses occurring in the behavior which the given individual shows in connection with the attitude object.

The probability conception of attitude is convenient and obviously quite simple. For one thing, this type of definition *anchors the attitude concept* firmly to observable events. By defining attitude as the probability of particular types of responses, the need to worry about the nature of "underlying mechanisms" operative within the individual organism is absent. The researcher can turn to an analysis of the kinds of past experiences, normative systems, peer groups, or to the types of social systems from which individuals with different response probabilities have come. Presumably, such analyses will lead to understanding of the part played by such factors in shaping the probabilities for given individuals.

The probability conception of attitude makes measurement a rather straightforward task. This is particularly true when the definable set of behaviors is verbal behavior. With the aid of various scaling techniques, the individual can be confronted with graded sets of statements which are representative selections from the universe of possible (verbal) responses to the attitude stimulus. If the individual clearly endorses only statements of a very complimentary nature regarding the attitude object, his probability of favorable verbal responses outside the measurement situation (or in a later repetition of the measurement situation) is thought to be high and he is characterized as having a favorable attitude. If one starts an investigation of attitude variables with the probability definition in mind, the measurement task can logically be conceived of as a determination of response probabilities. The measurement of attitude need not be restricted to verbal behavior. With the aid of standardized behavioral settings, other overt forms of response can be scaled or graded to determine response probabilities. However, inferences from response consistency in verbal behavior to other forms of response are treacherous. This topic will be discussed presently.

While in some ways the probability definition simplifies the task of measurement, and, while it avoids the necessity of complex inferences concerning underlying variables, at the same time it places certain limitations on the use of the attitude concept in the development of behavior theory. To illustrate the point, Cohen and Nagel[15] in their discussion of the nature of theory, comment on several types of theories which have been developed in the various sciences. One classification of interest to us is a rather loose dichotomy by means of which a distinction is made between *abstractive* theories and *hidden mechanism* theories.

Theories of the abstractive variety are actually statements of very stable empirical regularities among the phenomena they relate to. Theories concerning the attraction of bodies are of this nature. It is a general law that bodies attract each other directly in proportion to their masses and inversely proportional to the square of their distance. Many theorems and consequences can be deduced from this general law—propositions concerning the tides, the trajectories of cannon balls, and the paths of artificial satellites. The theory does not state *why* these regularities occur. There is no suggestion that there are hidden mechanisms inside the bodies which somehow work to bring them together. Theories of this type are broad laws of the behavior of similar phenomena, regularities that apparently hold true (under ideal conditions) everywhere and at all times. And, they more or less hold true under less than ideal conditions, depending upon the number and intensity of disturbing variables.

Explanations in terms of abstractive theories proceed in a relatively simple way. For example, the falling of particular bodies, or other forms of attraction between specific objects are referred to as "special cases" or "empirical instances" of the general laws that govern the entire class of similar events. These are often related in systems of laws.

On the other hand, hidden mechanism theories account for the behavior of phenomena on the basis of the action of some internal process which is not immediately observable. The diffusion of one gas into another, the manifestations of virus pneumonia, or the precipitation of a salt from a solution, are all explained on the basis of structures or mechanisms which operate to produce the observable events. There is no implication intended here that one of these two types of theory is somehow better or more legitimate.

But what does all this have to do with attitudes? Clearly, attitudes, as defined in terms of probabilities, can be used as explanatory concepts only in a very restricted sense. If an individual is observed more or less uniformly to reject the attitude stimulus, and we seek to explain this fact, it is not a legitimate answer simply to say "it is because he has a negative attitude." This would be, of course, completely tautological. The uniformity of his behavior (that is, his attitude or high probability of negative response) cannot legitimately be used to explain itself. Explanations for attitudinal behavior must come from more general propositions which describe broad empirical regularities between attitudes (high probabilities of negative response) and *other phenomena,* say, a membership in certain groups, present or past, which perhaps have been learning environments of a particular sort. This, then, is one limitation of the probability type definition—it requires that explanatory formulations rely upon propositions relating attitudes to other independent sets of variables.

The extent to which latent process definitions of attitude "explain" behavior also needs to be discussed. However, let us first examine such conceptions in more detail and then note the implications for the explanation issue.

"LATENT PROCESS" DEFINITIONS

Some of the underlying assumptions, limitations, and logical consequences of the latent process conception can be illustrated by two examples from current writers:

> (Allport) "An attitude is a mental and neural state of readiness *exerting a directive influence* upon the individual's response to all objects and situations to which it is related."
> (italics ours)[16]
>
> (Doob) "An attitude refers to an implicit response that is both *anticipatory* and *mediating* in reference to patterns of overt responses, that is evoked by a variety of stimulus patterns, and that is considered as socially significant in the individual's society."
> (italics ours)[17]

Clearly, these definitions include the stimulus-response framework and the notion of consistency or probability. However, here we see the *additional* idea that the individual's behavior is somehow "shaped," "guided," or "mediated" by some *underlying process.* That is, the probabilities of obtaining responses of a given type from an individual to a specified attitude stimulus are related to the action of some "inner mechanism," some unobservable "something" that constrains, influences, mediates, or otherwise determines that consistency will appear among the individual's responses to the attitude stimulus.

Lindesmith and Strauss offer another example of this type of inference in summarizing what they feel are the "generally accepted" meanings the concept attitude has for social scientists. They maintain that a distinction has been made between the "true attitude" and the behavior from which such an attitude is inferred:

> . . . . the idea developed that attitudes are separate from behavior and are more general than their specific overt expressions. Hence a distinction came to be made between attitudes and opinions, the latter being taken to mean verbal reports from which attitudes can be inferred.[18]

We agree with Lindesmith and Strauss that "the concept of attitude still carries these meanings today, and social scientists have pretty generally accepted them." However, the implications in terms of the use of the concept (defined in this manner) for the task of explanation needs to be traced out.

It is important to have a clear understanding of exactly what is meant by the notion of a latent variable, because some modern methods for the measurement of attitudes depend upon relating covariations among responses to inferred variations of the postulated underlying variable.

This relationship between the observable behavior and the latent variable is stated by Green:

> In general terms a latent variable *is used to describe the consistency* or covariation of a number of different responses to stimuli of the same general class. The variable is viewed as mediating the stimuli and the responses. The responses are said to covary because *they are all mediated by the same hypothetical variable.* (italics ours)[19]

Thus, if an individual shows consistency in his verbal and overt behavior toward a stimulus object—for example, if he is consistently negative toward Jews in both word and deed—this "covariation" among his responses can be "explained" or "accounted for" by the mediating action of the latent variable. This "hidden mechanism" feature of the second type of attitude conception makes attitude seem to be useful as an explanatory concept in a very direct way. Defined in this way, attitude is a process which occurs inside an individual which determines more or less immediately and directly the way in which he responds to an attitude stimulus. An example of this kind from recent work by Angus Campbell illustrates the point:

> Responses toward most objects are *prefaced by* attitudes toward those objects which in a proximal sense *determine* the response. (italics ours)[20]

The latent process conception of attitude, then, has been used as a simple sort of explanatory device. Also, it has permitted somewhat more complex thinking about problems of measuring attitudes. The task of measurement under such a conception is one of classifying the individual on a hypothetical quantitative continuum, i.e. the latent variable.

Like many such "dispositional" concepts[21] which postulate latent processes or structures to account for manifest functioning, this conception is not without difficulties. The whole idea of a latent variable is awkward in a behavioral science which stresses *observability.* A latent variable is by definition un-observable. There is the vague implication that somehow the organic processes of the individual may be involved, but in unspecified ways. Such a conception bears a disconcerting resemblance to certain theories and explanations in the early physical sciences. To cite an oft-quoted example, theories of combustion of an earlier day attributed observable burning to the action of an unobservable "something" called *phlogiston,* released from wood or other material during the fire. Such reified latent variables are no longer found useful in the physical sciences. Champions of the latent variable idea could counter such criticism by pointing out that currently physical scientists widely employ concepts such as "atom," "electron," etc., which are not observable either, but are inferred or hypothetical variables. This is, of course, true. However, these physical science concepts are supported by impressive empirical evidence in the nature of controlled demonstrations that show that the phenomena behave *precisely* as if these postulated conceptions were correct. The burden of such adequate demonstration with respect to attitudes rests directly upon those who advance the proposition that attitudinal behavior is caused (mediated, influenced, governed) by the action of a latent variable. Until such time that convincing empirical evidence is forthcoming, *the latent process conception of attitude must be entertained as most tentative.* In posing such an entity it is not precisely clear, at least at the present time, whether the advocates have named a discovery, or discovered a name. Until the mechanisms involved in this internal latent process can be described more fully, the latent variable must remain "an unknown something."

Our discussion of latent process conceptions requires certain qualifications. It would appear that there are two types of latent process conceptions: (1) those which impute the empirical existence of a hidden mechanism, and (2) those which postulate a hypothetical mediating variable which is not regarded as having empirical referents, counterparts, or existence but which is simply a construction which serves as a convenient tool for analysis. Green's conception of attitude appears, especially when considered in the context in which he presents it, to be an instance of a hypothetical construct involving no imputation of an empirically existent underlying mechanism:

> Like many psychological variables, attitude is a hypothetical or latent variable, rather than an immediately observable variable. The concept of attitude does not refer to any one specific act or response of an individual, but is an abstraction from a large number of related acts or responses. For example, when we state that individual A has less a favorable attitude toward labor organizations than individual B, we mean that A's many different statements and actions concerning labor organizations are consistently less favorable to labor than are B's comparable works and deeds. We are justified in using a comprehensive concept like attitude when the man's related responses are consistent.[22]

While Green speaks of a "latent variable," he says that it is "hypothetical" and that it is "an abstraction from a large number of responses." Thus, we must not assume that the user or similar analysts are guilty of naive reification or the fallacy of misplaced concreteness.

Both of these conceptions of attitudes (latent process and hypothetical construct) have been posed as aids in the construction of mathematical models specifying the relationship between a sample of verbal scale items and some "attitude universe" from which they are presumably drawn. However, regardless of their mathematical elegance and symbolic sophistication, these scaling models are but techniques for assigning numbers to the postulated underlying variable. In the final analysis, such measuring techniques themselves can be no more valid than the foundation of concepts upon which they rest. There is some possibility that this foundation contains at least some concepts, the referents of which cannot adequately be demonstrated at present.

THE FALLACY OF EXPECTED CORRESPONDENCE

Of the two major conceptions of attitude examined in the previous section, the type which we termed the latent process conception is by far the most popular. But, in spite of its popularity, there has been associated with this conception a traditional problem concerning the degree to which people behave in "real life" situations consistently with their verbal attitudes, as measured by modern attitude scales. This difficulty arises from the logical implications of making the assumption that a set of responses can be said to "covary" because they are all mediated by the *same* hypothetical attitude variable. That is, the latent process conception of attitude is premised upon the idea that an individual's response patterns (toward some attitude stimulus) are made consistent by the "mediating action" of that latent, underlying variable. The individual's observable behaviors are said to be "manifestations" of this inner and latent process. This notion poses a problem concerning the relationship among various dimensions of attitudinal behavior.

Attitudinal responses can be classified into three main dimensions (sometimes called "attitude universes"). Attitudinal responses include both verbal behavior and other overt non-verbal forms of action. In addition to these two dimensions, attitudinal responses include more complex affective processes which we can refer to "emotional-autonomic" behavior. These are not completely independent in every respect, but such a classification facilitates the discussion of the correspondence problem.

The essential point is that, given the latent process conception, not only are responses within a *given* behavioral dimension or category expected to show consistency over time, there must also logically be an expectation or covariation *between* one category and another *if each is mediated by the same general latent attitude* (frequently called the "true attitude"). The individual is expected to show consistency between his verbalizations and other forms of action toward the attitude object. It is this expectation of correspondence *between* various universes or categories of responses toward the attitude stimulus in question which we have called "the fallacy of expected correspondence."

There is ample evidence, however, to show that subjects do not always behave consistently in their verbal and action behavior. Those who subscribe to the latent process view have recognized this problem. Widespread indeed is the uneasy recognition, noted by Lindesmith and Strauss that

> [verbal behavior] is not an altogether reliable index of attitude, because the person expressing it can be concealing true attitudes, or may honestly say one thing but do another when the time comes to act.[23]

The sociological literature documents this difficulty clearly. An early study of LaPiere[24] showed that there can be a marked discrepancy between what people say they will do regarding members of a minority group, and what they actually *do* when confronted with an opportunity for action regarding that same minority group. In the company of a Chinese couple, LaPiere made a motor trip across the United States and along the Pacific coast. The party stopped at 184 eating establishments and 66 places for overnight accommodations. They were refused service only once, and this under rather unusual circumstances. Later, LaPiere sent a questionnaire to the proprietors of the various establishments to determine their stated verbal policy of accepting Chinese guests. More than 90 percent of the respondents indicated they would not accept Chinese persons. Clearly, there was a distinct lack of correspondence between the *verbal* attitude universe, at least as represented by the questionnaire, and the *action* opportunity described.

A somewhat analogous study regarding attitudes toward Negroes has been conducted by Kutner, Wilkins, and Yarrow.[25] A Negro woman accompanied by two white women visited a total of 11 restaurants in an urban community in the Northeast. In each establishment, the women were served without question or incident. Two weeks after these visits, each restaurant manager received a letter requesting reservations for a "social affair" for a group, some of the members of which were to be Negroes. None of the restaurant managers responded to this request for accommodations for a racially mixed group. After more than two weeks had passed, each of the managers was telephoned and the same request made for reservations. Several did finally agree with reluctance to accept the party, but not on a reservation basis. As a check, the same restaurants were called to make reservations for a group whose racial composition was not mentioned. All but one complied without hesitation. Clearly again, there was no one-to-one correspondence between behavior of the verbal variety and behavior of a more overt nature.

In these studies of the relationship between verbal and overt behavior, which of these behaviors represented the "true" manifestation of the latent attitude? Such a question has considerable theoretical importance if one has adopted the latent process definition of attitude. It might be very tempting to regard the verbal behavior as revealing the "true" latent attitude and to depreciate overt manifestations as a somehow less worthy basis for inference, or the reverse might be proposed. However, there is no strong theoretical foundation for such a choice in either direction and one is left with a dilemma. (Note that this issue becomes a meaningless question with the probability conception of attitude. Each universe of behavior can be regarded as equally legitimate and the probability of each occurring under various circumstances, or their possible correlation, becomes an empirical problem.)

There are clearly situational factors such as group norms, roles, definitions of situations, and other *social constraints* which materially "mediate" responses in situations involving either verbal behavior or overt action. Such "mediating" social constraints appear to explain lack of correspondence better than such a conception as "true attitudes" conceived of as latent variables.

The presumed "mediating" action of the latent process can be called into serious question on other, even more simple grounds. If such a process were in fact operative within the individual, it should at least show internal consistency within itself. That is, if an individual's response patterns toward a given attitude object were governed or mediated *solely* by a latent process, it would be logically difficult to imagine it operating in one direction on one day and in another direction on a different occasion. The behavior of an individual *within a given dimension of attitude behavior* should show consistency from one time to another, from one social situation to another, etc. For example, if an individual overtly rejects Negroes on one occasion due to the operation of an inner latent attitude process, he could not accept them overtly on another occasion due to the *same* latent process. However, it is not difficult to show situations where individuals behave in this grossly inconsistent fashion from one situation to the next. In a study by Lohman and Reitzes, 151 residents of an urban neighborhood were located who were also members of a particular labor union.[26] These individuals overtly behaved with conspicuous inconsistency toward Negroes under two different circumstances. The subjects were members of a property owner's association whose goals included resistance of penetration by Negro dwellers into their neighborhood. With respect to having a Negro for a neighbor, these subjects clearly behaved overtly in an anti-Negro fashion. At the same time, these 151 neighborhood residents were members of a labor union with a clear and well-implemented policy of granting Negroes equality and fair treatment on the job. With respect to having a Negro work companion, these subjects behaved overtly in a pro-Negro manner. It is difficult to square such data with the conception of attitudinal behavior as mediated by a single latent process. To account for such dramatic shifts of behavior solely in terms of inner or latent psychological processes, one would need at least two latent processes, one predisposed to negative action and one to positive behavior. Then one might also need one for verbal as well as overt *negative* behavior and another for verbal as well as overt *positive* behavior. This type of accounting for action bears an alarming resemblance to the instinct concept, which, shortly before its demise, was used to account for absurdly specific acts.

To add to this confusion, we can briefly examine the findings of Minard[27] who compared the behavior of white Southern coal miners toward Negroes while down in the mine, with their behavior outside the mine. While the workers of both races were in the mine there was a high degree of acceptance and integration, and even an equality of status among the ordinary workers. Outside the mine, however, the majority of white workers rejected Negroes, in the pattern characteristic of traditional Southern Negro-white relations. It is difficult to imagine a latent process which mediates behavior only above ground, and becomes *dormant* when the white Southerner descends below the surface.

But how can we proceed to clarify the attitude concept in the face of such confusion? A realistic conception of attitude must fit with these various findings regarding inconsistency. Such a conception should avoid the fallacy of expected correspondence, as there is ample evidence to indicate that such correspondence between verbal behavior and other forms of action can be conspicuously lacking.[28] Such a conception should also permit inconsistencies between an individual's behavior within one set of norms, or other social constraints, and another set of norms. Again, there is ample evidence to suggest that as the normative system about the individual changes, as his group memberships change, or as he moves from one role to another, his behavior toward an attitude object will undergo corresponding alterations. These variables are apparently the mediating factors which change and alter response patterns. A latent something interposed between attitudinal behavior patterns and the social variables which mediate them is *simply unnecessary.*

Thus far we have cautioned against expected correspondence in terms of consistency between one behavioral dimension and another. Given the fact that one of the primary characteristics of modern society is normative conflict—inconsistent demands on the individual from one group situation to another—plus the possibility of increased other-directedness, there is another kind of correspondence that can be expected: we can legitimately expect a *great deal* of correspondence between the "normative requirements" of a situation, and the kind of behavior a given individual will exhibit in that situation, regardless of past behavior or disposition. For example, an individual who acts in a liberal fashion as part of his informal role as a graduate student in a sociology department may conform to norms and demands of quite another sort when he moves to the role of guest at the home of conservative friends. He may shift his behavioral anchorages to the new set of norms appropriate to the new situation. The same can be said for the worker within the mine as compared to the same individual out of the mine and in the larger community.

We do, then, expect people to behave consistently under some circumstances. We expect them to behave more or less consistently, if the normative processes of the groups within which they are interacting are consistent. This is not to say that we can regard individuals as but mirror reflections of the particular norms they happen to be surrounded by at the moment. In spite of the obvious impact of social norms on action, there undoubtedly remains for each individual a pattern of learned responses toward any attitude object that is more likely under some standard set of circumstances than any other pattern. Also, two individuals caught up in exactly the same norms, roles, and social control processes will vary from one another in their patterns of response toward the same attitudinal stimulus. A useful conception of attitude, then, must be prepared to take into account both consistency and variability, uniformity and individuality, and at the same time remain a logical inference from observable behavior. Before suggesting concrete steps for clarification of the concept, a final issue must be taken into account.

UNDERLYING ASSUMPTIONS IN MODERN ATTITUDE MEASUREMENT

We have seen the two basic types of attitude conceptions, and some of the problems that are attendant with each. Closely coupled with the conceptual process is the problem of measurement. In modern behavioral science, concept formation and measurement are inseparable problems which in fact become identical under a strictly operational point of view.

The measurement of attitude has generally proceeded as a kind of quasi-psychophysical problem. That is, it is assumed that attitudes are latent hypothetical variables that cannot be measured directly, but can only be inferred from observations of a subject's responses to a selected set of graded statements (verbal behavior) or from his responses in other sets of graded behavior opportunities. The attitude, or "subjective" psychological variable, is inferred from the "objective" scale of behavioral items. Several techniques of some mathematical sophistication are available for making such inferences from observable behavior to the presumed underlying latent process.[29]

The methods developed by Likert, Thurstone, Guttman, Edwards, and others are techniques for classifying human beings along hypothetical attitude continua on the basis of what they do, or rather what they say they "would do" under hypothetical conditions posed in the statements or items of the attitude measuring instrument.

The basic techniques for attitude measurement were worked out in the late 1920's, or the early 1930's (with the exception of Guttman's technique which is a product of the 1940's). Roughly speaking, these techniques have been in use for more than a quarter century on the average. It seems appropriate, then, to inquire into the progress made in improvement in measurement during the intervening period. This line of inquiry is of particular importance because such measurement lies at the heart of research. Both conceptual and measurement problems must be clarified before intelligent research can be conducted in the important areas of the *etiology* of a given attitude pattern, its *distribution* in a given population, techniques for *changing* attitudinal responses through a variety of procedures, or the role of attitudes with respect to various classes of social behavior.

It has been the hope of measurement theorists, that through the improvement of existing scaling techniques, that is by developing new mathematical models for inferring underlying attitudes from responses to increasingly refined scale items, that certain of the difficulties involved in current conceptions of attitude will vanish. Such attitude theorists hope that improved scales will yield more precise measurement and lead to higher correspondence between responses to verbal scales and behavior in other contexts. Generally, this search for increased precision has concentrated on the invention of improved scaling methods based on psychophysical principles. The goal is to produce "unambiguous items," "unidimensional measures," "high reproducibility," or other measurement improvement which will make more tenable the underlying assumption that both verbal behavior and other response systems are structured because they are all manifestations of the underlying latent variable.

There are impressive reasons why we may not realize any great gain in either understanding attitudinal phenomena or in greater measurement precision by further travel along this route. There may be a serious limitation in the degree to which improvement in verbal scales can be successful as long as the subject is required to engage in an introspective process of weighing his self conception against the samples of attitudinal behavior posed in the items of the verbal scales. That is, the subject must compare the attitudinal "position" offered in a given scale item (statement) with his own "position" (on an underlying latent continuum) *perceived as part of his self conception.* A discriminating comparison of these two points on the continuum must be made before the subject can either endorse or reject the scale item.

Such a quasi-psychophysical process can yield precise discriminations only when two further assumptions are met. The first of these is that the subject has a sufficiently clear understanding of his own inner processes so that *he can formulate a precise self conception* concerning his orientation or "position" regarding how he would behave toward the attitude object under the hypothetical circumstances posed. This implies that the latent variable presumably mediating his behavior is at least in part open to introspection by the individual. The general inadequacy of the method of introspection as a tool for analyzing human conduct led to its abandonment in classical psychology before the turn of the century, but it lurks as the basic process upon which verbal attitude scales rest. The plain fact is that human beings simply are incapable of the degree of self-understanding that is assumed for precise measurement with current techniques that we now have.

The second assumption underlying present verbal measurement techniques is the proposition that the human being *can* make precise discriminations between his self concept (if he *could* formulate it clearly) and sample behaviors or beliefs posed in scale items. This assumption can be shown to be unrealistic. A large body of psychophysical literature is available which testifies to the imperfect nature of the human being as a discriminal mechanism. These facts have been understood since the astronomers first discovered the "personal equation." Even in such a relatively uncomplicated matter as judging which is the heavier of two physical weights, the ordinary human being produces a "discriminal dispersion," or normal distribution of judgments. It is somewhat idle to hope, then, that in an analogous judging process with the vastly more complicated stimuli of scale items and self-conceived attitude orientations, that these difficulties will vanish.

In short, because of inadequate, self-analysis powers, and limitations in discriminal ability, we must not hope for great advances in our ability to measure and understand attitudinal phenomena insofar as such attempts employ traditional verbal attitude measurement technology.[30]

STEPS FOR THE REFINEMENT OF THE ATTITUDE CONCEPT

In order to resolve some of the issues reviewed in the present paper, it appears that researchers who employ the attitude concept in their thinking, investigating, and writing must be prepared to alter their conception to fit some of the facts and realities which research on attitudes has revealed to us. One possible step for furthering our understanding of attitudinal phenomena and for clarification of the concept would be to abandon the awkward intervening or latent variable concept, including more complicated versions of the same idea. We have successfully abandoned, without serious loss, other conceptual tools such as "instinct" when their utility came to an end. Such an abandonment would leave us with definitions of attitudinal phenomena of the more observable sort we have called probability definitions.

But, this *alone* would prove to be of little help. While probability conceptions of attitudes have the virtue of simplicity and are easily translated into behavioral terms, they have certain potential disadvantages. As posed in the literature, such definitions are ordinarily very general, in that they do not specify the exact behavior forms whose probabilities are to be observed. Furthermore, they do not indicate clearly the observable operations which constitute the operational definition of the concept. This form of conceptualization does not distinguish "attitude behavior" from other consistent modes of acceptance-avoidance responses to objects.

A second step, then, for refinement of our conceptual apparatus in this area would be to *link our definitions more firmly to the methods we employ in measurement.* We must start with the concept of attitude defined as specified probabilities of a syndrome of responses and then carefully specify three things: (1) the *exact* "social object" which presumably provides the stimulation for these responses, (2) the *exact* nature and number of different classes or dimensions of responses, and (3) the *exact* measuring or observational operations employed to obtain a quantitative statement of an individual's response probability for each class of responses. Through adherence to these specifics we may be able to communicate clearly to each other, and to ourselves, just what we mean when we use the term "attitude."

With regard to the first recommendation above, this goal of increasing "stimulus specificity" has already directed research into exploring the effects on verbal attitudes by posing Negroes of *specific occupational categories* as the attitude objects. It has been found that verbal responses, regarding conceptions of social distance, vary significantly for white subjects as the "attitude objects" are Negroes of varying occupational statuses as opposed to simply Negroes in general.[31]

Another research direction is suggested by the second recommendation above. Many kinds of responses other than verbal responses can be used to make inferences concerning attitudes. A group of studies which have attempted to assess attitudes from overt behavior has been mentioned.[32] It has been noted elsewhere that attitudes have correlates within the autonomic-physiological responses of the individual. Inferences concerning the emotional dimension of attitudes can be made from measures of variations in such behaviors as galvanic skin responses and other autonomic responses such as heart activity.[33]

Exact specification of the class of response (verbal, overt, emotional autonomic) would aid considerably in the clarification of thinking concerning the degree to which predictions can be made from one class of response to another. The fallacy of expected correspondence resulted historically from the conception of attitudes as *general* response tendencies which implied that consistency should appear from one class of behavior to another, that verbal attitudes "should" predict over behavior. It has taken a quarter century of research, some of which has been summarized in previous sections, to refute this conception. Attitudes appear to be most usefully conceptualized as *specific,* in the sense that they may be viewed as probabilities of specific forms of response to specific social objects, or specific classes of social objects.

What are the implications of these claims regarding the specificity of attitudes for such general orientations as "the authoritarian attitude"? From our point of view there is no such thing as an "authoritarian attitude" because it is not derived as an inference from observation of responses to any specific object or class of objects. Rather, it is a rubric representing a higher level of abstraction referring to a system of attitudes toward more specific objects. The specific conception of attitude in no way invalidates the utility of such higher level abstractions.

The issues and research directions discussed in the present paper point to an obvious conclusion. The concept attitude is still in a surprisingly crude state of formulation considering its widespread use. At best it barely qualifies as a scientific concept. However, in the history of science crudely developed concepts have at times produced surprisingly useful results. The fact that attitude, like such concepts as "social organization," "class," "intelligence," and "motivation," has been ambiguous has not prevented the accumulation of a large body of research findings in a wide variety of disciplines. We do not share the view of those critics who maintain that because the concept has been (and still is) imprecise it should be abandoned. We feel that the history of the concept needs now to be moved into another stage in its development and it is hoped that the analysis and the suggestions above will aid in this transition.

NOTES

[1]See some of the archaic definitions of attitude quoted in *The Oxford English Dictionary*, Vol. 1 (The Oxford University Press, 1933), p. 553.

[2]Alexander Bain, *Mental Science* (New York: Appleton and Co., 1868), p. 158.

[3]A quotation cited from Herbert Spencer. See: The *Oxford English Dictionary*, *op. cit.*

[4]Edwin G. Boring, *A History of Experimental Psychology* (New York: Appleton-Century-Crofts, Inc., 1929). See especially Chapter 15, "Wilhelm Wundt," pp. 310-344.

[5]*Ibid.*, pp. 310-344.

[6]Gordon Allport, "Attitudes," in Carl Murchison (ed) *A Handbook of Social Psychology* (Worcester, Mass.: Clark University Press, 1935), p. 800.

[7]W. I. Thomas and Florian Znaniecki, *The Polish Peasant in Europe and America* (Boston: Badger, 1918).

[8]L. L. Thurstone and E. J. Chave, *The Measurement of Attitude* (Chicago: The University of Chicago Press, 1929). Also: Emory S. Bogardus, "Measuring Social Distance," *Journal of Applied Sociology*, Vol. 9, 1925, pp. 299-308.

[9]The interested reader is referred to Torgeson's comprehensive survey of scaling techniques for the measurement of psychological attributes (including attitudes). Cf. Warren W. Torgeson, *Theory and Methods of Scaling* (New York: John Wiley and Sons, 1958). Another work more specifically dealing with applications of scaling techniques to attitude measurement is Allen L. Edwards, *Techniques of Attitude Scale Construction* (New York: Appleton-Century-Crofts, Inc., 1957).

[10]Erland Nelson, "Attitudes," *The Journal of General Psychology*, Vol. 21, 1939, pp. 367-436.

[11]To be sure, a variety of elements have been included in attitude definitions by one writer or another. Some call attention to motivational processes, cognitive elements, perceptual orientations, or other additional features which they feel are important. We do not imply that such phenomena have no importance or may not be essential. We are focusing attention on the logical structure of the concept and the general framework within which attitudes are treated as inferences from behavior.

[12]Quoted in Bert F. Green, "Attitude Measurement," in Gardner Lindzey (ed), *Handbook of Social Psychology* (Cambridge, Mass.: Addison-Wesley, 1954), p. 335. The authors wish to acknowledge their indebtedness to Green's article, which, in the view of the present authors, is unexcelled in the literature on attitudes.

[13]*Ibid.*

[14]*Ibid.*

[15]Morris Cohen and Ernest Nagel, *An Introduction to Logic and Scientific Method* (New York: Harcourt, Brace, 1934). See especially Chapter 20.

[16]Quoted in Green, *op. cit.*, p. 335.

[17]*Ibid.*

[18]Alfred R. Lindesmith and Anselm Strauss, *Social Psychology* (New York: Dryden, 1956), p. 494.

[19]Green, *op. cit.*, p. 335

[20]Angus Campbell, et. al., *The American Voter* (New York: Wiley, 1960), p. 28.

[21]For a discussion of such concepts see: Carl Hempel, "Concept Formation in Empirical Science," *International Encyclopedia of Unified Science*, Vol. 2, No. 7 (Chicago: University of Chicago Press).

[22]Green, *op. cit.*, p. 335.

[23]Lindesmith and Strauss, *op. cit.*, p. 494.

[24]R. T. LaPiere, "Attitudes vs. Action," *Social Forces*, Vol. 13, 1934, pp. 230-237.

[25]Bernard Kutner, Carol Wilkins, and Penny Yarrow, "Verbal Attitudes and Overt Behavior Involving Race Prejudice," *Journal of Abnormal and Social Psychology*, Vol. 47, 1952, pp. 649-652.

[26]Joseph Lohman and Dietrich Reitzers, "Deliberately Organized Groups and Racial Behaviors," *American Sociological Review,* Vol. 19, June 1954, pp. 342-344.

[27]R. D. Minard, "Race Relations in the Pocahontas Coal Fields," *Journal of Social Issues,* Vol. 8, No. 1. 1952, pp. 29-44.

[28]The "expectation of inconsistency" advocated by the present authors poses serious problems for the determination of the validity of attitude scales. Ubiquitous indeed are the demands that those who construct attitude scales show the validity of their instruments by demonstrating that people behave overtly in a manner consistent with their verbal attitude scale scores. But if, as we aver, *inconsistency* between verbal scale scores and other overt actions is to be expected, then the use of *external* criteria for testing validity is ruled out. Bert Green explicitly recognizes this problem, maintaining: "by definition, an attitude scale for one universe cannot measure a second universe." (Green, *op. cit.*, p. 340). Green suggests the use of Gulliksen's tests of "intrinsic validity" as a possible solution to the problem. The typical test of intrinsic validity involves the rating of items by a "group of experts."

[29]See Warren W. Torgeson, *op. cit*; also Allen L. Edwards, *op. cit.*

[30]See Melvin DeFleur and William R. Catton, Jr., "The Limits of Determinacy in Attitude Measurement," *Social Forces*, Vol. 35, No. 4, 1957, pp. 295-300.

[31]Frank R. Westie, "Negro-White Status Differentials and Social Distance," *American Sociological Review,* Vol. 17, October 1952, pp. 550-558.

[32]See also the discussion of this issue in Melvin L. DeFleur and Frank R. Westie, "Verbal Attitudes and Overt Acts," *American Sociological Review,* Vol. 23, 1958, pp. 667-673.

[33]Research exploring this area of "behavior" is summarized in Frank R. Westie and Melvin L. DeFleur, "Autonomic Responses and Their Relationship to Race Attitudes," *Journal of Abnormal and Social Psychology,* Vol. 58, 1959, pp. 340-347.

2

ATTITUDES VS. ACTIONS

Richard T. LaPiere

By definition, a social attitude is a behaviour pattern, anticipatory set or tendency, predisposition to specific adjustment to designated social situations, or, more simply, a conditioned response to social stimuli.[1] Terminological usage differs, but students who have concerned themselves with attitudes apparently agree that they are acquired out of social experience and provide the individual organism with some degree of preparation to adjust, in a well-defined way, to certain types of social situations if and when these situations arise. It would seem, therefore, that the totality of the social attitudes of a single individual would include all his socially acquired personality which is involved in the making of adjustments to other human beings.

But by derivation social attitudes are seldom more than a verbal response to a symbolic situation. For the conventional method of measuring social attitudes is to ask questions (usually in writing) which demand a verbal adjustment to an entirely symbolic situation. Because it is easy, cheap, and mechanical, the attitudinal questionnaire is rapidly becoming a major method of sociological and socio-psychological investigation. The technique is simple. Thus from a hundred or a thousand responses to the question "Would you get up to give an Armenian woman your seat in a street car?" the investigator derives the "attitude" of non-Armenian males towards Armenian females. Now the question may be constructed with elaborate skill and hidden with consummate cunning in a maze of supplementary or even irrelevant questions yet all that has been obtained is a symbolic response to a symbolic situation. The words "Armenian woman" do not constitute an Armenian woman of flesh and

Reprinted from *Social Forces* (Vol. 13, December, 1934, pp. 230-237) by permission of *Social Forces* and the University of North Carolina Press.

blood, who might be tall or squat, fat or thin, old or young, well or poorly dressed—who might, in fact, be a goddess or just another old and dirty hag. And the questionnaire response, whether it be "yes" or "no," is but a verbal reaction and this does not involve rising from the seat or stolidly avoiding the hurt eyes of the hypothetical woman and the derogatory stares of other streetcar occupants. Yet, ignoring these limitations, the diligent investigator will jump briskly from his factual evidence to the unwarranted conclusion that he has measured the "anticipatory behavior patterns" of non-Armenian males towards Armenian females encountered on streetcars. Usually he does not stop here, but proceeds to deduce certain general conclusions regarding the social relationships between Armenians and non-Armenians. Most of us have applied the questionnaire technique with greater caution, but not I fear with any greater certainty of success.

Some years ago I endeavored to obtain comparative data on the degree of French and English antipathy towards dark-skinned peoples.[2] The informal questionnaire technique was used, but, although the responses so obtained were exceedingly consistent, I supplemented them with what I then considered an index to overt behavior. The hypothesis as then stated *seemed* entirely logical. "Whatever our attitude on the validity of 'verbalization' may be, it must be recognized that any study of attitudes through direct questioning is open to serious objection, both because of the limitations of the sampling method and because in classifying attitudes the inaccuracy of human judgment is an inevitable variable. In this study, however, there is corroborating evidence on these attitudes in the policies adopted by hotel proprietors. Nothing could be used as a more accurate index of color prejudice than the admission or nonadmission of colored people to hotels. For the proprietor must reflect the group attitude in his policy regardless of his own feelings in the matter. Since he determines what the group attitude is towards Negroes through the expression of that attitude in overt behavior and over a long period of actual experience, the results will be exceptionally free from those disturbing factors which inevitably affect the effort to study attitudes by direct questioning."

But at that time I overlooked the fact that what I was obtaining from the hotel proprietors was still a "verbalized" reaction to a symbolic situation. The response to a Negro's request for lodgings might have been an excellent index of the attitude of hotel patrons towards living in the same hotel as a Negro. Yet to ask the proprietor "Do you permit members of the Negro race to stay here?" does not, it appears, measure his potential response to an actual Negro.

All measurement of attitudes by the questionnaire technique proceeds on the assumption that there is a mechanical relationship between symbolic and nonsymbolic behavior. It is simple enough to prove that there is no *necessary* correlation between speech and action, between response to words and to the realities they symbolize. A parrot can be taught to swear, a child to sing "Frankie and Johnny" in the Mae West manner. The words will have no meaning to either child or parrot. But to prove that there is no *necessary* relationship does not prove that such a relationship may not exist. There need be no relationship between what the hotel proprietor says he will do and what he actually does when confronted with a colored patron. Yet there may be. Certainly we are justified in assuming that the verbal response of the hotel proprietor would be more likely to indicate what he would actually do than would the verbal response of people whose personal feelings are less subordinated to economic expediency. However, the following study indicates that the reliability of even such responses is very small indeed.

Beginning in 1930 and continuing for two years thereafter, I had the good fortune to travel rather extensively with a young Chinese student and his wife.[3] Both were personable, charming, and quick to win the admiration and respect of those they had the opportunity to become intimate with. But they were foreign-born Chinese, a fact that could not be disguised. Knowing the general "attitude" of Americans towards the Chinese as indicated by the "social distance" studies which have been made, it was with considerable trepidation that I first approached a hotel clerk in their company. Perhaps that clerk's eyebrows lifted slightly, but he accommodated us without a show of hesitation. And this in the "best" hotel in a small town noted for its narrow and bigoted "attitude" towards Orientals. Two months later I passed that way again, phoned the hotel and asked if they would accommodate "an important Chinese gentleman." The reply was an unequivocal "No." That aroused my curiosity and led to this study.

In something like ten thousand miles of motor travel, twice across the United States, up and down the Pacific Coast, we met definite rejection from those asked to serve us just once. We were received at 66 hotels, auto camps, and "Tourist Homes," refused at one. We were served in 184 restaurants and cafes scattered throughout the country and treated with what I judged to be more than ordinary consideration in 72 of them. Accurate and detailed records were kept of all these instances. An effort, necessarily subjective, was made to evaluate the overt response of hotel clerks, bell boys, elevator operators, and waitresses to the presence of my Chinese friends. The factors entering into the situations were varied as far and as often as possible. Control was not, of course, as exacting as that required by laboratory experimentation. But it was as rigid as is humanly possible in human situations. For example, I did not take the "test" subjects into my confidence fearing that their behavior might become self-conscious and thus abnormally affect the response of others towards them. Whenever possible I let my Chinese friend negotiate for accommodations (while I concerned myself with the car or luggage) or sent them into a restaurant ahead of me. In this way I attempted to "factor" myself out. We sometimes patronized high-class establishments after a hard and dusty day on the road and stopped at inferior auto camps when in our most presentable condition.

In the end I was forced to conclude that those factors which most influenced the behavior of others towards the Chinese had nothing at all to do with race. Quality and condition of clothing, appearance of baggage (by which, it seems, hotel clerks are prone to base their quick evaluations), cleanliness and neatness were far more significant for person to person reaction in the situations I was studying than skin pigmentation, straight black hair, slanting eyes, and flat noses. And yet an air of self-confidence might entirely offset the "unfavorable" impression made by dusty clothes and the usual disorder to appearance consequent upon some hundred miles of motor travel. A supercilious desk clerk in a hotel of noble aspirations could not refuse his master's hospitality to people who appeared to take their request as a perfectly normal and conventional thing, though they might look like tin-can tourists and two of them belong to the racial category "Oriental." On the other hand, I became rather adept at approaching hotel clerks with that peculiar crab-wise manner which is so effective in provoking a somewhat scornful disregard. And then a bland smile would serve to reverse the entire situation. Indeed, it appeared that a genial smile was the most effective password to acceptance. My Chinese friends were skillful smilers, which may account, in part, for the fact that we received but one rebuff in all our experience. Finally, I was impressed with the fact that even where some tension developed due to the strangeness of the Chinese it would evaporate immediately when they spoke in unaccented English.

The one instance in which we were refused accommodations is worth recording here. The place was a small California town, a rather inferior auto-camp into which we drove in a very dilapidated car piled with camp equipment. It was early evening, the light so dim that the proprietor found it somewhat difficult to decide the genus *voyageur* to which we belonged. I left the car and spoke to him. He hesitated, wavered, said he was not sure that he had two cabins, meanwhile edging towards our car. The realization that the two occupants were Orientals turned the balance or, more likely, gave him the excuse he was looking for. "No," he said, "I don't take Japs!" In a more pretentious establishment we secured accommodations, and with an extra flourish of hospitality.

To offset this one flat refusal were the many instances in which the physical peculiarities of the Chinese served to heighten curiosity. With few exceptions this curiosity was considerately hidden behind an exceptional interest in serving us. Of course, outside of the Pacific Coast region, New York, and Chicago, the Chinese physiognomy attracts attention.

It is different, hence noticeable. But the principal effect this curiosity has upon the behavior of those who cater to the traveler's needs is to make them more attentive, more responsive, more reliable. A Chinese companion is to be recommended to the white traveling in his native land. Strange features when combined with "human" speech and action seem, at times, to heighten sympathetic response, perhaps on the same principle that makes us uncommonly sympathetic towards the dog that has a "human" expression in his face.

What I am trying to say is that in only one out of 251 instances in which we purchased goods or services necessitating intimate human relationships did the fact that my companions were Chinese adversely affect us. Factors entirely unassociated with race were, in the main, the determinant of significant variations in our reception. It would appear reasonable to conclude that the "attitude" of the American people, as reflected in the behavior of those who are for pecuniary reasons presumably most sensitive to the antipathies of their white clientele, is anything but negative towards the Chinese. In terms of "social distance" we might conclude that native Caucasians are not averse to residing in the same hotels, autocamps, and "Tourist Homes" as Chinese and will with complacency accept the presence of Chinese at an adjoining table in restaurant or cafe. It does not follow that there is revealed a distinctly "positive" attitude towards the Chinese, that whites prefer the Chinese to other whites. But the facts as gathered certainly preclude the conclusion that there is an intense prejudice towards the Chinese.

Yet the existence of this prejudice, very intense, is proven by a conventional "attitude" study. To provide a comparison of symbolic reaction to symbolic social situations with actual reaction to real social situations, I "questionnaired" the establishments which we patronized during the two-year period. Six months were permitted to lapse between the time I obtained the overt reaction and the symbolic. It was hoped that the effects of the actual experience with Chinese guests, adverse or otherwise, would have faded during the intervening time. To the hotel or restaurant a questionnaire was mailed with an accompanying letter purporting to be a special and personal plea for response. The questionnaires all asked the same question, "Will you accept members of the Chinese race as guests in your establishment?" Two types of questionnaire were used. In one this question was inserted among similar queries concerning Germans, French, Japanese, Russians, Armenians, Jews, Negroes, Italians, and Indians. In the other the pertinent question was unencumbered. With persistence, completed replies were obtained from 128 of the establishments we had visited; 81 restaurants and cafes and 47 hotels, auto-camps, and "Tourist Homes." In response to the relevant question 92 per cent of the former and 91 per cent of the latter replied "No." The remainder replied "Uncertain; depend upon circumstances." From the woman proprietor of a small auto-camp I received the only "Yes," accompanied by a chatty letter describing the nice visit she had had with a Chinese gentleman and his sweet wife during the previous summer.

A rather unflattering interpretation might be put upon the fact that those establishments who had provided for our needs so graciously were, some months later, verbally antagonistic towards hypothetical Chinese. To factor this experience out responses were secured from 32 hotels and 96 restaurants located in approximately the same regions, but uninfluenced by this particular experience with Oriental clients. In this, as in the former case, both types of questionnaires were used. The results indicate that neither the type of questionnaire nor the fact of previous experience had important bearing upon the symbolic response to symbolic social situations.

It is impossible to make direct comparison between the reactions secured through questionnaires and from actual experience. On the basis of the above data it would appear foolhardy for a Chinese to attempt to travel in the United States. And yet, as I have shown, actual experience indicates that the American people, as represented by the personnel of hotels, restaurants, etc., are not at all averse to fraternizing with Chinese within the limitations which apply to social relationships between Americans themselves. The evaluations which follow are undoubtedly subject to the criticism which any human judgment must withstand. But the fact is that, although they began their travels in this country with considerable trepidation, my Chinese friends soon lost all fear that they might receive a rebuff. At first somewhat timid and considerably dependent upon me for guidance and support, they came in time to feel fully self-reliant and would approach new social situations without the slightest hesitation.

TABLE I

DISTRIBUTION OF RESULTS FROM QUESTIONNAIRE STUDY OF ESTABLISHMENT "POLICY" REGARDING ACCEPTANCE OF CHINESE AS GUESTS

Replies are to the question: "Will you accept members of the Chinese race as guests in your establishment?"

	Hotels, etc., Visited		Hotels, etc., not Visited		Restaurants, etc., Visited		Restaurants, etc., not Visited	
Total	47		32		81		96	
	1*	2*	1	2	1	2	1	2
Number replying	22	25	20	12	43	38	51	45
No	20	23	19	11	40	35	37	41
Undecided: depend upon circumstances	1	2	1	1	3	3	4	3
Yes	1	0	0	0	0	0	0	1

*Column (1) indicates in each case those responses to questionnaires which concerned Chinese only. The figures in columns (2) are from the questionnaires in which the above was inserted among questions regarding Germans, French, Japanese, etc.

The conventional questionnaire undoubtedly has significant value for the measurement of "political attitudes." The presidential polls conducted by the *Literary Digest* have proven that. But a "political attitude" is exactly what the questionnaire can be justly held to measure; a verbal response to a symbolic situation. Few citizens are ever faced with the necessity of adjusting themselves to the presence of the political leaders whom, periodically, they must vote for—or against. Especially is this true with regard to the president, and it is in relation to political attitudes towards presidential candidates that we have our best evidence. But while the questionnaire may indicate what the voter will do when he goes to vote, it does not and cannot reveal what he will do when he meets Candidate Jones on the street, in his office, at his club, on the golf course, or wherever two men may meet and adjust in some way one to the other.

The questionnaire is probably our only means of determining "religious attitudes." An honest answer to the question "Do you believe in

TABLE II

DISTRIBUTION OF RESULTS OBTAINED FROM ACTUAL EXPERIENCE IN THE SITUATION SYMBOLIZED IN THE QUESTIONNAIRE STUDY

Conditions	Hotels, etc.		Restaurants, etc.	
	Accompanied by investigator	Chinese not so accompanied as inception of situation*	Accompanied by investigator	Chinese not so accompanied at inception of situation
Total	55	12	165	19
Reception very much better than investigator would expect to have received had he been alone, but under otherwise similar circumstances	19	6	63	9
Reception different only to extent of heightened curiosity, such as investigator might have incurred were he alone but dressed in manner unconventional to region yet not incongruous	22	3	76	6
Reception "normal"	9	2	21	3
Reception perceptibly hesitant and not to be explained on other than "racial" grounds	3	1	4	1
Reception definitely, though temporarily, embarrassing	1	0	1	0
Not accepted	1	0	0	0

*When the investigator was not present at the inception of the situation the judgments were based upon what transpired after he joined the Chinese. Since intimately acquainted with them it is probable that errors in judgment were no more frequent under these conditions than when he was able to witness the inception as well as results of the situation.

God?" reveals all there is to be measured. "God" is a symbol; "belief" a verbal expression. So here, too, the questionnaire is efficacious. But if we would know the emotional responsiveness of a person to the spoken or written word "God" some other method of investigation must be used. And if we would know the extent to which that responsiveness restrains his behavior it is to his behavior that we must look, not to his questionnaire response. Ethical precepts are, I judge, something more than verbal professions. There would seem little to be gained from asking a man if his religious faith prevents him from committing sin. Of course it does—on paper. But "moral attitudes" must have a significance in the adjustment to actual situations or they are not worth the studying. Sitting at my desk in California I can predict with a high degree of certainty what an "average" business man in an average Mid-Western city will reply to the question "Would you engage in sexual intercourse with a prostitute in a Paris brothel?" Yet no one, least of all the man himself, can predict what he would actually do should he by some misfortune find himself face to face with the situation in question. His moral "attitudes" are no doubt already stamped into his personality. But just what those habits are which will be invoked to provide him with some sort of adjustment to this situation is quite indeterminate.

It is highly probable that when the "Southern Gentleman" says he will not permit Negroes to reside in his neighborhood we have a verbal response to a symbolic situation which reflects the "attitudes" which would become operative in an actual situation. But there is no need to ask such a question of the true "Southern Gentleman." We knew it all the time. I am inclined to think that in most instances where the questionnaire does reveal non-symbolic attitudes the case is much the same. It is only when we cannot easily observe what people do in certain types of situations that the questionnaire is resorted to. But it is just here that the danger in the questionnaire technique arises. If Mr. A adjusts himself to Mr. B in a specified way we can deduce from his behavior that he has a certain "attitude" towards Mr. B and, perhaps, all of Mr. B's class. But if no such overt adjustment is made it is impossible to discover what A's adjustment would be should the situation arise. A questionnaire will reveal what Mr. A writes or says when confronted with a certain combination of words. But not what he will do when he meets Mr. B. Mr. B is a great deal more than a series of words. He is a man and he acts. His action is not necessarily what Mr. A "imagines" it will be when he reacts verbally to the symbol "Mr. B."

No doubt a considerable part of the data which the social scientist deals with can be obtained by the questionnaire method. The census reports are based upon verbal questionnaires and I do not doubt their basic integrity. If we wish to know how many children a man has, his income, the size of his home, his age, and the condition of his parents, we can reasonably ask him. These things he has frequently and conventionally converted into verbal responses. He is competent to report upon them, and will do so accurately, unless indeed he wishes to do otherwise. A careful investigator could no doubt even find out by verbal means whether the man fights with his wife (frequently, infrequently, or not at all), though the neighbors would be a more reliable source. But we should not expect to obtain by the questionnaire method his "anticipatory set or tendency" to action should his wife pack up and go home to Mother, should Elder Son get into trouble with the neighbor's daughter, the President assume the status of a dictator, the Japanese take over the rest of China, or a Chinese gentleman come to pay a social call.

Only a verbal reaction to an entirely symbolic situation can be secured by the questionnaire. It may indicate what the responder would actually do when confronted with the situation symbolized in the question, but there is no assurance that it will. And so to call the response a reflection of a "social attitude" is to entirely disregard the definition commonly given for the phrase "attitude." If social attitudes are to be conceptualized as partially integrated habit sets which will become operative under specific circumstances and *lead to* a particular pattern of adjustment they must, in the main, be derived from a study of humans behaving in actual social situations. They must not be imputed on the basis of questionnaire data.

The questionnaire is cheap, easy, and mechanical. The study of human behavior is time consuming, intellectually fatiguing, and depends for its success upon the ability of the investigator. The former method gives quantitative results, the latter mainly qualitative. Quantitative measurements are quantitatively accurate; qualitative evaluations are always subject to the errors of human judgment. Yet it would seem far more worth while to make a shrewd guess regarding that which is essential than to accurately measure that which is likely to prove quite irrelevant.

NOTES

[1]See Daniel D. Droba, "Topical Summaries of Current Literature," *The American Journal of Sociology,* 1934, p. 513.

[2]"Race Prejudice: France and England," *Social Forces,* September, 1928, pp. 101-111.

[3]The results of this study have been withheld until the present time out of consideration for their feelings.

II

DISCOVERY OF ATTITUDE—BEHAVIOR INCONSISTENCY

3

BEHAVIORAL SUPPORT FOR OPINION CHANGE

Leon Festinger

The last three decades have seen a steady and impressive growth in our knowledge concerning attitudes and opinions—how they are formed, how they are changed, and their relations to one another. For example, we now know a good deal about the effects on opinion change of varying the structure of a persuasive communication—whether it is one-sided or two-sided, whether it is fear-arousing or not, whether pro arguments precede or follow con arguments, and whether it is attributed to trustworthy or untrustworthy sources. Phenomena such as sleeper effects, immunization to counterpropaganda, assimilation and contrast effects, are beginning to be understood. We have also learned a great deal about attitude and opinion change in small face-to-face groups, about the relationship between personality variables and opinion change, about factors affecting resistance to persuasive communications, and so on. I do not intend to review seriously all this work. Anyone who wants to has only to start looking for the names of Hovland, Janis, Kelley, McGuire, Newcomb, Katz, Peak, Kelman—there are many others but these would do for a start.

There is, however, one important gap in our knowledge about attitude and opinion change—a gap that is doubly peculiar when seen in relation to the strong behavioral emphasis in psychology in the United States. I first realized the existence of this gap on reading a manuscript by Arthur R. Cohen. Let me read to you the paragraph that startled me. Cohen's manuscript focuses on the ". . . ways in which persuasive communicators and members of one's social group come to influence the attitudes of the individual." In his concluding remarks he says:

Reprinted from *The Public Opinion Quarterly* (Vol. 28, Fall, 1964, pp. 404-417) by permission of the author and *The Public Opinion Quarterly*.

> Probably the most important and long-range research problem in the sphere of attitude theory has to do with the implications of attitude change for subsequent behavior. In general, most of the researchers whose work we have examined make the widespread psychological assumption that since attitudes are evaluative predispositions, they have consequences for the way people act toward others, for the programs they actually carry out and the manner in which they perform these programs. Thus attitudes are always seen to be a precursor to behavior, a determinant of what behaviors the individual will actually go about doing in his daily affairs. However, though most psychologists assume such a state of affairs, very little work on attitude change has explicitly dealt with the behavior that may follow upon a change in attitudes. Most researchers in this field are content to demonstrate that there are factors which affect attitude change and that these factors are open to orderly exploration, without actually carrying through to the point where they examine the links between changed attitudes and changes in learning, performance, perception and interaction. Until a good deal more experimental investigation demonstrates that attitude change has implications for subsequent behavior, we cannot be certain that our change procedures do anything more than cause cognitive realignments, or even, perhaps, that the attitude concept has any critical significance whatever for psychology.[1]

I was, at first reading, slightly skeptical about the assertion that there is a dearth of studies relating attitude or opinion change to behavior. Although I could not think of any offhand, it seemed reasonable that many of them would be scattered through the journals. Consequently, I started looking for such studies and asked others if they knew of any. (After prolonged search, with the help of many others, I succeeded in locating only three relevant studies, one of which is of dubious relevance and one of which required re-analysis of data. The absence of research, and of theoretical thinking, about the effect of attitude change on subsequent behavior is indeed astonishing.)

Before telling you about these three studies I would like to make sure that the problem is clear. I am not raising the question of whether or not attitudes are found to relate to relevant behavior. Let us accept the conclusion that they are related, at least to some extent, although even here relatively few studies in the literature address themselves to this question. A fairly recent study by De Fleur and Westie provides a good example of the kind of relationship between existing attitudes and relevant overt behavior that may be found under controlled conditions with good measurement.[2]

The investigators obtained measures of attitudes toward Negroes from 250 college students. The particular attitude measure employed was apparently reliable, test-retest measures over a five-week interval yielding a correlation of +.96. They selected, from these 250 students, 23 who had scored in the upper quartile and 23 who had scored in the lower quartile, matching the two groups on a number of other variables. These two extreme groups were then compared on a rather clever measure of overt behavior with respect to Negroes. A situation was constructed in which it was believable to ask each of them to sign an authorization permitting use of a photograph of himself sitting with a Negro. The subject was free not to permit the photograph to be taken at all, or, if he signed the authorization, to permit any of a number of possible uses of the photograph ranging from very limited use in laboratory experiments to, at the other extreme, use in a nationwide publicity campaign. The signing of the authorization was real, and may be regarded as an instance of overt commitment. As the authors say: "In American society, the affixing of one's signature to a document is a particularly significant act. The signing of checks, contracts, agreements, and the like is clearly understood to indicate a binding obligation on the part of the signer to abide by the provisions of the document."

What, then, is the relationship found between the measure of general attitudes toward Negroes and the behavioral measure? Table 1 presents a summary of the data. Clearly, there is a relationship between the attitude and the behavior. Those who are prejudiced are less willing to have the photograph taken and widely used. True, it is a relatively small relationship, although highly significant statistically. The smallness of the relationship is emphasized when we recall that we are comparing extreme groups. But nevertheless, it is comforting to know that a relation does exist. One can understand the smallness of the relationship by realizing that overt behavior is affected by many other variables in addition to one's own private attitude.

But data such as this do not answer the question we wish to raise here. The fact that existing attitudes relate to overt behavior does not tell us whether or not an attitude *change* brought about by exposure to a persuasive communication will be reflected in a *change* in subsequent behavior. To answer this question we need studies in which, after people have been exposed to a persuasive communication, a measure of attitude or opinion is obtained on the basis of which attitude change can be assessed. Such studies must also, some time later, provide an indication of behavior change relevant to the opinion or attitude, so that one can see whether the cognitive change had any effect on subsequent behavior. We may even be content with studies in which overt behavior is not actually observed. If the subjects are asked questions about what they actually did, this may suffice.

As I mentioned before, we were able to locate only three studies reasonably close to meeting these requirements. One of these, the data from which I reanalyzed, was part of a larger series of studies conducted by Maccoby et al.[3] These investigators selected a sample of mothers whose only child was between three and twelve months old. Each of these mothers was interviewed and was asked, among other questions, at what age she believed toilet training of the child should begin. Three weeks later, each of these women was again interviewed. This time, however, two different procedures were followed. Half the mothers, selected at random, were designated as a control group and were simply re-interviewed. In this second interview they were again asked the age at which they thought toilet training of the child should begin. The other half of the sample, the experimental group, were first exposed to a persuasive communication and then re-interviewed with the same interview used in the control group. The persuasive communication was a specially prepared, illustrated pamphlet entitled "When to Toilet Train Your Child." Each mother in the experimental group was handed this pamphlet and asked to read it, then and there, while the interviewer waited. The pamphlet argued strongly for starting toilet training at the age of twenty-four months. The re-interview occurred immediately after the mother had read the pamphlet. Thus, a comparison of the results of the two groups on the first and second interviews indicated how successful the pamphlet was in changing their opinion concerning when toilet training should start.

TABLE 1

RELATIONSHIP BETWEEN RACE ATTITUDES AND LEVEL OF SIGNED AGREEMENT TO BE PHOTOGRAPHED WITH NEGRO

Signed Level of Agreement	*Prejudiced Group*	*Unprejudiced Group*
Below mean	18	9
Above mean	5	14

In order to assess the persistence of the change in opinion brought about by the pamphlet, both groups of mothers were again interviewed about six months later and were again asked at what age they thought toilet training should begin. Finally, and most importantly for our present concern, about a year after the initial interviews, on the assumption that most of the mothers would have started toilet training already, they were interviewed again and asked at *what age they had actually started*. This last may certainly be regarded as a simple, and probably truthful, report of their actual behavior. Consequently, one can look at the relationship between attitude change and behavior.

In any study in which people are interviewed and re-interviewed over a period of a year, there is an inevitable attrition. Some mothers left the area, others simply could not be reached for one or another interview, and the like. Actually, in this study the drop-out rate was remarkably small. About 80 per cent of the initial sample was actually interviewed all four times, 45 mothers in the experimental group and 47 mothers in the control group. At the time of the fourth interview 34 mothers in each of the two groups had begun toilet training their child and, consequently, it is only for these 68 mothers that we have a measure of actual behavior. The other 24 mothers (11 in the experimental group and 13 in the control group) who had not yet started toilet training by the time of the last interview were asked when they intended to start. Although for these we cannot say that we have a measure of actual behavior, we will present the results for them also.

First, however, let us look at the data presented in Table 2 for those who had started toilet training. The data are rather startling to contemplate—although perhaps not too startling. It is clear that the persuasive communication was quite effective in immediately changing the opinions of the mothers in the experimental group. The change, on the average, was to advocate toilet training 2.3 months later than on the initial interview. The control group did not change materially—actually moving slightly in the direction of advocating earlier toilet training.

Six months later the change was still maintained, although somewhat reduced in magnitude. The experimental group still advocated that toilet training begin 1.6 months later than they had on the initial interview. The control group, however, also now advocated somewhat later toilet training. Nevertheless, there was still a clear difference between the two groups.

When we examine when these mothers actually started to toilet train their child, however, we are met with a surprise. There is, if anything, a reverse relationship between attitude change and behavior. The mothers in the experimental group actually started toilet training 1.2 months later on the average than they had initially advocated. But the mothers in the control group, who had never been subjected to any experimental persuasive communication to change their opinion, started toilet training 2.0 months later than their initial opinion would have indicated. Apparently, in the usual American home, as the child gets older, events conspire to delay toilet training somewhat beyond what the mothers think is probably desirable. But the opinion change in the experimental group clearly did not carry over to affect behavior.

We can also see evidence of the same thing in the data for those mothers who had not as yet started to toilet train their children at the time of the fourth interview. These are presented in Table 3. Here again it is clear that the persuasive communication had a strong immediate effect on the opinions of the mothers in the experimental group and that, six months later, this effect had been maintained. The difference between the control and the experimental groups was almost as large after six months as it was immediately after the persuasive communication. It is also clear that events conspired to make these mothers delay the actual onset of toilet training and conspired equally for both groups. The changed opinion had no effect on the actual behavior of these mothers. The difference between their initial opinion and their intention at the time of the fourth interview was high because these data are for a selected group who had not yet started to toilet train their children. The important thing, however, is that there was no difference between the experimental and control groups.

TABLE 2

ATTITUDE CHANGE AND BEHAVIOR OF MOTHERS WHO HAD STARTED WITH RESPECT TO TOILET TRAINING
(*data in months*)

	Control (*N=34*)	*Experimental* (*N=34*)
Immediate opinion change (Interview 2—Interview 1)	–0.2	+2.3
Delayed opinion change (Interview 3—Interview 1)	+0.8	+1.6
Effect of opinion change on behavior (Interview 4—Interview 1)	+2.0	+1.2

TABLE 3

ATTITUDE CHANGE AND INTENTIONS OF MOTHERS WHO HAD NOT STARTED WITH RESPECT TO TOILET TRAINING
(*data in months*)

	Control (*N*=13)	*Experimental* (*N=11*)
Immediate opinion change (Interview 2—Interview 1)	–1.2	+2.2
Delayed opinion change (Interview 3—Interview 1)	+0.3	+3.0
Effect of opinion change on intention (Interview 4—Interview 1)	+5.1	+5.2

Another way to look at the data is as follows. Both Table 2 and Table 3 show that the persuasive communication was effective for the experimental group and that the impact of the persuasive communication was still present six months later. If this opinion change had had any effect on behavior, we would expect that, by the time of the fourth interview, a larger percentage of the mothers in the control group would have already started to toilet train their children. More of the mothers in the experimental group, having become convinced that toilet training should start later, would *not* yet have started. Actually, the difference was negligible and slightly in the reverse direction. Thirty-four out of 45 mothers in the experimental group and 34 out of 47 mothers in the control group had already started toilet training by the time of the fourth interview. All in all, we can detect no effect on behavior of a clear and persistent change in opinion brought about by a persuasive communication.

Let us proceed to examine another relevant study. This study, reported by Fleishman, Harris, and Burtt, attempted to measure the effects of a two-week training course for foremen in industry.[4] This training course stressed principles of human relations in dealing with subordinates. Clearly, we are not faced here with the impact of one short persuasive communication but rather with a series of such communications extending over a two-week period. These persuasive communications took the form of lectures and group discussions, assisted by visual aids and role playing. For our purposes here, we may, perhaps, safely regard this two-week training session as a concerted attempt to persuade the foremen that mutual trust, warmth, and consideration for the other person are important aspects of effective leadership. (Before anyone misinterprets what I have said, let me hasten to add that undoubtedly other things went on during the two weeks. I have simply abstracted the aspect of the training session that resembles a persuasive communication.)

Given such a prolonged exposure to such a heavy dose of persuasion, we can well imagine that the opinions of the trainees would change from before to after the two-week session. The investigators attempted to measure any such opinion change in the following way. Before the training session and on its last day, the foremen were given a questionnaire measuring their opinions concerning leadership on the part of foremen. The major dimension on the questionnaire of interest to us here is one the authors label "consideration," made up of questions on such things as friendship, mutual trust, and warmth between the leader and his group. As one would expect, the investigators found a clear, appreciable, and significant change on this dimension from before to after the training session. The two weeks of persuasion were effective and the foremen now thought that the dimension of "consideration" was more important than they had previously believed.

This study is relevant for our present purposes because the investigators proceeded to obtain a subsequent on-the-job behavioral measure relevant to the dimension of "consideration." They compared the behavior of those foremen who had attended the training session with a comparable group of foremen who had not. The results are rather surprising. In general, there were no very consistent differences in behavior between the group of foremen who had, and the group who had not, been exposed to the two-week training session. This, in itself, is worrisome. Significant opinion change brought about as a result of a two-week exposure to a series of persuasive communications shows no relationship to behavior. But the results are actually even more surprising than this. The investigators divided their group of "trained" foremen into subgroups according to how recently they had completed the training course. After all, it might be reasoned that the effect of the training disappears with time. If so, one should at least be able to observe an effect on behavior among those who had most recently completed their two-week training course. The results show that the "most recently trained sub-group" was actually *lower* in consideration *behavior* than the group that had never been exposed to any training—had never been exposed to the impact of the persuasive communications. Once more we see the hint of a slightly inverse relationship between attitude change and behavior.

We will now proceed to examine the only other study we were able to find bearing on the question of the relation between opinion change and behavior. This is the well known study by Janis and Feshbach on the effects of fear-arousing communications.[5] Because the authors of this study did not interpret their data as bearing on this question, we will have to put a different interpretation on their experiment in order to make it relevant. Perhaps this different interpretation is not justifiable. But since so few published studies could be found that bear on our problem at all, I will proceed with the re-interpretation.

Of four groups of high school students used in the experiment, one, the control group, was not exposed to the relevant persuasive communication. The other three groups each heard an illustrated lecture about proper care of teeth and gums that attempted to persuade them that it was important to care for the teeth properly in order to avoid unpleasant consequences. The lectures each of the three groups heard differed in their emphasis on the painful consequences of improper oral hygiene. In the words of the authors:

> One of the main characteristics of the *Strong* appeal was the use of personalized threat-references explicitly directed to the audience, i.e., statements to the effect that "this can happen to you." The *Moderate* appeal, on the other hand, described the dangerous consequences of improper oral hygiene in a more factual way using impersonal language. In the *Minimal* appeal, the limited discussion of unfavorable consequences also used a purely factual style.

One might expect that the more emphasis put upon the importance of proper oral hygiene, and the more personal the importance is made, the more effective the communication would be in making the listener feel that proper oral hygiene is something to be concerned about. Thus, we might expect that the Strong appeal would be most effective, and the Minimal appeal least effective, in persuading people to be concerned about proper oral hygiene. One week before hearing the lecture, and immediately after hearing the lecture, all the subjects were asked two questions about how concerned or worried they were about the possibility of developing diseased gums and decayed teeth. The authors interpret these questions as indicating the degree of emotionality aroused by the persuasive communication, but, for the sake of our reinterpretation, let us look at the answers as reflecting opinion change. After all, the communications attempted to concern the listeners about these things. Let us see how well they succeeded. The data are shown in Table 4.

As one might expect, the persuasive communications were all effective to some extent—they all succeeded in creating more change in concern about oral hygiene than appeared in the control group. Within the experimental conditions we find that the Strong appeal was, plausibly, most effective. The Moderate and Minimal appeals seem to have been about equally effective.

TABLE 4

PERCENTAGE WHO FELT "SOMEWHAT" OR "VERY" WORRIED ABOUT DECAYED TEETH AND DISEASED GUMS

	Before	*After*
Strong appeal (N=50)	34	76
Moderate appeal (N=50)	24	50
Minimal appeal (N=50)	22	46
Control group (N=50)	30	38

The three persuasive communications, in addition to attempting to persuade the listeners of the importance of oral hygiene, also attempted to persuade them about the proper way to brush one's teeth and the characteristics of a "proper" type of toothbrush. Here, however, the three communications were equal. Before and after measures were obtained concerning the beliefs in the desirability of the recommended characteristics of a toothbrush. On these issues, where the communications did not differ, the authors state, ". . . all three experimental groups, as compared with the Control group, showed a significant change in the direction of accepting the conclusions presented in the communication. Among the three experimental groups, there were no significant differences with respect to net changes."

In other words, the three experimental groups were equally persuaded about the proper procedures to use in caring for the gums and teeth, but the Strong appeal group was made to feel these procedures were more important. If there were a simple, straightforward relationship between opinion or attitude change and behavior, one would expect the control group to change their behavior least (or not at all) and the Strong appeal group to change their behavior most.

On the initial questionnaire, given one week before the students heard the persuasive communications, five questions asked them to describe the way they were currently brushing their teeth—in other words, asked them to report their behavior. A week after having been exposed to the persuasive communications they were again asked these same five questions, covering aspects of tooth brushing that were stressed in the persuasive communications as the proper way to brush one's teeth. The answers were scored in terms of whether the student did or did not use the recommended practice. Since these questions asked the students about what they actually did when they brushed their teeth, perhaps it is legitimate to regard their answers as truthful reports concerning their actual behavior. This may or may not be a valid interpretation of their responses, but, assuming that it is, let us see what the relationship is between attitude change and their reported behavior. Table 5 presents the data on the percentage of subjects in each group who changed in the direction of increased use of the practices recommended in the persuasive communication.

It is clear from even a cursory glance at the data that the results do not represent a simple relation between attitude change and behavior. It is true that those who heard any of the persuasive communications reported more change in their behavior than the control group. This, however, may simply reflect the fact that subjects in the experimental conditions learned the proper terminology and what is approved. The interesting comparison is among the experimental groups. Within the experimental conditions, the relation between behavior and the degree to which students were made to feel concerned about oral hygiene was actually in the reverse direction from what one would expect from any simple relationship between attitude change and behavior.

The authors offer as an explanation for the inverse relationship the hypothesis that the Strong appeal created strong fear and, hence, subjects exposed to this communication were motivated to avoid thinking about it. Perhaps this is the correct explanation, although little evidence is presented in the study to support the assertion that strong fear was aroused in the Strong appeal condition. And it is certainly not clear why people who are more concerned about something are not more likely to take action. If we think of the results of this study together with the results of the previous studies I described (and let me stress again that these are the only three studies I have been able to find that are at all relevant to the issue at hand), it seems clear that we cannot glibly assume a relationship between attitude change and behavior. Indeed, it seems that the absence of research in this area is a glaring omission and that the whole problem needs thinking through.

Let us, for the sake of the present discussion, put aside the possibility that responses to a questionnaire after having been exposed to a persuasive communication may reflect nothing more than "lip service"; that is, the person's real opinions and attitudes may not have changed at all but his responses may simply reflect a desire not to appear unreasonable in the eyes of the experimenter. This kind of thing may affect responses to questionnaires to some extent, but it seems unreasonable to imagine that it is a dominant effect or that it could account for differences among experimental conditions. Undoubtedly, to a major extent, a person's answers to a questionnaire reflect how he really feels about the issue at that moment. Then why should one not observe a clear relationship with behavior?

I would like to suggest one possible reason for a complex relationship between attitude or opinion change and behavior. I have no data to support this suggestion, but perhaps it may offer some conceptual basis for future research that will clarify the problem. I want to suggest that when opinions or attitudes are changed through the momentary impact of a persuasive communication, this change, all by itself, is inherently unstable and will disappear or remain isolated unless an environmental or behavioral change can be brought about to support and maintain it.

To illustrate and amplify this suggestion, let us imagine a person who held the unlikely opinion that giving speeches was a productive and worthwhile thing to do. Undoubtedly, such an opinion would have been developed over many years on the basis of his own experience, what other people say about it, and also his own needs and motives. For example, he has observed that many people engage in the practice of giving speeches and from this it seems clear that it must have some desirable aspects. He has even read that at A.P.A. conventions papers are held to short periods of time because so many people (more than can be accommodated) want to make speeches. Surely, giving a speech must be a good thing to do. What is more, he has observed that many people actually go to listen to such speeches—a fact that certainly supports his opinion.

There is even more to the "reality" basis he has for this opinion. Once when he gave a speech, two people came up to him afterward and told him how wonderful they thought it was. What better evidence could he have that it was indeed worthwhile to engage in this activity? Furthermore, no one ever came up to him to tell him it was a waste of time. In addition, he found that he got quite a bit of personal satisfaction out of having all those people listening to what he said. All in all, the opinion became rather well established. There was considerable evidence to support it, none to contradict it, and it was a pleasant opinion to hold.

Needless to say, such a well-established opinion would affect the person's behavior. This does not mean that at every possible opportunity he would give a speech, but rather that he would be more likely to do so than someone who did not hold the opinion that such speeches were very worthwhile. It would not be a perfect relationship, since many other factors would affect his behavior, for example, the availability of time and whether or not he really had anything to say. But, by and large, one would observe a positive relationship.

Let us now imagine that the following unhappy incident occurs in the life of this contented speechmaker. One day, shortly before he is to leave town to go to some distant place to deliver a speech, he happens to engage in conversation with a few of his friends. One of them, on learning about the imminent trip, raises the question as to why it is necessary or valuable to do this kind of thing. After all, the monetary cost and the time spent are rather large. What does an audience get out of a personally delivered speech that they couldn't get just as well out of reading it?

TABLE 5

PERCENTAGE WHO CHANGED TOWARD INCREASED USE OF RECOMMENDED DENTAL PRACTICES

	Per Cent Who Changed
Strong appeal	28
Moderate appeal	44
Minimal appeal	50
Control group	22

Let us imagine the highly unlikely event that, in the ensuing discussion, no one is able to come up with a good answer to this question and so a real impact is made on the speechmaker's opinion. If one were to give this person a questionnaire at this moment, one would discover that a change in his opinion had been brought about. He would feel less certain that it was a good thing to do. But what are the implications for the future of this change in his opinion? After this friendly but unsettling discussion, our speechmaker returns to the same environment that produced his opinion initially, and, we can consequently assume, there will be pressures to return to his former opinion. Pressures, indeed, that he has not felt in a long time. Furthermore, he is about to leave to make a speech and he goes ahead with what he is already committed to doing. This obviously further helps to restore his former opinion. The world he encounters remains the same, his experiences remain the same, and so his opinion will tend to revert. His behavior will remain the same or perhaps even intensify in an effort to restore his former opinion. The exact content of his opinion may indeed have changed somewhat and become more differentiated. He may buttress his original opinion by the notion that many people will listen to a speech who would not read it and that it is important to communicate to many people; he may persuade himself that the personal contact is in some unspecified way very important; he may even tell himself that a practice so widespread must be good even if he, at the moment, cannot see its good aspects clearly.

It is my present contention that, in order to produce a stable behavior change following opinion change, an environmental change must also be produced which, representing reality, will support the new opinion and the new behavior. Otherwise, the same factors that produced the initial opinion and the behavior will continue to operate to nullify the effect of the opinion change.

Thus far we have speculated mainly about some possible reasons for the *absence* of a relationship between opinion change following a persuasive communication and resulting behavior. We have not grappled with the perplexing question raised by the persistent hint of a slightly inverse relationship (if three times may be called persistent). I must confess that I have no very good or interesting speculations to offer here. Let me also emphasize that the data certainly do not warrant assuming that such an inverse relationship really does exist: they do no more than raise a possible suspicion. If this inverse relation is found not to exist, there is, of course, nothing to explain. If, however, it does exist, we must find some explanation for it.

What I want to stress is that we have been quietly and placidly ignoring a very vital problem. We have essentially persuaded ourselves that we can simply assume that there is, of course, a relationship between attitude change and subsequent behavior and, since this relationship is obvious, why should we labor to overcome the considerable technical difficulties of investigating it? But the few relevant studies certainly show that this "obvious" relationship probably does not exist and that, indeed, some nonobvious relationships may exist. The problem needs concerted investigation.

NOTES

[1]Arthur R. Cohen, *Attitude Change and Social Influence,* New York, Basic Books, in press.

[2]M. L. De Fleur and F. R. Westie, "Verbal Attitudes and Overt Act: An Experiment on the Salience of Attitudes," *American Sociological Review,* Vol. 23, 1958, pp. 667-673.

[3]N. Maccoby, A. K. Romney, J. S. Adams, and Eleanor E. Maccoby, *"Critical Periods" in Seeking and Accepting Information,* Paris-Stanford Studies in Communication, Stan-

ford, Calif., Institute for Communication Research, 1962.

[4]E. Fleishmann, E. Harris, and H. Burtt, *Leadership and Supervision in Industry: An Evaluation of a Supervisory Training Program,* Columbus, Ohio State University, Bureau of Educational Research, 1955.

[5]I. Janis and S. Feshbach, "Effects of Fear-arousing Communications," *Journal of Abnormal and Social Psychology,* Vol. 48, 1953, pp. 78-92.

4

WORDS AND DEEDS: SOCIAL SCIENCE AND SOCIAL POLICY

Irwin Deutscher

The Society for the Study of Social Problems was established by and continues to attract sociologists with a dual commitment. We seek, on the one hand, to achieve a better understanding of the problems society creates for some of the people within it and, on the other, more effective application of socially relevant knowledge to the solution of those problems. Ultimately most of us are concerned with finding ways to alter this world in such a manner that more people may find it a better place in which to live. Our orientation leads us to search for effective alterations of the society rather than effective adjustments of individuals to the society. We tend, therefore, to shun efforts to improve treatment of individuals who reflect symptomatically the malfunctionings of the society whether they be defined as sick, deviant, pathological, nonconformists, outsiders, or whatever. Since our focus is upon the society rather than the individual, whatever changes we have to recommend, whatever advice and criticism we have to offer, must be directed toward those who make or influence policy in our society. I will conclude this address with some comments on our increasing responsibility in the arena of public policy, but I will start elsewhere.

My point of departure is the basic research, the evaluative studies, and the demonstration projects which are the "scientific" materials from which social scientists generally derive their recommendations to policy makers. Our scientific conclusions, for the most part, are based on analyses of verbal responses to questions put by an interviewer. Those responses may be written or oral and the questions may range from forced

Reprinted from *Social Problems* (Vol. 13, No. 3, 1966, pp. 235-254) by permission of the author and The Society for the Study of Social Problems.

choice to open ended, but the fact remains that what we obtain from such methods are statements of attitude, opinion, norms, values, anticipation, or recall. The policy maker is interested in none of these things; as a man of action, he is interested in overt *behavior*. Although we rarely study such behavior, we do insist that the object of our discipline is to understand and even to predict it. Therefore, to oblige the policy maker, as well as ourselves, the assumption must be made that verbal responses reflect behavioral tendencies.

In his definitive volume on interviewing, Hyman makes this assumption explicit: "If one could wait around indefinitely," he writes, "the natural environment would ultimately liberate behavior relevant to a given inference. However, practical limitations preclude such lengthy procedures. As Vernon puts it: 'Words are actions in miniature. Hence by the use of questions and answers we can obtain information about a vast number of actions in a short space of time, the actual observation and measurement of which would be impracticable.' "[1] This inferential jump from verbal behavior to overt behavior appears to be tenuous under some conditions.

Acting out a relationship is not necessarily the same as talking about a relationship. We have known this for a long time and we have known why for a long time, but we proceed as if we did not know. With the advantage of hindsight, I intend to suggest that we began to make incorrect choices in the early 1930's, and once having begun, managed easily to build error upon error. Although we have frequently proceeded with rigor and precision, we have, nevertheless, been on an erratic course. In retrospect, we may well have had a thirty-year moratorium in social science.

Symbolizing the period during which we had the choice to make is a classic experiment designed by Richard LaPiere and reported in 1934 under the simple title, "Attitude vs. Actions."[2] Since this address has the reactionary intent of picking up where LaPiere left off, I will review some of the events leading to his experiment and refresh you on its details.

THE LAPIERE EXPERIMENT

Richard LaPiere's quest for answers to a haunting methodological problem can be traced through a trilogy of his papers, the last of which is "Attitudes vs. Actions." If such quests can be thought of as being initiated at a specific point in time, LaPiere's probably began while he was attending a seminar with Malinowski at the London School in 1927.[3] During the course of that seminar, the term "verbalization" was employed to indicate a distinction between what informants may say and what may be the actual custom of the primitive society. LaPiere was formulating a comparative survey of race prejudice in France and England.[4] Interested in the concept of "verbalization," he attempted to check his questionnaire findings against actual practices. This he accomplished by questioning hotel proprietors about their policy. The results left LaPiere satisfied at the time that he had found a fair concordance between verbal responses and nonverbal responses and, consequently, that his survey results were sufficiently valid.

Upon his return to the United States, LaPiere undertook a study of an Armenian community,[5] as a result of which he writes, "I began again to doubt the certain value of verbal evidence."[6]

Perhaps as a result of this doubt, LaPiere reconsidered the evidence from his French study and realized that "at that time I overlooked the fact that what I was obtaining from the hotel proprietors was still a 'verbalized' reaction to a symbolic situation."[7] He had not compared verbal and nonverbal behavior. What he had done was to compare attitudes with self-reports of behavior. His concern resulted in the carefully designed and controlled experiment which consumed two years in the field and over ten thousand miles of driving and culminated in the publication of "Attitudes vs. Actions."

Traveling with a Chinese couple, twice across country and up and down the West Coast, the investigator recorded the treatment they received in hotels, auto camps, tourist homes, and restaurants.[8] *Of the 251 establishments approached in this manner, one auto camp refused to accommodate them.* Here then was an estimate of Caucasian-Oriental intergroup *behavior*.

Allowing a time-lapse of six months after being served by an establishment, a questionnaire was sent to each. Half of them were asked only, "Would you accept members of the Chinese race as guests in your establishment?" The other half were asked additional questions about other ethnic groups. *Only one "yes" response was received*—this from a lady who reminisced about the nice Chinese couple she had put up six months earlier.[9] Here then was an estimate of Caucasian "attitudes" toward Orientals.

Most important is the juxtapositioning of these two estimates. We have then, in 1934, strong empirical evidence, not only that there may be no relationship between what people say and what they do, but that under some conditions there may be a high inverse relationship between the two.

LaPiere's conclusions are primarily theoretical and methodological. With scientific caution he restricts *empirical* conclusions to the empirical data and warns against careless generalization. He reminds us that the conventional questionnaire is a valuable tool for identifying such phenomena as political or religious *beliefs*.[10] But, he continues, "if we would know the extent to which [his belief] restrains his behavior, it is to his behavior that we must look, not to his questionnaire response:

. . . . Sitting at my desk in California I can predict with a high degree of cer-

> tainty what an "average" businessman in an average Mid-Western city will reply to the question, "Would you engage in sexual intercourse with a prostitute in a Paris brothel? Yet no one, least of all the man himself, can predict what he would actually do should he by some misfortune find himself face-to-face with the situation in question.[11]

In LaPiere's work we find a line of continuity leading toward new theoretical insights into human behavior, new methods for attaining knowledge, and new kinds of evidence which could be used with confidence by policy makers bent on reducing some of the problems of the contemporary world. But that line of continuity has hardly extended beyond the publication of "Attitudes vs. Actions" in March, 1934. Some of the occasional and discontinuous efforts to proceed along this path are mentioned in the pages which follow. For the most part social science proceeded in other directions.

LaPiere contends that no one has ever challenged his argument that what men say and what they do are not always in concordance. "On the other hand," he writes, "it seems to have had no effect at all on the sociological faith in the value of data gathered via opinion, attitude, and other kinds of questionnaires. The 'Attitude vs. Action' paper was," he continues, "cited for years by almost everyone who wrote on attitudes or opinions as a sort of caution not to take their data too seriously; whereupon each author promptly ignored the caution and proceeded to assume that his data was indicative of what people would actually do in real-life circumstances."[12]

LaPiere was certainly not alone; there were other voices crying in the wilderness. In the late thirties some of the best young minds in American sociology were clearly concerned with the problem. Reading a paper at the 1938 meetings of the American Sociological Society, Robert K. Merton was critical of his own recently-acquired survey data on attitudes toward Negroes. He wondered if it wasn't possible that Northerners treat Negroes less favorably than they talk about them and that Southerners talk about Negroes less favorably than they treat them. He asks, "May we assume the amount and direction of spread between opinion and action to be relatively constant for members of different groups? To my knowledge," Merton continues, "no systematic research on this problem has been carried out."[13]

At about the same time, C. Wright Mills argued, "Perhaps the central methodological problem of the social sciences springs from recognition that often there is a disparity between lingual and social-motor types of behavior." Mills suggested that we need to know *"how much* and *in what direction* disparities between talk and action will probably go."[14]

Herbert Blumer has been the most consistent spokesman for the point of view suggested by LaPiere's data. For the past 35 years in at least a half-dozen articles, Blumer has argued the logic of this position, in terms of theory,[15] in terms of method,[16] and in terms of substantive fields such as Industrial Relations[17] and Public Opinion Polling.[18] In his presidential address to the American Sociological Society in 1956, Blumer suggests that, not only do we know nothing about behavior or the relation between attitudes and behavior, but that we don't know much about attitudes either: "The thousands of 'variable' studies of attitudes, for instance, have not contributed to our knowledge of the abstract nature of an attitude; in a similar way the studies of 'social cohesion,' 'social integration,' 'authority,' or 'group morale' have done nothing, so far as I can detect, to clarify or augment generic knowledge of these categories."[19] Yet, in the closing lines of his address, after 35 years of persistence, Blumer acknowledges defeat with the wistful hope that people at least know what they are doing. He concludes, "In view, however, of the current tendency of variable analysis to become the norm and model for sociological analysis, I believe it important to recognize its shortcomings and its limitations."[20]

Why have both the empirical evidence and the theoretical rationale been ignored? There is adequate reason to suspect that behavior toward words about social or cultural objects (i.e., responses to questions) may not provide an adequate basis for imputing behavior toward the objects themselves (i.e., responses to the people or situations to which the words refer). Three decades ago LaPiere's explanation was couched in terms of economy and reliability: "The questionnaire," he observed, "is cheap, easy, and mechanical. The study of human behavior is time consuming, intellectually fatiguing, and depends for its success upon the ability of the investigator. The former method gives quantitative results, the latter mainly qualitative. Quantitative measurements are quantitatively accurate; qualitative evaluations are always subject to the errors of human judgment. Yet," he concludes, "it would seem far more worthwhile to make a shrewd guess regarding that which is essential than to accurately measure that which is likely to prove quite irrelevant."[21]

Others, like Mills, have assumed a more cynical explanation. Turning to the sources of research finance, he suggests that: "Many foundation administrators like to give money for projects that are thought to be safe from political or public attack, that are large-scale, hence easier 'to administer' than more numerous handicraft projects, and that are scientific with a capital S, which often only means made 'safe' by trivialization. Accordingly," Mills concludes, "the big money tends to encourage the large-scale bureaucratic style of research into small-scale problems as carried on by The Scientists."[22]

These explanations have persisted and most of them remain as valid today as they were in the past, but I suspect that they reflect a deeper and perhaps more basic problem. It is possible that the apparent anomaly of acknowledging the correctness of one position while pursuing another can best be explained in terms of the sociology of knowledge.

EPISTEMOLOGY AND RESEARCH METHODS

It has been suggested that the sociology of knowledge "is devoted to digging up the social roots of knowledge, to searching out the ways in which knowledge and thought are affected by the environing social structure."[23] We may indeed have some roots to dig in our attempt to understand the directions taken by American sociology during the last three or four decades. The perceptions of knowledge—notions of the proper or appropriate ways of knowing—which were fashionable during the late twenties and early thirties, when sociology had its choices to make, surely impinged upon those choices.

Men like LaPiere and Blumer and, later, Mills were arguing from a basically antipositivistic position at a time when a century of more of cumulative positivistic science was resulting in a massive payoff in our knowledge and control of physical forces. And sociology had its alternatives. L. L. Thurstone was giving birth to what was to become modern scaling. Emory Bogardus was translating some of these ideas into sociological scales of contemporary relevance. And the intellectual brilliance of men like George Lundberg and Stuart Chapin was creating the theoretical and methodological rationale for the new "science." Incisive critiques of the new sociology and the logic of its quantitative methods were plentiful,[24] but if we listen to Richard LaPiere's recollections of the temper of the times it becomes apparent that logic may not have been the deciding factor:

> . . . . What you may not know, or at least not fully appreciate, is that well into the 1930's the status of sociology and hence of sociologists was abominable, both within and outside the academic community. The public image of the sociologist was of a blue-nosed reformer, ever ready to pronounce moral judgments, and against all pleasurable forms of social conduct. In the universities, sociology was generally thought of as an uneasy mixture of social philosophy and social work . . . . Through the 1920's the department at Chicago was the real center of sociology in the United States [but] . . . . The men who were to shape sociology during the 1930's were, for the most part, products of one or two-men departments (e.g., Columbia) of low status within their universities; they were, therefore, to a considerable degree self-trained and without a doctrinaire viewpoint, and they were exceedingly conscious of the low esteem in which sociology was held. Such men, and I was one among them, were determined to prove—at least to themselves—that sociology is a science, that sociologists are not moralists, and that sociology deserves recognition and support comparable to that being given psychology and economics. It was, I think, to this end that toward the end of the 20's, scientific sociology came to be identified with quantitative methods . . . and by the mid-thirties American sociologists were split into two antagonistic camps—the moralists . . . and the scientists . . . Now as to my own uncertain part in all this. I was one of the Young Turks, and I shared with Lundberg, Bain, Stouffer, etc., the distaste for sociology as it had been and the hurt of its lowly status. But unlike the majority of the rebels, I did not

share their belief that the cure for bad sociology was quantification [although] I did set off in that direction . . . .

LaPiere sees the history of American sociology between the two world wars as an effort, not to build knowledge, but to achieve respectability and acceptability. In terms of this goal we have been successful. "For it has in considerable measure been sociological reliance on quantitative methods that has won for sociology the repute and financial support that it now enjoys. That in gaining fame, sociology may have become a pseudo-science is another, and quite different, matter. Now that sociology is well-established, it may be possible for a new generation of Young Turks to evaluate the means through which sociology has won respectability."[25]

With the security of respectability perhaps now we can afford to take a more critical look at alternatives which were neglected at other times for reasons which are no longer cogent. Perhaps now we can begin again to achieve some understanding of the tenuous relationships between men's thoughts and their actions. One strategic point of departure for such a reevaluation is an examination of some of the consequences of the choices we have made. In attempting to assume the stance of physical science, we have necessarily assumed its epistemology—its assumptions about the nature of knowledge and the appropriate means of knowing, including the rules of scientific evidence. The requirement of clean empirical demonstration of the effects of isolated factors or variables, in a manner which can be replicated, led us to create, by definition, such factors or variables. We knew that human behavior was rarely if ever directly influenced or explained by an isolated variable; we knew that it was impossible to assume that any set of such variables was additive (with or without weighting); we knew that the complex mathematics of the interaction among any set of variables, much less their interaction with external variables., was incomprehensible to us. In effect, although we knew they did not exist, we defined them into being.

But it was not enough just to create sets of variables. They had to be stripped of what little meaning they had in order that they might be operational, i.e., that they have their measurement built into their definition. One consequence, then, was to break down human behavior in a way that was not only artificial but which did not jibe with the manner in which that behavior was observed.

Having laid these foundations and because the accretion of knowledge is a cumulative affair, we began to construct layer upon layer. For example, in three decades we "advanced" from Bogardus to Guttman.[26] Merton suggests that the cumulative nature of science requires a high degree of consensus among scientists and leads, therefore, to an inevitable enchantment with problems of reliability.[27] Merton is wrong in his equation of scientific method with maximum concern for problems of reliability: *all* knowledge, whether scientific or not, is cumulative and all men who think or write stand on the shoulders of those who have thought or have written before. It does, nevertheless, appear that the adoption of the scientific model in the social sciences has resulted in an uncommon concern for methodological problems centering on issues of reliability and to the concomitant neglect of problems of validity.

We have been absorbed in measuring the amount of error which results from inconsistency among interviewers or inconsistency among items on our instruments. We concentrate on consistency without much concern with what it is we are being consistent about or whether we are consistently right or wrong. As a consequence we may have been learning a greal deal about how to pursue an incorrect course with a maximum of precision.

It is not my intent to disparage the importance of reliability *per se*; it is the obsession with it to which I refer.[28] Certainly zero reliability must result in zero validity. But the relationship is not linear, since infinite perfection of reliability (zero error) may also be associated with zero validity. Whether or not one wishes to emulate the scientist and whatever methods may be applied to the quest for knowledge, we must make estimates of, allowances for, and attempts to reduce the extent to which our methods distort our findings.

This is precisely why C. Wright Mills identifies the "disparities between talk and action" as "the central *methodological* problem of the social sciences."[29] Mills' plea for systematic investigations into the differences between words and deeds is based on the need for the "methodologist to build into his methods standard margins of error"—to learn how to appropriately discount variously located sources of data. Just as Mills is concerned about reliability in the historical method, Hyman has documented the need for estimates of reliability in social anthropological and clinical psychiatric observations. He reminds us, for example, that the village of Tepoztlan as described by Lewis is quite different from the same village as it was described earlier by Robert Redfield.[30] Hyman cites Kluckhohn's lament that "the limited extent to which ethnologists have been articulate about their field techniques is astonishing to scholars in other disciplines."[31]

One of the few positive consequences of our decades of "scientific" orientation is the incorporation into the sociological mentality of a self-consciousness about methods—regardless of what methods are employed. As a result, those few sociologists who bring ethnological field techniques to bear on their problems are constrained to contemplate methodological issues and to publish methodological observations. I have in mind, specifically, the continuing series of articles by Howard S. Becker and Blanche Geer.[32] Regardless of the importance of reliability, there remains a danger that in our obsession with it, the goals—the purposes for which we seek knowledge—and the phenomena about which we seek knowledge, may become obscured.

One of the more regretful consequences of our neglect of the relationship between words and deeds has been the development of a technology which is inappropriate to the understanding of human behavior, and conversely, the almost complete absence of a technology which can facilitate our learning about the conditions under which people in various categories do or do not "put their monies where their mouths are." We still do not know much about the relationship between what people say and what they do—attitudes and behavior, sentiments and acts, verbalizations and interactions, words and deeds. *We know so little that I can't even find an adequate vocabulary to make the distinction!*[33]

Under what conditions will people behave as they talk? Under what conditions is there no relationship? And under what conditions do they say one thing and behave exactly the opposite? In spite of the fact that all of these combinations have been empirically observed and reported, few efforts have been made to order such observations.[34] Furthermore, and perhaps of even greater importance, we do not know under what conditions a change in attitude anticipates a change in behavior or under what conditions a change in behavior anticipates a change in attitude. Again, both phenomena have been empirically observed and recorded.

It is important that my comments not be misunderstood as a plea for the simple study of simple behavioral items. This would be a duplication of the same kinds of mistakes we have made in the simple study of simple attitudinal items. Overt action can be understood and interpreted only within the context of its meaning to the actors, just as verbal reports can be understood and interpreted only within the context of their meaning to the respondents. And in large part, the context of each is the other. But the fact remains that one of the methodological consequences of our recent history is that we have not developed a technology for observing, ordering, analyzing, and interpreting *overt behavior*—especially as it relates to attitudes, norms, opinions, and values.

The development of a new technology could take any of a number of directions. Ideally, we should seek to refine the model provided by La Piere, whereby we obtain information from the same population on verbal behavior and interaction behavior under natural social conditions. Surely, the kind of cleverness which creates situational apparati for the psychological laboratory could also create refined situational designs for research under conditions which have meaning for the actors. The theoretical and methodological rationalization of participant-observer field techniques, begun by Becker and Geer, is a promising alternative. There may be as yet untapped possibilities in contrived laboratory experiments—if we can learn how to contrive them in such a way that their results are not denuded of any general meaning by the artificial specificity of the situations. If someday reliable and valid projective instruments are developed, we may have made a significant technological step forward. There is considerable developmental work under way at present on instruments which facilitate self-reporting of overt behavior and allow comparisons to be made between attitudes and behavior on the same people, although still on a verbal level.[35]

There was a time earlier in this century when we had a choice to make, a choice on the one hand of undertaking neat, orderly studies of measureable phenomena. This alternative carried with it all of the gratifications of conforming to the prestigious methods of pursuing knowledge then in vogue, of having access to considerable sums of monies through the granting procedures of large foundations and governmental agencies, of a comfortable sense of satisfaction derived from dealing rigorously and precisely with small isolated problems which were cleanly defined, of moving for 30 years down one track in an increasingly rigorous, refined, and reliable manner, while simultaneously disposing of the problems of validity by the semantic trickery of operational definitions. On the other hand, we could have tackled the messy world as we knew it to exist, a world where the same people will make different utterances under different conditions and will behave differently in different situations and will say one thing while doing another. We could have tackled a world where control of relevant variables was impossible not only because we didn't know what they were but because we didn't know how they interacted with each other. We could have accepted the conclusion of almost every variant of contemporary philosophy of science, that the notion of cause and effect (and therefore of stimulus and response or of independent and dependent variables) is untenable. We eschewed this formidable challenge. This was the hard way. We chose the easy way.

Yet the easy way provides one set of results and the hard way provides another. The easy way for LaPiere in 1934 would have been to conduct as rigorous as possible a survey of attitudes of hotel and restaurant managers toward Orientals. But this leads to a set of conclusions which are the opposite of what he finds when he does it the hard way, i.e., traveling thousands of miles in order to confront those managers with Orientals.[36] One of our graduate students, after reviewing some of the literature on the relationship between attitudes and overt behavior,[37] concluded that laboratory experimental studies such as those by Scott,[38] King and Janis,[39] and DeFleur and Westie[40] tend to show a positive correlation between attitude and behavior, while observational field studies such as those by Kutner, Wilkins, and Yarrow;[41] and Saenger and Gilbert,[42] tend to show no such correlation. Although there are important exceptions to this rule,[43] it serves as a reminder that our choice of methods may not be unrelated to our conclusions.

EMPIRICAL EVIDENCE AND THEORETICAL SUPPORT

Why do I fuss so, largely on the basis of a primitive field study on a Chinese couple done over thirty years ago and the stubborn polemics of a Herbert Blumer?[44] Frankly, that would be sufficient to cause me considerable concern! But there is other empirical evidence as well as a variety of theoretical support for the argument that more attention needs to be directed toward the relationship between what men say and what they do.[45]

There is reason to believe that this problem transcends *American* attitudes toward *Chinese tourists thirty years ago.* There is evidence that interracial attitudes and behavior are not identical *in Brazil,*[46] that sentiments about *Negroes* in northern American communities do not coincide with behavior toward Negroes in those communities,[47] that interracial attitudes and behavior between customers and department *store clerks* are inconsistent,[48] and that divergences between interracial attitudes and behaviors persist *in 1965* as they did in 1934.[49]

Perhaps of even greater importance are the bits of empirical evidence that *this discrepancy between what people say and what they do is not limited to the area of racial or ethnic relations:* it has been observed that trade union members talk one game and play another,[50] that there is no relationship between college students' attitudes toward cheating and their actual cheating behavior,[51] that urban teachers' descriptions of classroom behavior are sometimes unrelated to the way teachers behave in the classroom,[52] that what rural Missourians say about their health behavior has little connection with their actual health practices,[53] and that the moral and ethical beliefs of students do not conform to their behavior.[54]

It has also been reported that Kansans who vote for prohibition maintain and use well equipped bars in their homes,[55] that small time steel wholesalers mouth patriotism while undercutting the national economy in wartime,[56] that employers' attitudes toward hiring the handicapped are not reflected in their hiring practices,[57] and that the behavior of mothers toward their children is unrelated to their attitudes toward them.[58] If it were possible to observe bedroom behavior, I wonder what would be the relationship between Kinsey's survey results and such observations? I don't know, nor does anyone else, but a contemporary novelist has a confused fictional respondent muse about a sex survey, "But what do they expect of me? Do they want to know how I feel or how I act?"[59]

Students of aging suspect that what older people have to say about retirement has little relationship to their life during that stage of the life cycle.[60] A pair of industrial psychologists, interested in assessing the current state of knowledge regarding the relationship between employee attitudes and employee performance, covered all of the literature in that area through 1954.[61] Treating various classes of studies separately, they find in every category "minimal or no relationship between employee attitudes and performance."

It would be a serious selective distortion of the existing evidence to suggest that all of it indicates an incongruence between what people say and what they do. Consumers sometimes do change their buying habits in ways that they say they will,[62] people frequently do vote as they tell pollsters they will, urban relocation populations may accurately predict to interviewers the type of housing they will obtain,[63] local party politicians do in fact employ the campaign tactics which they believe to be most effective,[64] and youngsters will provide survey researchers with reports of their own contact or lack of contact with the police which are borne out by police records.[65]

The empirical evidence can best be summarized as reflecting wide variation in the relationships between attitudes and behaviors. As a result of their review of all of the studies on employee attitudes and performance, Brayfield and Crockett observe, "The scarcity of relationships, either positive or negative, demonstrated to date even among the best designed of the available studies leads us to question whether or not methodological changes alone would lead to a substantial increase in the magnitude of the obtained relationships."[66] Having arrived at the point where they are able to question the assumption that a relationship must obtain between what people say and what they do, these authors can now question whether or not the failure to observe such a relationship is necessarily a consequence of the inefficiency of the measuring instruments. This is an important breakthrough, since it permits them, and us, to look at alternative explanations—especially at conceptual considerations.

A cursory review of the conceptual frameworks within which most of us work suggests that *no matter what one's theoretical orientation may be, he has no reason to expect to find congruence between attitudes and actions and every reason to expect to find discrepancies between them.* The popular varieties of balance theory in current social science, such as functionalism in sociology and anthropology and cognitive dissonance in psychology, posit a drive or strain toward consistency. This image of man and society must carry with it the assumption that at any given point in time a condition of imbalance or dissonance or inconsistency obtains.

The psychoanalytic concepts of the unconscious and the subconscious assume that people cannot themselves know how they might behave under specified conditions and such mechanisms as repression suggest that they may not be able to tell an interviewer how they have behaved in the past. Such dissimilar sociological ancestors as Charles H. Cooley and Emile Durkheim built their conceptions of man in society around the assumption that human nature is such that it requires the constraints of society. Under such conditions there is an inherent conflict between man's private self and his social self and the area of role theory is developed to help us understand some of the mechanisms by which man is constrained to act as he "ought."

On the gross societal level, such concepts as social disorganization and cultural lag suggest that people can be caught up in discrepant little worlds which make conflicting demands upon them. The immigrant to a new world has been described as assuming new forms of behavior while clinging to older attitudes and beliefs. In the developing countries of Africa, the idea of cultural lag leads us to expect that the rapid acceptance of new behaviors may outrun, at least for a while, the rejection of old norms. Or perhaps behavioral changes may not be able to keep pace with the rapid acceptance of new norms. Either way, the outcome must be inconsistent attitudes and behaviors!

When we consider the behavior of individuals in groups smaller than societies, we frequently think in such terms as situational contingencies, the definition of the situation, public and private behavior, or reference-group theory—all of which relate what one does or what one says to the immediate context, both as it exists objectively and as it exists in the mind of the actor. Do we not expect attitudes and behaviors to vary as the definition of the situation is altered or as different reference groups are brought to bear?

The symbolic interactionists have traditionally exhibited the greatest sensitivity to this problem in sociology. Among others, both Blumer and LaPiere have insisted that we act, either verbally or overtly, in response to the symbolic meaning the confronting object has for us in the given situation. A question put to me by an interviewer concerning how I feel about Armenian women forces me to respond to the words and to the interviewer; standing face-to-face with a real flesh and blood Armenian woman, I find myself constrained to act toward a very different set of symbols. Is there any reason to assume that my behavior should be the same in these two radically different symbolic situations? Arnold Rose has developed a vigorous symbolic interactionist argument regarding the theoretical independence of attitudes and behaviors.[67]

One conceptual framework which we tend to neglect lies in the undeveloped field of sociolinguistics. Although it may be many other things, sociolinguistics should also deal with an analysis of the meanings of verbal communications.[68] It provides an untapped potential for understanding the relation between what people say and what they do. What differences in meaning can be conveyed by different people with the same words? The eloquent teen-age Negro prostitute, Kitten can find herself involved in a $100 misunderstanding only becuase she thinks she is listening to someone who speaks the same language.[69] The truth of the matter is that, unfortunately, she and her Babbitt-like college sophomore protagonist employ the same vocabulary to speak different languages. Might this not also occur occasionally between interviewer and interviewee? What is the relationship between language and thought and between language and action? Should we assume that a response of "yah," "da," "si," "oui," or "yes" all really mean exactly the same thing in response to the same question? Or may there not be different kinds of affirmative connotations in different languages? And, of course, can we assume that the question itself means the same thing simply because it translates accurately?

We have a great deal to learn from comparative linguistics if we can bring ourselves to view language from the perspective of the symbolic interactionist—as social and cultural symbolism—rather than from the perspective of those psycholinguists who reduce language to mathematical symbols and thus effectively denude it of its socio-cultural context. I would suggest that it is impossible to translate any word in any language to any word in any other language. Words are fragments of linguistic configurations; they mean nothing in isolation from the configuration. The basic linguistic problems of cross-cultural and cross-class survey research have hardly been recognized, much less dealt with.

Let me suggest that, as an intellectual exercise, you take whatever other conceptual frameworks you may be partial to or comfortable with and determine whether or not they permit you to assume that you can expect people to act in accordance with their words. Meanwhile, I will return to Brayfield and Crockett, who helped me earlier with the transition from method to theory: "Foremost among [the] implications," of their review of research, "is the conclusion that it is time to question the strategic and ethical merits of selling to industrial concerns an assumed relationship between employee attitudes and employee performance."[70] It is but a slight extension of this conclusion to question the strategic and ethical merits of selling anything to anyone or to any establishment based on the dubious assumption that what people say is related directly to what they do.

SOCIAL RESEARCH AND SOCIAL POLICY

If I appear to have belabored some obvious points, it is because it is necessary to build as strong a backdrop as possible to the implications of all of this for the role of social science research in policy recommendations. Research aimed at demonstration and evaluation tends to make precisely the assumption which I have been challenging: the notion that what people *say* is a predictor of what they will *do*.

Thus far, I have tried to restrict my attention to the relatively simple question of the relations between attitudes and behaviors—simple as compared to the issues raised when we turn to the relationship between attitudinal and behavioral *changes*. If we are to be relevant to social policy, then we must consider this more complex question. Can we assume that if we are attempting to alter behavior through a training program, an educational campaign, or some sort of information intervention, a measured change in attitude in the "right" direction results in a change in behavior?

Leon Festinger, encountering a statement in an unpublished manuscript, reports that he was "slightly skeptical about the assertion that there is a dearth of studies relating attitude or opinion change to behavior."[71] Although no examples occurred to him, he was certain that there must be many such studies. "After prolonged search," he writes, "with the help of many others, I succeeded in locating only three relevant studies, one of which is of dubious relevance and one of which required reanalysis of data. The absence of research and of theoretical thinking, about the effect of attitude change on subsequent behavior is," Festinger concludes, "indeed astonishing."[72]

The three relevant studies all involve study and control populations and pre- and post-tests of attitude. Some form of persuasive communication was injected into the study groups and either self-reports or behavioral observations are obtained. The studies deal with attitudes of mothers of infants toward the age at which toilet training should begin; the training of industrial foremen in human relations; and attitudes of high school students toward proper dental care.[73] *In all three cases the process of persuasive communication resulted in a significant change of attitude in the desired direction. In all three cases there is no evidence of a change in behavior in the desired direction.* To the contrary, Festinger concedes that he has not "grappled with the perplexing question raised by the persistent hint of a slightly inverse relationship," and he confesses his inability to explain the possibility of such a reversal.[74]

It seems to me that we have sufficient grounds to reject any evaluation of an action program which employs attitudinal change as a criterion of "success," except in the unlikely event that the goal of the program is solely to change attitudes without concern for subsequent behavioral changes. And even under these conditions, the validity of our attitudinal measurements can be seriously challenged. For example, Ehrlich and Rinehart recently reported the results of their analysis of a stereotype measuring instrument which has been used in identical or slightly modified form in dozens of studies since 1933. They observe that the results achieved in these studies have all been roughly consistent and then proceed to demonstrate that these reliable results are of doubtful validity.[75] In effect, we have achieved over thirty years' worth of cumulative, consistent, and misleading information about prejudice.

If we do not know enough about the behavioral consequences of attitude change to make policy recommendations with confidence in their validity, what do we know about the attitudinal consequences of behavioral change? There is some evidence in the American Soldier studies that the integration of army units may lead to more favorable attitudes toward Negroes on the part of the integrated white soldiers.[76] Integrated public housing projects are reported to increase friendly contacts between races and to reduce stereotyping and prejudice among the white occupants.[77] In Yarrow's report of a controlled experiment in a children's camp, the experimental (desegregated) cabins did produce a significant reduction in prejudice as measured by pre- and post-sociometric interviews.[78] But another study in an integrated camp concludes that four weeks of intimate contact on the part of the children produced no change in attitude.[79] Similarly, Bettelheim and Janowitz found in their study of veterans that intimate contact with members of the minority group does not seem to disintegrate prejudices.[80]

These bits of evidence concerning the attitudinal consequences of behavioral change are all limited to the specific case of coercively integrated residential enclaves, i.e., army units, public housing projects, and childrens' camps. Although it has been reported that interracial occupational contacts may also result in changed attitudes, the evidence is limited.[81] The invasion-succession process which occurs when people are not coerced in their residential arrangements suggests that, by and large, they prefer flight (avoidance) to attitudinal change. Furthermore, there is some evidence that even when attitudinal changes appear to have occurred in one area, such as the work situation or the housing situation, they are not necessarily generalized to other interactional areas.[82]

Aside from the case of interracial attitudes and behaviors, there are an infinite number of situations where attitudinal consequences of behavioral change can be studied. In a country such as Britain where employers are coerced by law under certain conditions to employ handicapped workers, do their attitudes toward such workers change? If a group of Jaycees can be induced to undertake work with delinquent boys, does the experience alter their attitude toward such boys? Does a relatively indifferent adolescent drafted and shipped to Viet Nam consequently develop hostile attitudes toward the Viet Cong?

There can, of course, be no simple "yes" or "no" answer to such simple questions. To polarize attention upon two variables labeled "attitude" and "behavior" and to operationally define them so that we can measure their relationship is to continue down the same track. It is what goes on in between—the process—toward which we must direct our attention. We need to ask what intervenes between the change in behavior and the change in attitude.[83] Such questions need to be reformulated and qualified so that we ask "under what conditions do what kinds of people change their attitudes as a consequence of induced behavior?" We need to recognize that change probably occurs in both directions—from thought to act and from act to thought—sometimes separately, sometimes simultaneously, and sometimes sequentially.

Taking such a balanced position, Bettelheim and Janowitz reject on theoretical grounds "the view that social practice must invariably precede attitude or personality changes." They argue, "It is a serious oversimplification to assume that changes in overt behavior necessarily bring about desired changes toward increased tolerance," and that "attitude changes often anticipate overt political and social behavior. Thus," they conclude, "it becomes necessary to assess the policy implications of our research on both the levels of social and personal controls."[84]

It would seem that, in spite of our facile use of such concepts as socialization, internationalization, re-enforcement—all of which imply attitudinal development as a consequence of behavioral experience—we cannot blandly suggest to the policy maker that if he changes behavior, a change in attitude will follow. Nor can we lead him to assume that if he can alter attitudes, he need only wait patiently for the appropriate behavior to develop.

In view of the arguments and evidence reviewed, I should allude to the possibility that changes in policy are not necessarily related to subsequent changes in behavior. It follows that the process of influencing policy makers may at times have negligible impact on the resolution of social problems.[85] Nevertheless, I am concerned with the consequences of doling out to policy makers wrong advice, based on bad research and justified in the name of science. How many good programs are halted and bad ones continued because of "scientific" evaluations? There are increasing demands being made upon social science. There are expectations that we can be helpful—and we ought to be. We do not know the current extent of our influence or its future limits. No doubt it will incease. It may be that as consultants or advisors or sources of information we are used by policy makers only when our knowledge is expedient to bolster positions they have already arrived at for other reasons. But the fact remains that we are used.

You are all aware of the psychological, sociological, and anthropological documentation of the Supreme Court's historic decisions on segregated education in 1954. You know of the intimate involvement of sociologists as architects of President Kennedy's Committee on Juvenile Delinquency and Youth Crime. You must realize the multiple influences of social scientists on President Johnson's "War on Poverty." And our role in local school systems, urban renewal and relocation programs, social agency programs, hospitals, and prisons is probably more pervasive than anyone—including ourselves—realizes.

There are new terms in the language we use to describe ourselves and we ought to be self-conscious about their implications. To what new phenomenon are we referring when we invent the phrase "behavioral science"—and why? What are the implications of beginning to refer to selected disciplines as the "policy sciences?" Why is a new magazine launched in 1965 which is described as concerning itself with "problems of public policy especially," on the grounds "that the social sciences (particularly economics, politics and sociology) have become inextricably linked to issues of public policy . . . ?"[86]

The myth of a value-free social science was exploded with finality by a recent past president of this society.[87] To make such a pretext reflects either hypocrisy or self-delusion. As social scientists, we have responsibility for encouraging and working for social change. The theme of these meetings is based in part upon that assumption and upon the consequent requirement we place upon ourselves to ask, "change for what and why?" The sacred political documents of the United States refer repeatedly to certain kinds of equality and freedoms from constraints in our kind of democracy. There is a discrepancy between the words which most of us honor and the deeds which we all observe. I have no reluctance—in fact, feel an obligation—to bring about a maximum congruence between the word and the deed.

I think that, in large part, this is what the so-called current social revolution in the United States (and probably elsewhere) is all about. It is not a revolution in the sense of seeking to replace existing political and social values with new ones; it is the opposite—a conservative movement which demands that we live by old values. It is rebellion, if at all, only against an hypocrisy which claims that there are no inequitable social, political, education, or economic barriers in our kind of democracy, while in fact there are. It is rebelling against an hypocrisy which claims that universities are establishments where highest values are placed upon teaching and learning, while in fact they are not.

Actually, it makes no difference whether we view the nature of man through the dark lenses of a Hume or a Hobbes—"beastly," with each warring against all others—or through the rose colored glasses of a Locke or Rousseau—as essentially "good" but corrupted by society. It makes no difference since either way man is constrained to behave in ways which are contrary to his supposed nature; either way, the dialectic between man's private self and his social self must create occasional and sometimes radical inconsistencies between what he says and what he does; either way, inconsistency between attitudes and behavior may be assumed.

The dilemma of words and deeds is not peculiarly American, as Gunnar Myrdal would have it, nor is it peculiar to the race question. It is a universal condition of human nature. If our inability to recognize and contend with this condition between World War I and World War II was largely a consequence of the scientific temper of the times, perhaps one day it will be written that in the temper of the new times between World War II and World War III, sociology did flourish and come of age.

NOTES

Presidential address presented at the annual meetings of the Society for the Study of Social Problems, August 28, 1965. I am grateful to my colleagues, Blanche Geer, Warren C. Haggstrom, and Alphonse Sallett, for their critical analyses of an earlier draft of this paper.

[1] Herbert Hyman *et al., Interviewing in Social Research,* Chicago: University of Chicago Press, 1954, pp. 17-18. The quotation is from P. E. Vernon, *The Assessment of Psychological Qualities by Verbal Methods,* Medical Research Council, Industrial Health Research Board, Report No. 83, London: H. M. Stationery, 1938.

[2] Richard T. LaPiere, "Attitudes vs. Actions," *Social Forces,* 13 (March, 1934), pp. 230-237.

[3] In addition to the three *Social Forces* articles (1928, 1934, 1936), I was fortunate to receive a lengthy communication from Professor LaPiere in which he reminisces about some of his early research experiences and about the general state of American sociology in the twenties and thirties. Many of my observations in this section are derived from that communication (dated October 23, 1964).

[4] Richard T. LaPiere, "Race Prejudice: France and England," *Social Forces,* 7 (September, 1928), pp. 102-111.

[5] Richard T. LaPiere, "Type-Rationalizations of Group Antipathy," *Social Forces,* 15 (December, 1936), pp. 232-237.

[6] Personal communication.

[7] LaPiere, "Attitudes vs. Actions," *op. cit.,* p. 231.

[8] LaPiere employed a variety of methodological precautions; for example, in order to control for abnormal behavior or self-consciousness on the part of the Chinese couple, he did not inform them about the experiment in which they were participating. He made it a practice to hang back so that the Chinese undertook all negotiations. He also recorded such things as the condition of his and his subjects' clothing in relation to the quality of the establishment.

[9] With "persistence," responses were obtained from 128 establishments. Ninety-two per cent of the hotels and 91 per cent of the restaurants responded with an out-and-out "no." The rest were either uncertain or stated that it depended upon the circumstances. In order to control for the effect of the previous experience he had created, the investigator sent the same questionnaires to hotels and restaurants in the same areas but at which he and his subjects had not stopped. The distribution of responses from this control sample was the same.

[10] LaPiere, "Attitudes vs. Actions," *op. cit.,* p. 235.

[11] *Ibid.,* pp. 235-236.

[12] Personal communication.

[13] Robert K. Merton, "Fact and Factitiousness in Ethnic Opinionnaires," *American Sociological Review,* 5 (February, 1940), pp. 21-22.

[14] C. Wright Mills, "Methodological Consequences of the Sociology of Knowledge," *American Journal of Sociology,* 46 (November, 1940), pp. 316-330. Reprinted in Irving L. Horowitz (ed.), *Power, Politics and People: The Collected Essays of C. Wright Mills,* New York: Ballantine Books, 1963, p. 467.

[15] Herbert Blumer, "What is Wrong With Social Theory," *American Sociological Review,* 19 (February, 1954), pp. 3-10; "The Problem of the Concept in Social Psychology," *American Journal of Sociology,* 45 (May, 1940), pp. 707-719; "Science Without Concepts," *ibid.,* 36 (May, 1931), pp. 515-533.

[16] Herbert Blumer, "Sociological Analysis and the Variable," *American Sociological Review,* 21 (December, 1956), p. 683.

[17] Herbert Blumer, "Sociological Theory in Industrial Relations," *ibid.,* 12 (February, 1947), pp. 271-277.

[18] Herbert Blumer, "Public Opinion and Public Opinion Polling," *ibid.,* 13 (March, 1948), pp. 542-549.

[19] Herbert Blumer, "Sociological Analysis and the Variable," *op. cit.,* p. 684.

[20] *Ibid.,* p. 690.

[21] LaPiere, "Attitudes vs. Actions," *op. cit.,* p. 237.

[22] C. Wright Mills, "IBM Plus Reality Plus Humanism = Sociology," *Saturday Review,* May 1, 1954; reprinted in Irving L. Horowitz (ed.), *Power, Politics and People: The Collected Essays of C. Wright Mills, op. cit.,* p. 570. I have reason to believe that "the big money" may be more tolerant now than it was when Mills was writing. My suspicion is based in part on the fact that I have received fellowships independently from the National Science Foundation and the National Institute of Mental Health to pursue the questions raised in this paper over the next two years.

[23] Robert K. Merton, *Social Theory and Social Structure* (rev. ed.), Glencoe, Ill.: The Free Press, 1957, p. 440.

[24] *Cf.* Merton, "Fact and Factitiousness in Ethnic Opinionnaires," *op. cit.* Among the sources cited by Merton (n. 9, pp. 15-16) are Morris Cohen and Ernest Nagel, *An Introduction to Logic and Scientific Method,* ch. 15, New York, 1934; H. M. Johnson, "Pseudo-Mathematics in the Mental and Social Sciences," *American Journal of Psychology,* 48 (1936), pp. 342-351; Clifford Kirkpatrick, "Assumptions and Methods in Attitude Measurements," *American Sociological Review,* 1 (1936), pp. 75-88.

[25] Personal communication from LaPiere. That this defensiveness persisted well into the 1940's is evidenced in the "Discussion" of Blumer's "Public Opinion and Public Opinion Polling" in which he challenges the empirical relevance of sampling procedures. Newcomb completely misses the point and with a comparison to "our older-brother sciences" bemoans the fact that "Blumer's stand is one which delays scientific progress" (p. 551). Woodward, the second discussant, gets the point and even makes a number of positive suggestions for implementing it. But his ultimate reaction is one of self-conscious dismay at the image of sociology Blumer may be projecting both within academia and among pollsters. Woodward concludes that "this is too bad" (p. 554).

[26] Louis Guttman, "A Structural Theory for Intergroup Beliefs and Action," *American Sociological Review,* 24 (June, 1959), pp. 318-328.

[27] Merton, *Social Theory and Social Structure, op. cit.,* p. 448.

[28] My references to reliability here and on the following pages have to do with inter-rater, inter-item, interviewer, informant, or observer reliability. The notion of test-retest or any other "reliability" measure involving a time sequence is antithetical to social science since it must make the incorrect assumption that human thought and behavior is static and, therefore, that any change in response is a reflection of either instrument error or deception. In fact, such recorded changes are more likely to reflect shifts in attitude or behavior on the part of the respondent.

[29] Mills, "Methodological Consequences of the Sociology of Knowledge," in Horowitz, *op. cit.,* p. 467 (underscoring added).

[30] Hyman *et al., Interviewing in Social Research, op. cit.,* pp. 4-5.

[31] Clyde Kluckhohn, "The Personal Document in Anthropological Science," in *Social Science Research Council Bulletin,* no. 53, New York: SSRC, 1945. Cited by Hyman, *ibid.,* pp. 5-6.

[32] See, for example, Howard S. Becker and Blanche Geer, "Participant Observation and Interviewing: A Comparison," *Human Organization,* 16 (Fall, 1957), pp. 28-32; Howard S. Becker, "Problems of Inference and Proof in Participant Observation," *American Sociological Review,* 23 (December, 1958), pp. 652-660; Howard S. Becker and Blanche Geer, "Participant Observation: The Analysis of Qualitative Field Data," in R. N. Adams and J. L. Preiss (eds.), *Human Organization Research,* Homewood, Ill.: The Dorsey Press, 1960; Blanche Geer, "First Days in the Field," in P. E. Hammond (ed.), *Sociologists at Work,* New York: Basic Books, 1964, pp. 322-344.

[33] Since what people write, say, or do, can all be viewed as different kinds of "behavior," it is possible to engage in the spurious operation of eliminating the distinctions by subsuming everything under this single rubric. I doubt that this is an adequate solution to the problems posed in this paper. It is possible that the conceptual problem can be broached by viewing verbal behavior and overt behavior as different segments of a single act in process. Apparent inconsistencies can then be conceptualized as resulting from errors in interpretation on the part of the actor or from re-interpretation of the meaning of the act during the interval between the moment of verbal expression and the moment of overt behavior. This formulation also sensitizes the investigator to the possibility that the apparent inconsistency is a result of the actor's perception of the verbalization and the overt behavior as segments of two different acts, i.e., regardless of the investigator's intent, the word and the deed may

be perceived by the actor as relating to different objects. This conceptual framework, and the behavioral theory which it forms, is spelled out in Herbert Blumer, "Sociological Implications of the Thought of George Herbert Mead," *American Journal of Sociology,* 71 (forthcoming, 1966).

[34] Examples of some very different attempts to make sense out of apparent inconsistencies between attitudes and behaviors include A. J. Diekema, "Some Postulates Concerning the Relationship Between Attitudes and Behavior," paper read at the Annual Meeting of the Ohio Valley Sociological Society, May, 1965 (mimeo.); Louis Guttman, "A Structural Theory for Intergroup Beliefs and Action," *American Sociological Review,* 24 (June, 1959), pp. 318-328; Ulf Himmelstrand, 'Verbal Attitudes and Behavior: A Paradigm for the Study of Message Transmission and Transformation," *Public Opinion Quarterly,* 24 (1960), pp. 224-250; Kiyoshi Ikeda, "Discriminatory Actions and Intergroup Attitudes: A Re-examination," ca. 1962 (ditto). Identifying the problem of apparent inconsistencies as one of the more important ones confronting social psychology, the Society for the Psychological Study of Social Issues devoted a full issue of the *Journal of Social Issues* to consideration of that problem as it relates to intergroup relations (vol. 5, no. 3, 1949). Although the intent of the editors was to encourage thinking and research, as far as I can determine their results were slim. See, for example, J. H. Mann, "The Relationship Between Cognitive, Affective, and Behavioral Aspects of Racial Prejudice," *Journal of Social Psychology,* 49 (1959), pp. 223-228.

[35] Robert H. Hardt and George E. Bodine, *Development of Self-Report Instruments in Delinquency Research,* Syracuse, N. Y.: Syracuse University Youth Development Center, 1964. Novel methodological innovations do lie buried in the literature. Kohn and Williams, for example, have suggested a method of deliberately introducing new factors into natural situations for observational purposes. See Melvin Kohn and Robin Williams, "Situational Patterning in Intergroup Relations," *American Sociological Review,* 21 (April, 1956), pp. 164-174. Occasionally a social psychologist devises a laboratory experiment of such diabolical cleverness that the situation must surely appear real to his subjects. See, for example, Stanley Milgram, "Group Pressure and Action Against A Person," *Journal of Abnormal and Social Psychology,* 69 (August, 1964), pp. 137-143. One group of psychologists has evolved a design which enables them to exploit the subject's definition of a dummy experimental situation in order to distract him from the actual experiment which appears as a natural event unrelated to the experiment. See, for example, Philip Himelstein and James C. Moore, "Racial Attitudes and the Action of Negro- and White-Background Figures as Factors in Petition-Signing," *The Journal of Social Psychology,* 61 (December, 1963), pp. 267-272.

[36] Cook and Selltiz have examined the different results which may be obtained by employing different methods of assessing attitudes—including both self-reports and behavioral observations. Stuart W. Cook and Claire Sellitz, "A Multiple Indicator Approach to Attitude Measurement," *Psychological Bulletin,* 62 (July, 1964), pp. 36-58.

[37] David J. Hanson, "Notes on a Bibliography on Attitudes and Behavior," 1965 (unpublished).

[38] W. A. Scott, "Attitude Change Through Reward of Verbal Behavior," *Journal of Abnormal and Social Psychology,* 55 (1957), pp. 72-75; "Attitude Change By Response Reinforcement: Replication and Extension, *Sociometry,* 22 (1959), pp. 328-335.

[39] B. T. King and I. L. Janis, "Comparison of the Effectiveness of Improvised Versus Non-improvised Role-Playing in Producing Opinion Changes," *Human Relations,* 9 (1956), pp. 177-186.

[40] Melvin L. DeFleur and Frank R. Westie, "Verbal Attitudes and Overt Acts: An Experiment in the Salience of Attitudes," *American Sociological Review,* 23 (December, 1958), pp. 667-673.

[41] B. Kutner, C. Wilkins, and P. B. Yarrow, "Verbal Attitudes and Overt Behavior Involving Racial Prejudice," *Journal of Abnormal and Social Psychology,* 47 (1952), pp. 649-652.

[42] Gerhart Saenger and Emily Gilbert, "Customer Reactions to the Integration of Negro Sales Personnel," *International Journal of Opinion and Attitude Research,* 4 (Spring, 1950), pp. 57-76.

[43] For example, a controlled laboratory study showing no relationship between attitude and behavior is reported in Michael Zunich, "Relationship Between Maternal Behavior

and Attitudes Toward Children," *Journal of Genetic Psychology* (March, 1962), pp. 155-165. On the other hand, behavior under natural conditions which has been observed to conform to expressed attitudes is reported in Irwin Deutscher and Laurence Cagle. "Housing Aspirations of Low Income Fatherless Families," Syracuse, N. Y.: Syracuse University Youth Development Center, 1964 (mimeo).

[44] Blumer may be a prophet with honor. In a review of a public opinion textbook published in 1964, Angus Campbell recollects Blumer's comments of two decades earlier with a touch of nostalgia and no little remorse: "It is curious that Blumer's hopes for the functional analysis of public opinion have been so little realized. The ability to conduct effective research on the problems he would have selected seems to elude us. The direction research has actually taken has been heavily influenced by the methods available." See Angus Campbell's review of Lane and Sears, *American Sociological Review,* 30 (August, 1965), p. 633. Cf. footnote 25 in this paper.

[45] The following series of references is selected from a bibliography of some 200 items I have found to be related to the central theme of this paper. See Irwin Deutscher, "Bibliography on the Relation Between Sentiments and Acts," Syracuse N.Y.: Syracuse University Youth Development Center, Jan., 1966 (mimeo). Available in limited quantity on request.

[46] R. Bastide and P. L. van den Berghe, "Stereotypes, Norms, and Interracial Behavior in Sao Paulo, Brazil," *American Sociological Review,* 22 (December, 1957), pp. 689-694.

[47] Wilbur B. Brookover and John B. Holland, "An Inquiry into the Meaning of Minority Group Attitude Expressions," *American Sociological Review,* 17 (April, 1952), pp. 196-202.

[48] Saenger and Gilbert, "Customer Reactions to the Integration of Negro Sales Personnel," *op. cit.*

[49] Lawrence S. Linn, "Verbal Attitude and Overt Behavior: A Study of Racial Discrimination," *Social Forces,* 43 (March, 1965), pp. 353-364.

[50] Lois Dean, "Interaction, Reported and Observed: The Case of One Local Union," *Human Organization,* 17 (Fall, 1958), p. 36.

[51] Linton C. Freeman and Turkoz Ataov, "Invalidity of Indirect and Direct Measures of Attitudes Toward Cheating," *Journal of Personality,* 28 (December, 1960), pp. 443-447.

[52] Jules Henry, "Spontaneity, Initiative, and Creativity in Suburban Classrooms," *American Journal of Orthopsychiatry,* 29 (1959), pp. 266-279. Reprinted in George D. Spindler (ed.), *Education and Culture: Anthropological Approaches,* New York: Holt, Rinehart and Winston, 1963, pp. 215-233. See esp. p. 228.

[53] Edward Hassinger and Robert L. McNamara, "Stated Opinion and Actual Practice in Health Behavior in a Rural Area," *The Midwest Sociologist* (May, 1957), pp. 93-97.

[54] Snell Putney and Russell Middleton, "Ethical Relativism and Anomia," *American Journal of Sociology,* 67 (January, 1962), pp. 430-438. "Religion, Normative Standards, and Behavior," *Sociometry,* 25 (1962), pp. 141-152.

[55] Charles K. Warriner, "The Nature and Functions of Official Morality," *American Journal of Sociology,* 64 (September, 1958), pp. 165-168.

[56] Louis Kriesberg, "National Security and Conduct in the Steel Gray Market," *Social Forces,* 34 (March, 1956), pp. 268-277.

[57] Vera Meyers Schletzer *et al.,* "Attitudinal Barriers to Employment," *Minnesota Studies in Vocational Rehabilitation: XI,* Industrial Relations Center, Bulletin no. 32, University of Minnesota, Minneapolis, 1961.

[58] Michael Zunich, "Relationship Between Maternal Behavior and Attitudes Toward Children," *op. cit.*

[59] Irving Wallace, *The Chapman Report,* New York: Signet Books, 1961, pp. 106-107.

[60] Leonard Z. Breen, "Retirement: Norms, Behavior, and Functional Aspects of Normative Behavior," in R. H. Williams, C. Tibbitts, and W. Donahue (eds.), *Processes of Aging,* vol. 2, New York: Atherton Press, 1963; William E. Henry and Elaine Cumming, *Growing Old: The Process of Disengagement,* New York: Basic Books, 1961. See esp. section dealing with normative responses.

[61] A. Brayfield and D. M. Crockett, "Employee Attitudes and Employee Performance," *Psychological Bulletin,* 52 (September, 1955), pp. 396-428.

[62] Harold H. Martin, "Why She Really Goes To Market," *Saturday Evening Post,* September 28, 1963, pp. 40-43.

[63] Deutscher and Cagle, "Housing Aspirations of Low Income Fatherless Families," *op. cit.*

[64] Richard T. Frost, "Stability and Change in Local Party Politics," *Public Opinion Quarterly,* 25 (Summer, 1961), pp. 221-235.

[65] Dramatic evidence of this is provided in Robert H. Hardt, "Juvenile Suspects and Violations: A Comparative Study of Correlates of Two Delinquency Measures," unpublished doctoral dissertation, Syracuse University, 1965, Table 8, p. 73ff. See also Maynard L. Erickson and Lamar T. Empey, "Court Records, Undetected Delinquency and Decision Making," *Journal of Criminal Law, Criminology and Police Science,* 54 (December, 1963), pp. 456-469; Harwin L. Voss, "Ethnic Differentials in Delinquency in Honolulu," *Journal of Criminal Law, Criminology and Police Science,* 54 (September, 1963), pp. 322-327; Hardt and Bodine, *Development of Self-Report Instruments in Delinquency Research, op. cit.,* pp. 19-25.

[66] Brayfield and Crockett, "Employee Attitudes and Employee Performance," *op. cit.,* p. 415.

[67] Arnold M. Rose, "Intergroup Relations Vs. Prejudice: Pertinent Theory For the Study of Social Change," *Social Problems,* 4 (October, 1956). For a symbolic interactionist approach to explaining inconsistencies, see footnote 33 in this paper.

[68] For a reflection of the current primitive state of Sociolinguistics see Charles A. Ferguson, "Directions in Sociolinguistics: Report on an Interdisciplinary Seminar," *Social Science Research Council Items,* 19 (March, 1965), pp. 1-4. The participants of the seminar described in that report appear to have skirted the central core of the relevance of linguistics to sociology and social psychology and concentrated instead on several marginal areas of mutual interest.

[69] Robert Gover, *The One-Hundred Dollar Misunderstanding,* New York: Ballantine Books, 1963.

[70] Brayfield and Crockett, "Employee Attitudes and Employee Performance," *op. cit.,* p. 421.

[71] Leon Festinger, "Behavioral Support for Opinion Change," *Public Opinion Quarterly,* 28 (Fall, 1964), p. 405.

[72] *Ibid.* For reasons which are unclear to me, Festinger insists that he is "not raising the question of whether or not attitudes are found to relate to relevant behavior." He accepts the conclusion that they are related and cites De Fleur and Westie to document the fact. See De Fleur and Westie, "Verbal Attitudes and Overt Acts: An Experiment in the Salience of Attitudes," *op. cit.*

[73] The first of these, data from which Festinger reanalyzed, is N. Maccoby *et al., "Critical Periods" In Seeking and Accepting Information,* Paris-Stanford Studies in Communication, Stanford, Calif., Institute for Communication Research, 1962. The other two are E. Fleishmann *et al., Leadership and Supervision in Industry: An Evaluation of a Supervisory Training Program,* Columbus, O.: Ohio State University, Bureau of Educational Research, 1955, and I. Janis and S. Feshback, "Effects of Fear-arousing Communications," *Journal of Abnormal and Social Psychology,* 48 (1953), pp. 78-92.

[74] Leon Festinger, "Behavioral Support For Opinion Change," *op. cit.,* p. 416.

[75] Howard J. Ehrlich and James W. Rinehart, "A Brief Report on the Methodology of Stereotype Research," *Social Forces,* 43 (May, 1965).

[76] Samuel A. Stouffer *et al., The American Soldier: Adjustment During Army Life,* Studies in Social Psychology in World War II, vol. 1, Princeton, N.J.: Princeton University Press, 1949, p. 594ff. For a more detailed analysis of these data see "Opinions About Negro Infantry Platoons in White Companies of Seven Divisions," in Guy E. Swanson *et al., Readings in Social Psychology,* New York: Holt, 1952, pp. 502-506.

[77] Morton Deutsch and May Evans Collins, "Interracial Housing," in William Petersen (ed.), *American Social Patterns,* New York: Doubleday Anchor Books, 1956, esp. pp. 19-46. See also Daniel M. Wilner, Rosabelle P. Walkley, and Stuart W. Cook, "Residential Proximity and Intergroup Relations in Public Housing Projects," *Journal of Social Issues,* vol. 8, no. 1 (1952), pp. 45-69.

[78] Marian Radke Yarrow, "Interpersonal Dynamics in a Desegregation Process," Special Issue, *Journal of Social Issues,* vol. 14, no. 1 (1958).

[79] Paul H. Mussen, "Some Personality and Social Factors Related to Changes in Children's Attitudes Toward Negroes," *Journal of Abnormal and Social Psychology,* 45 (July, 1950), pp. 423-441.

[80] Bruno Bettelheim and Morris Janowitz, *Social Change and Prejudice Including Dynamics of Prejudice,* New York: The Free Press of Glencoe, 1964.

[81] See, for example, Barbara K. MacKenzie, "The Importance of Contact in Determining Attitudes Toward Negroes," *Journal of Abnormal and Social Psychology,* 43 (October, 1948), pp. 417-441.

[82] Joseph Lohman and Dietrick C. Reitzes, "Deliberately Organized Groups and Racial Behavior," *American Sociological Review,* 19 (June, 1954), pp. 342-348; Arnold Rose, "Inconsistencies in Attitudes Toward Negro Housing," *Social Problems,* 8 (Spring, 1961), pp. 286-292; R. D. Minard, "Race Relationships in the Pocahontas Coal Field," *Journal of Social Issues,* 8 (1952), pp. 29-44.

[83] Kelman properly phrases the abstract question in his theoretical analysis which leads to a consideration of the variables which intervene between an action and a possible change in attitude: "What are the conditions under which the induction of action does lead to attitude change, and what are some of the mechanisms and processes that account for the phenomenon when it does occur?" See Herbert Kelman, "The Induction of Action and Attitude Change," *Proceedings of the XIV International Congress of Applied Psychology,* Copenhagen: Munksgaard, 1961, p. 82.

[84] Bettelheim and Janowitz, *Social Change and Prejudice Including Dynamics of Prejudice, op. cit.,* pp. 79-80.

[85] For an example of low level subversion of high level policy with the tacit approval of middle level management, see my chapter, "The Bureaucratic Gatekeeper in Public Housing," in Irwin Deutscher (ed.), *Among The People: Encounters With the Urban Poor,* New York: Basic Books, forthcoming, 1966.

[86] Undated memorandum from Daniel Bell and Irving Kristol to members of the American Economic, American Political Science, and American Sociological Associations announcing the quarterly magazine, *The Public Interest.*

[87] Alvin Gouldner, "Anti-Minotaur: The Myth of a Value-Free Sociology," *Social Problems,* 9 (Winter, 1962). No myth is ever exploded with absolute finality. There remain occasional protests that sociology is or should be a value-free science, *viz.,* Ernest Van den Haag, "On Mobilization for Youth," *American Sociological Review,* 30 (August, 1965), pp. 587-588.

III

METHODOLOGICAL REEXAMINATION

5

A STUDY OF THE ASSOCIATION AMONG VERBAL ATTITUDES, COMMITMENT AND OVERT BEHAVIOR IN DIFFERENT EXPERIMENTAL SITUATIONS*

James M. Fendrich

Studies examining racial attitudes and overt behavior have often reported inconsistency between the measure of verbal attitudes and overt behavior.[1] One explanation for the discrepancy is that characteristics of the overt situation, rather than attitudes, determine the action toward the attitude object.[2] Another way of interpreting the findings involves the recognition that situational factors influence behavior in both measurement situations. When measuring verbal attitudes, the situational characteristics can be markedly different than characteristics in the overt situation. The disparity between the situational characteristics which influence respondents' role-playing in each setting may contribute to the inconsistency.

The present study examines the relationship between expressed racial attitudes and overt behavior, looking at characteristics of the research setting which influence the expression of attitudes and affect the consistency between verbal attitudes and overt behavior. The objectives are: (1) to manipulate the definition of the situation while measuring verbal attitudes in order to explore the extent to which different definitions of the situation influence the degree of association between verbal attitudes and overt behavior; and (2) to compare the relative power of verbal attitudes and commitment in predicting overt behavior.

The definition of the situation is used to refer to the respondent's subjective attempt to orient himself to the context in which he finds himself, ascertain his interest, and then proceed to cope with the circumstances.[3] The definition of the situation is a process whereby present stimuli and past experience are synthesized in some meaningful whole

Reprinted from *Social Forces* (Vol. 45, March, 1967, pp. 347-355) by permission of the author, *Social Forces,* and the University of North Carolina Press.

to facilitate interaction. When a situation has been defined "decisions can be made as to what behavior and objects can be appropriately woven into the interaction sequence and what cannot."[4] Role-playing is considered to be the overt manifestation of a set of perceived normative expectations resulting from defining the situation.[5] By altering the definition of the research setting, the role-playing involved in expressing attitudes was expected to vary. Verbal attitudes were considered to be the outward manifestation of two internal processes. One is the acquired behavioral dispositions toward a class of objects. The other is the definition of the situation. Both processes shape the expression of attitudes. Commitment was considered as the act of making perceived voluntary decisions to participate in a consistent pattern of action that involves some risk.[6] The perceived voluntary decisions refer to the choices between a limited set of possible alternatives that will affect subsequent behavior. The consistent activity involves a series of acts which are not easily reversible. The risk of commitment results from making decisions to engage in a particular pattern of overt behavior. Thus, the committed person by acting out his decisions exposes himself to the sanctioning of significant others. Overt behavior refers to observable acts directed toward the attitude object.

A number of authors have suggested the usual testing situation has unique characteristics which influence respondents' role-playing. Hyman states the inconsistency between verbal attitudes and overt behavior results from inconsistencies between the interpretations researchers put upon attitude measurements and the measurements' relation to behavior. In attempting to account for the lack of a one-to-one relationship between verbal attitudes and overt behavior, Hyman states that in the typical testing situation respondents are not subject to the normal coercive forces of everyday life. In contrast, outside the testing situation respondents are held to account for what they have said or how they have acted.[7] Cicourel and Back *et al.,* outline game theory models to explain behavior in the testing situation. They stress the researcher tries to create a testing situation that is considered a special kind of interpersonal system, very similar to play.[8] The behavior is separate in time and space, uncertain, unproductive, free and governed by rules of make-believe.[9] Linn has described the characteristics of role-playing when measuring racial attitudes of students. While attending a university which has a reputation for being more politically and racially liberal than many other institutions, there is a social and cultural norm held by most *S*s to take a liberal position on racial integration. In the usual testing situation many *S*s actively play, or attempt to play, their social role of the liberal college student; consequently, they express favorable attitudes toward Negroes.[10] Linn's description of active role-playing suggests that *S*s in trying to cooperate, may bias the results of the attitude measure.

The association between verbal attitudes and overt behavior was not expected to be highly correlated in the usual research setting due to its play-like characteristics. In this type of setting it was assumed that subjects would define the situation as an attempt to find out how prejudiced they were toward Negroes. In actively trying to cooperate some subjects would try to demonstrate they were not prejudiced while others would cooperate in revealing how they *felt* toward Negroes. In neither interpretation would they be revealing how they would *act* toward the attitude object.

Hyman states if the aim is to predict a given kind of behavior in a given social setting, tests should be designed to incorporate the fundamental aspects of the overt setting into the testing situation.[11] One of the most important characteristics of overt behavior is the sanctioning of significant others.[12] A commitment measure was designed to incorporate this fundamental aspect of the overt setting into the testing situation. Since committing one's self involves volunteering to engage in future acts that will be sanctioned by significant others, it was hypothesized the commitment would be significantly related to overt behavior.

Measurement of verbal attitudes does not normally tap commitment. Verbal attitudes are statements of preference that have no specific consequences for subsequent behavior. Definite decisions are not made to interact with the attitude object outside the testing situation. Therefore, attitudes can be expressed without consideration of the sanctioning of significant others. Thus, the relationship between commitment and overt behavior was expected to be greater than verbal attitudes and overt behavior.

If expressed commitment preceded verbal attitudes in the testing situation, the role-playing in the research setting was expected to change. Role-playing in the measurement of verbal attitudes would no longer retain its play-like characteristics, but would be played within a framework of previous commitment. When the attitude measurement immediately followed the measurement of commitment, verbal attitudes were expected to be consistent with the expressed level of commitment. Therefore, the relationship between verbal attitudes and overt behavior was expected to be greater in the research setting involving previous commitment to the attitude object. In summary, three hypotheses were tested:

1. *The greater the degree of favorable commitment, the greater the degree of overt behavior.*

2. *The degree of relationship between commitment and overt behavior will be greater than the relationship between verbal attitudes and overt behavior.*

3. *The greater the extent to which attitudes are expressed in a research setting involving previous commitment to the attitude object, the greater the relationship between verbal attitudes and overt behavior.*

EXPERIMENTAL METHODOLOGY

Research Design

The attitude and commitment data were gathered in face-to-face interviews. There were two experimental treatments. The two treatments were designed to create different definitions of the attitude measure-situation. Treatment A was similar to the usual testing situation. Students were asked to express their attitudes toward Negroes. They were not told they would later be asked to commit themselves to interaction with Negroes. In essence a playlike environment was created. In Treatment B *S*s were asked to commit themselves to interaction with Negroes before they responded to the attitude items. Commitment involved interacting with Negroes in the future, creating the risk of being sanctioned by significant others. The commitment scale was designed to reduce sharply the play-like conditions of the testing situation. After taking the risk of committing themselves, *S*s were asked to respond to the attitude scale. In Treatment B role-playing was expected to be consistent with commitment.

After responding to both the attitude and commitment questions, respondents were asked if they would be willing to attend a small group discussion with Negro and white members of a campus chapter of the "National Association For The Advancement of Colored People" (NAACP).[13] The discussions were planned for the week following the administration of the instruments. The expressed purpose of the discussions was to improve interracial understanding in the college community.

Sample

The interview data were gathered by sampling from the undergraduate population at a large "Big Ten" university. The university was not considered solely as an institution of higher learning; it was considered to be a community. Within this community *S*s interact with people directly and indirectly involved with the academic institution. Sampling criteria were used to select those most likely to be participants in the university community. Freshmen were excluded because they were relatively new arrivals on campus and were not familiar with the prevalent attitudes and sanctions governing the patterns of interracial interaction. With the assistance of the university's Data Processing Center a small representative sample of 65 sophomores, juniors and seniors was drawn. From this sample *S*s were selected if they were U.S. citizens, white, full-time students who lived on campus or in the community surrounding the university. Foreign *S*s were excluded because their familiarity with interracial activities in the United States was considered to be either limited or viewed from a different perspective. Students who lived outside the community and *S*s who were not attending the university on a full-time basis were excluded because of their often minimal contact with other *S*s outside of the classroom. Six *S*s who did not complete all of the scales were excluded. The remaining 46 *S*s were interviewed at their place of residence. Randomization procedures were used in order that each *S* would have the same probability of falling into either treatment.

Attitude Scale

The operational definitions consist of scales designed to measure three variables—verbal attitudes, commitment and overt behavior. A 32-item scale was developed to measure verbal attitudes toward Negro *S*s.[14] A variety of campus experiences were included in the items, e.g., dating, student government, housing, athletics, academic abilities, militancy, etc. Thirteen items expressed a favorable attitude toward Negro *S*s and 19 expressed an unfavorable attitude. To be consistent *S*s had to both agree and disagree with items. All of the attitude scale items had a range of five possible responses—"strongly agree," "agree," "undecided," "disagree," and "strongly disagree." The estimated split-half reliability of the study was .91. Item-total score correlations indicated that the scale was internally consistent. Twenty-eight of the 32 items were significantly correlated with the total score. The remaining four approached significance. The following 32 items were used to construct the attitude scale:

1. I think there are Negroes qualified to be class presidents.
2. Negro students all look alike.
3. I think research would show that Negroes definitely get much poorer grades than white students.
4. I wouldn't want Negroes in positions of responsible student leadership on campus.
5. I wouldn't mind at all if I lived in an area that was integrated.
6. I find some Negroes attractive.
7. Negroes on campus want too much.
8. I would like to go on a double date with a Negro couple.
9. I would feel extremely uncomfortable dancing with a Negro student.
10. Negroes are better in sports because they come from more primitive backgrounds.
11. Eating at the same table with a Negro wouldn't bother me.
12. It would be a good experience to get to know more Negroes on campus.
13. Negro students don't take care of their personal hygiene.
14. I'd hate to be seen walking across campus alone with a Negro.
15. Negroes should stick to themselves.
16. Any white student is better than a Negro student.
17. No one forgets so easily as a Negro student.

18. When given a chance Negroes can do just as well in school as anyone else.
19. I wouldn't want to see a Negro president of student government.
20. Only unprincipled students would go on an interracial date.
21. I would like to see Negroes get equal treatment in all areas of campus life.
22. Negroes want the same things out of life that I do.
23. The more Negroes come to this university the lower the standards get.
24. I wouldn't mind working with Negroes on some campus project.
25. I hate to see a white and Negro going steady together.
26. I would prefer sharing living quarters with any white rather than with a Negro student.
27. I think the only thing that Negroes can contribute to campus life is better athletics.
28. The only way that Negro students can obtain full equality on campus is through the help of white students.
29. The more Negro professors we get on campus the lower will be the quality of teaching.
30. The reason why Negroes want fraternities and sororities of their own is so they can stay by themselves.
31. I think there are Negroes on campus who will be more successful in the future than I will.
32. Some Negro students are smarter than I am.

Commitment Scale

A 10-item scale was developed to measure commitment.[15] Questions were designed to imply participation in interracial activities with Negro *S*s. The interviewer stated the questions involved possible interaction with Negro *S*s in the future. Following this introduction, *S*s were asked if they would be willing to commit themselves to nine different forms of activities. If they committed themselves to any of the nine activities, they were then asked to give their phone number. This last item was included in the scale to reinforce the idea of being committed to future interaction. Care was taken to construct items that would appear realistic to the *S*s. Items varied in the extent of personal involvement in the interracial activities. The following 10 items were used to construct the commitment scale:

1. Would you agree to go to coffee or lunch with a mixed racial group of students to talk about interracial problems on campus?
2. Would you agree to have a Negro as a roommate next year or next term?
3. Would you agree to spend a weekend at the home of a Negro attending the university if he or she invited you?

4. Would you agree to invite a Negro at the university to spend a weekend at your home?
5. Would you agree to participate in a small group discussion on the topic of white students' social relations with Negroes on campus?
6. Would you agree to attend a lecture or conference on the topic of white students' social relations with Negroes on campus?
7. Would you agree to protest against segregated housing in the city with Negro students?
8. Would you agree to attend a meeting of the Campus Chapter of the NAACP?
9. Would you, if asked, agree to contribute $1.00 to help finance the activities of a Negro action group, (SNCC) (NAACP) or (CORE)?
10. (If respondent says yes to any of the above items) Would you give your phone number? No. ....

The *S*s were given three choices of responses to each of the ten items—"yes," "maybe," and "no." Since the primary interest was the degree of positive commitment, it was decided to score the "yes" responses as one and the remaining two responses as zero. The estimated split-half reliability was .82. Every item was significantly correlated to the total score.

Overt Behavior Scale

The overt behavior scale was developed to measure behavior congruent with verbal attitudes and commitment toward Negro *S*s. After responding to the attitude and commitment scales, *S*s were asked if they were willing to attend small group discussions with members of the NAACP that were scheduled in the near future. During the five-day period following the administration of the attitude and commitment scales, *S*s were contacted to determine if they still definitely planned to attend the discussions. The NAACP representatives tried to obtain firm decisions and answer any questions. The *S*s were given the opportunity to attend one of four discussions.[16] If the *S*s declined, the representatives did not force the issue and noted either a refusal or acceptance to attend the discussions. At the small group discussions every *S* was asked to give his name in order that name-tags could be used to facilitate interaction. This information was used to associate *S*s with their interview data. At the beginning of each meeting the researcher defined himself as a member of the NAACP and he introduced other members who had previously volunteered to take part in the discussions. At each session the campus history of the organization was presented, particular areas of discrimination on- and off-campus were cited, and future activities were brought to the students' attention. Afterwards *S*s participated in lively and pointed conversation with the members of the NAACP. At the end of the discussions they were asked if they were willing to sign up to participate further in interracial activities. The activities involved a number of committees of the NAACP, e.g., publicity, program of research, entertainment, membership, direct action, housing, and the NAACP Newsletter. Besides these activities *S*s were given the opportunity to help organize a talent show to raise money for projects in southern states, volunteer to work in Mississippi during the summer, or recruit students for summer work, take part in a civil rights program sponsored by student government, assist in a campus fund raising drive students volunteering for summer projects and circulate a petition in the local community to obtain signatures of residents which would be used as evidence to support a "Fair Housing Ordinance" being considered by the City Council.

The overt behavior scale measures behavior outside of the research setting. The scale has four discrete points:

0 = Refusing invitation to attend small group discussions designed to improve race relations on campus.
1 = Accepting invitation to attend small group discussions designed to improve race relations on campus.
2 = Participating in small group discussions.
3 = Signing up for ongoing civil rights activities.

Inspection of the scale revealed very few inconsistencies. The time ordering of responses that increased in degree of involvement in interracial activities reduced the possibility of inconsistency. Using scalogram analysis procedures, resulted in a coefficient of reproducibility of .99.

Table 1 reports the scores of the *S*s on the three scales. The *S*s in both treatments had favorable attitudes toward Negro *S*s. The commitment scores were widely dispersed and the overt behavior scores were more varied in Treatment B than Treatment A.

Statistical Treatment

In contrast to other studies on verbal attitudes and overt behavior, this study does not employ a theoretical model that posits there will be a linear one-to-one association between the independent and dependent variables. This type of model for testing hypotheses is artificially stringent. It was felt that a better theoretical and methodological approach would be to consider verbal attitudes and commitment as contributory causes of overt behavior, i.e., they are important independent variables but not the sole determinants of overt behavior. The most useful measures for testing the consistency hypothesis are measures reporting the "predictability" of the dependent variable from known values of the independent variable.

Since interest was primarily in the proportional-reduction-in-error variance of overt behavior from knowledge of attitude and commitment, a measure was chosen that meets Costner's criteria for proportional-reduction-in-error measures.[17] The overt behavior scale was an ordinal

TABLE 1.
SCORES ON THE ATTITUDE, COMMITMENT AND OVERT BEHAVIOR SCALES, BY STUDENT

Treatment A				Treatment B			
Student	Attitude	Commitment	Overt Behavior	Student	Attitude	Commitment	Overt Behavior
1.......	131	5	3	23	118	4	0
2.......	127	7	2	24	118	4	0
3.......	138	2	1	25	108	0	0
4.......	118	6	1	26	141	8	2
5.......	106	3	0	27	127	5	1
6.......	113	6	1	28	131	10	1
7.......	113	4	0	29	110	4	1
8.......	118	4	0	30	144	8	3
9.......	149	8	0	31	144	10	3
10.......	131	10	3	32	132	6	1
11.......	118	6	1	33	159	10	2
12.......	143	8	1	34	126	5	0
13.......	137	7	0	35	116	3	0
14.......	123	6	0	36	139	6	1
15.......	117	10	0	37	124	6	0
16.......	146	9	1	38	136	6	2
17.......	137	7	0	39	129	8	0
18.......	127	8	1	40	133	6	1
19.......	124	5	0	41	128	10	1
20.......	149	10	0	42	136	10	2
21.......	124	6	0	43	113	7	1
22.......	132	3	0	44	123	5	0
				45	111	7	1
				46	123	7	1

scale and the data were not normally distributed. Therefore, *gamma* was chosen as the measure of association. If the explained variance was -.50 the independent variable was considered a good predictor of overt behavior.

RESULTS

Test of Hypothesis 1

Table 2 reports the results of the measures of association by treatment. In Treatment A the attitude scale preceded the commitment scale. The order was reversed in Treatment B. Hypothesis 1 states that the level of commitment is an effective predictor of overt behavior. In Treatment B the relationship between commitment is significant beyond the .01 confidence level. The level of commitment explains .72 of the variance of overt behavior scores. In Treatment B *S*s responded to the experimental design, engaging in acts of commitment that were consistent with their overt behavior.

In Treatment A the relationship was not significant at the .05 level of confidence. The level of commitment explains only .18 of the variance of overt behavior scores. The proportion of explained variance in Treat-

TABLE 2.
ASSOCIATION AMONG VERBAL ATTITUDES, COMMITMENT AND OVERT BEHAVIOR, BY TREATMENT

Relationship	Treatment A: Attitude Measured Before Commitment *gamma*	Treatment B: Commitment Measured Before Attitude *gamma*
Attitude-Commitment	.37*	.66†
Attitude-Overt Behavior	.12	.69†
Commitment-Overt Behavior.....	.18	.72†
	N=22	N=24

*P<.05
†<.01

ment A did not meet perceived expectations. It was felt that the threat of sanctions from significant others would make acts of commitment consistent with overt behavior. Evidently there were two major types of social pressures operating in the interview situation. The first was to respond in a consistent manner to the interviewer. The second social pressure was to be consistent with the expectations of significant others outside of the testing situation. Recent research on cognitive dissonance theory has demonstrated the extent to which respondents strain to act consistently in a voluntary experimental situation.[18] This strain to act consistently was expected to be greater in Treatment B when measuring attitudes after commitment, but it was not expected to operate as strongly in Treatment A when measuring commitment after verbal attitudes. Thus, the strain to give consistent response patterns within the testing situation was underestimated in Treatment A. One conclusion that can be drawn is that commitment is a useful predictor of overt behavior if the research setting is not contaminated by previous acts unrelated to overt behavior with which the respondent is forced to be consistent.

Test of Hypothesis 2

Hypothesis 2 states commitment will be a better predictor of overt behavior than verbal attitudes. Since the pressure to be consistent with the first expression of either commitment or verbal attitudes strongly influenced the second expression, the measure of association between verbal attitudes and overt behavior in Treatment A and commitment and overt behavior in Treatment B were used to test the hypothesis. The research situations in which these two measures were obtained were comparable. Both measures were presented first in the respective treatments, and therefore, were unaffected by interaction with the second variable. In Treatment B the level of commitment explains .69 of the variance of overt behavior. In Treatment A the degree of favorable attitudes explains only .12 of the variance of overt behavior. Under comparable research conditions commitment is a much stronger predictor of overt behavior than verbal attitudes.

Test of Hypothesis 3

Hypothesis 3 states the greater the extent to which attitudes are expressed in a research setting involving previous commitment to the attitude object, the greater the relationship between verbal attitudes and overt behavior. In Treatment B, verbal attitudes were expected to be consistent with commitment, and therefore, significantly related to overt behavior. Data from Treatments A and B support the hypothesis. The difference between $gamma_1$-$gamma_2$ was .57, i.e., verbal attitudes in Treatment B explained 57 percent more of the variance in overt behavior than verbal attitudes in Treatment A. This great a difference of *gammas* was considered to be significant. The results suggest the definitions of the research settings were markedly different, producing one set of responses that were consistent with overt behavior and one set of inconsistent responses.

DISCUSSION

The results of this study caution against simplistic explanations of either consistency or inconsistency between verbal attitudes and overt behavior. The expression of attitudes is not simply an expression of an orientation toward action with the attitude object, and thus, consistent with overt behavior. The definition of the measurement situation influences the way respondents express their attitudes. Previous research that explains the inconsistency between verbal attitudes and overt behavior as being due to different situational factors in the overt situation and the attitude measurement situation appears to be correct. The researchers, however, did not recognize the flexibility of the research setting. Verbal attitudes can be useful predictors of overt behavior, if the artificial play atmosphere of the testing situation is reduced. Hyman's suggestion that fundamental aspects of the overt setting should be incorporated in the testing situation, which is designed to predict behavior, is useful advice. In this study a measure of commitment to interaction with the attitude object did incorporate the fundamental aspects of overt behavior. When the expression of attitudes immediately followed the measured commitment, attitudes were consistent with overt behavior.

The findings of this study add to the growing body of literature on social behavior in the research process.[19] It is dangerous to assume that participants are willing, but docile subjects in social research, rather, they are active agents who define a social situation and play what they perceive to be the appropriate role. The results of this study suggest that recognition of the social psychology of the research process can contribute to designing experiments to collect reliable and valid predictors of overt behavior. Lacking this knowledge researchers may draw false conclusions from their findings.

In criticizing a recent article that tended to polarize conceptualizations of attitudes into "probability conceptions" and "latent process conceptions," Weissberg made a point that is well taken. The effects of attitudes in behavior should not be considered from a perspective of theoretical monism. Verbal attitudes are, "simply one of the terms in the complex regression equation we use to predict behavior."[20] One possible way of solving this equation is to adopt a field theory orientation, considering behavior both in and outside an experimental environment as being a function of both personality and environmental factors. Such an approach prevents positing theories of contemporaneity or theories of predispositional determinism.

SUMMARY

The data for this study were gathered from 46 randomly selected college sophomores, juniors and seniors at a "Big Ten" university. The *S*s were randomly distributed between two experimental treatments. Under Treatment A *S*s were encouraged to define the research setting as the usual play-like experiment. In Treatment B *S*s were encouraged to define the research setting as a situation where current acts would have consequences for future behavior. In Treatment A verbal attitudes toward Negroes were not found to be good predictors of the degree of involvement in a campus chapter of the NAACP. In contrast verbal attitudes in Treatment B were good predictors of the same overt behavior.

This study demonstrates the importance of the social psychology of the research process. The way respondents define a situation, and consequently, play the corresponding role, significantly affects the relationship between independent and dependent variables. *Verbal attitudes can be either consistent or inconsistent with overt behavior, depending upon the way respondents define the attitude measurement situation.* The results caution against simplistic interpretations of verbal attitudes relationship to overt behavior. As Hyman has stated the inconsistency between verbal attitudes and overt behavior frequently results from inconsistencies between the interpretations researchers put upon attitude measurements and the measurements' relationship to behavior, rather than from evidence of measures of association.

Data also suggest that measures of commitment may be better predictors of overt behavior than measures of attitude, if the measurement situation is not contaminated by role-playing unrelated to overt behavior with which respondents feel forced to be consistent. Unlike attitude measures, commitment incorporates in the measurement situation the fundamental aspect of overt behavior—the possible sanctioning of significant others. Since the measurement of commitment involves the reduction of the play-like atmosphere of the usual testing situation, it serves the function of providing a good predictor for overt behavior.

NOTES

* The author is indebted to Santo F. Camilleri and Archie O. Haller for their valuable advice and criticism in the designing and carrying out of this study. This investigation was supported by a Public Health Service predoctoral fellowship 1-F1-MH-28, 021-01 from NIMH.

[1] There are numerous articles on this topic: Douglas W. Bray, "The Prediction of Behavior From Two Attitude Scales," *Journal of Abnormal and Social Psychology*, 45 (1950), pp. 64-84; Wilber Brookover and John Holland, "An Inquiry into the Meaning of Minority Group Attitude Expressions," *American Sociological Review*, 17 (April 1952), pp. 196-202; Lewis M. Killian, "The Adjustment of Southern White Migrants to Northern Urban Norms," *Social Forces*, 32 (October 1953), pp. 66-69; Bernard Kutner, Carol Wilkins and Penny Yarrow, "Verbal Attitudes and Overt Behavior Involving Racial Prejudice," *Journal of Abnormal and Social Psychology*, 47 (1952), pp. 649-652; Richard T. LaPiere, "Attitudes vs. Actions," *Social Forces*, 13 (December 1934), pp. 230-237; Lawrence S. Linn, "Verbal Attitudes and Overt Behavior: A Study of Racial Discrimination," *Social Forces*, 45 (1965), pp. 353-364; Milton Malof and Albert Lott, "Ethnocentrism and the Acceptance of Negro Support in a Group Situation," *Journal of Abnormal and Social Psychology*, 65 (October 1962), pp. 254-258; Gerhart H. Saenger and Emily Gilbert, "Customer Reactions to the Integration of Negro Sales Personnel," *Public Opinion Quarterly*, 4 (1950), pp. 57-76.

[2] Herbert Blumer, "Research on Race Relations in the United States of America," *International Social Science Journal*, 10 (1958), pp. 403-447; Melvin L. DeFleur and Frank A. Westie, "Attitude as a Scientific Concept," *Social Forces*, 42 (October 1963), pp. 17-31; Earl Raab and Seymour Martin Lipset, "The Prejudiced Society," *American Race Relations Today*, (ed.) Earl Raab (New York: Doubleday & Co., 1962), pp. 29-55; Dietrich C. Reitzes, "Institutional Structures and Race Relations," *Phylon* (Spring 1959), pp. 48-66; and Arnold M. Rose, "Intergroup Relations vs. Prejudice: Pertinent Theory for the Study of Social Change," *Social Problems*, 4 (1956), pp. 173-176.

[3] Tamotsu Shibutani, *Society and Personality* (Englewood Cliffs, New Jersey: Prentice-Hall, 1961), pp. 41-42.

[4] Glenn M. Vernon, *Human Interaction* (New York: The Ronald Press, 1965), p. 154.

[5] Shibutani, *op. cit.*, pp. 46-50.

[6] This short definition was derived from Jack W. Brehm and Arthur Cohen, *Explorations in Cognitive Dissonance* (New York: John Wiley & Sons, 1962), pp. 8-9, 198, 217; Amitai Etzioni, *A Comparative Analysis of Complex Organizations* (New York: The Free Press of Glencoe, 1961), pp. 8-11; Kurt Lewin, "Frontiers in Group Dynamics," *Field Theory in Social Science*, (ed.) Dorwin Cartwright (New York: Doubleday & Co., 1965), pp. 227-235; Carl I. Hovland, Enid H. Campbell and Timothy Brock, "The Effects of 'Commitment' on Opinion Change Following Communication," *The Order of Presentation in Persuasion* (New Haven: Yale University Press, 1957), pp. 23-32; Harold B. Gerald, "Deviation, Conformity and Commitment," *Current Studies in Social Psychology*, (ed.) Ivan D. Steiner and Martin Fishbein (New York: Holt, Rinehart & Winston, 1965), pp. 263-276; Leon Festinger, *Conflict, Decision, and Dissonance* (Stanford: Stanford University Press, 1964), pp. 155-156.

[7] Herbert H. Hyman, "Inconsistencies as a Problem of Attitude Measurement," *Journal of Social Issues*, 5 (1959), pp. 38-42.

[8] Aaron V. Cicourel, *Method and Measurement in Sociology* (New York: The Free Press of Glencoe, 1964), pp. 203-209; Kurt W. Back, Thomas C. Hood, and Mary L.

Brehm, "The Subject Role in Small Group Experiments," *Social Forces,* 43 (December 1964), pp. 181-187.

[9] Back, Hood, and Brehm, *op. cit.*, p. 181.

[10] Linn, *op. cit.,* p. 359.

[11] Hyman, *op. cit.,* p. 40.

[12] DeFleur and Westie, *op. cit.,* p. 672 and Linn, *op. cit.,* pp. 363-364 have indicated that the overt behavior toward members of minority groups is strongly influenced by significant others. As another part of this study it was found that perceived support from significant others was significantly related to attitude, commitment and overt behavior. See James M. Fendrich, "A Study of White Attitudes, Commitment and Overt Behavior Toward Members of a Minority Group," unpublished Ph.D. dissertation, Michigan State University, 1965.

[13] The NAACP was chosen for its saliency to the respondents. At the time the study was conducted, the NAACP was the only effective civil rights organization on campus. It held regular meetings and the group activities were frequently reported in the school daily. Membership in the organization varied from timid support to advocators of strong militancy.

[14] It was felt that the class of social objects should be clearly specified and they should be similar to the object of the commitment and overt behavior.

[15] It was unrealistic to create a longer scale. The longer the scale, the more students would have become skeptical of the manifest function of the commitment items.

[16] The scheduling of the small group discussions was designed to provide every student the opportunity to attend; however, the students independently selected the evening discussions. Some of the students brought friends who did not take part in the interviews.

[17] Herbert L. Costner, "Criteria for Measures of Association," *American Sociological Review,* 30 (June 1965), pp. 341-353. Computation of a confidence interval for *gamma* takes ties into account. The magnitude of *gamma* is not affected by ties, but a large proportion of ties affects sampling variability. For more information on *gamma* see, Leo A. Goodman and William H. Kruskal, "Measures of Association for Cross-Classification: III Approximate Sampling Theory," *Journal of the American Statistical Association,* 58 (1963), pp. 322-330.

[18] Brehm and Cohen, *op. cit.,* p. 303.

[19] Cicourel, *op. cit.,* pp. 39-72; Back, Hood, and Brehm, *op. cit.,* pp. 181-187; M. T. Orne, "On the Social Psychology of the Psychological Experiment: With Particular Reference to Demand Characteristics and Their Implications," *American Psychologist,* 17 (1962), pp. 776-783; Robert Rosenthal, "On the Social Psychology of the Psychological Experiment," *American Scientist,* 51 (1963), pp. 268-283; and William H. Form, "On the Sociology of Social Research," *Rassegna di Sociologia* (September 1963), pp. 463-481.

[20] Norman C. Weissberg, "On DeFleur and Westie's 'Attitude as a Scientific Concept,' " *Social Forces,* 43 (March 1965), p. 422.

6

ATTITUDE MEASUREMENT AND PREDICTION OF BEHAVIOR: AN EVALUATION OF CONDITIONS AND MEASUREMENT TECHNIQUES

Charles R. Tittle
and
Richard J. Hill

The degree of relationship between measured attitude and other behavior continues to be investigated and debated.[1] Some social scientists now conclude that accurate prediction of behavior from attitude measures is not possible with the techniques generally employed. Green, for instance, states that "many investigations have found that specific acts or action attitudes often cannot be predicted very accurately from elicited verbal attitudes."[2] Deutscher recently reintroduced the issue in most general terms when he again questioned the assumption that verbal responses reflect behavioral tendencies.[3] However, if the issue is examined on the basis of available evidence, no conclusion can be reached with a satisfactory degree of confidence.

In addition to conventional standards of research, adequate investigation of the problem appears to require that several methodological conditions be fulfilled. First, it would seem obvious that a particular attitude should be measured using a multi-item instrument constructed according to a replicable set of procedures and resulting in at least the objective ordering of respondents. The general superiority of multi-item instruments over single-item measures and introspective orderings of data has been discussed at length. The argument will not be reviewed here.[4]

Second, derivation of an appropriate criterion of non-attitudinal behavior would appear to necessitate consideration of action taking place under typical social circumstances. Preferably, a behavioral measure or index should refer to sets of acts indicative of consistent or patterned

Reprinted from *Sociometry* (Vol. 30, June, 1967, pp. 199-213) by permission of the authors and the American Sociological Association.

action. The concept of attitude usually implies some form of cognitive and affective organization in terms of which an individual responds to an aspect of the world.[5] Further, if attitudes are cognitive and affective organizations which result from normal socialization processes, it seems reasonable to assume that the correspondence between attitude and other behavior will be highest in those situations which the individual has come to define as normal and common. The individual encountering a situation which is characterized by unfamiliar contingencies is not likely to have a well-structured attitudinal organization relevant to behavior in that situation. Attitudinally influenced response is not seen as the equivalent of a deterministic reflex. Many situational contingencies enter into any particular action situation in ways which influence response. Given these considerations, attitude measures should be least predictive of behaviors occurring in situations which (1) are alien to the subject's customary behavioral context or (2) call for aberrant behavior in a familiar action context.[6] Attitude measures should be most predictive of behavior in situations which occur repetitively within the common behavioral context of the individual. With respect to the general relationship, then, the criteria of most relevance should reflect those behaviors which are repetitious and which take place under usual social circumstances.

When studies designed specifically to evaluate the relationship between measured attitude and other behavior are examined with these considerations in mind, the degree of discrepancy is found to be partially a function of the methodological strategies employed. Table 1 summarizes the results of a review of previous research.[7] Studies were classified by the measurement instrument employed, the kind of behavioral criterion which was used, and the type of situation under which the behavior occurred. For purposes of this classification, several behaviors occurring over time, or the same behavior repetitively engaged in, were considered to constitute a configuration of patterned behavior. With respect to the behavioral circumstances, the studies were categorized into two groups—those that utilized a behavioral criterion representing normal action alternatives and those that employed unusual options. In some cases the research report indicated that the subjects probably defined the situation as atypical. For example, in the Kutner study, it was graphically illustrated that the subjects were dealing with an undefined situation. In instances where no detailed information was provided, we used our own judgment following the general prescription that laboratory situations represented unusual behavior contexts or options.

In addition, the studies were classified as to whether a low, moderate, or high relationship between attitude and the behavioral criterion was observed. In cases where no actual measures of association were provided, the reported conclusions were taken as the basis of classification. Where measures of association were available, association below .35 were classified as showing little relationship, associations between .35 and .59 were considered to represent moderate association, and associations of .60 or above were classified in the high category.

Obviously, the results reported in Table 1 do not include all investigations concerned with the relationship between attitudes and other behaviors. For example, several consistency tests using "known groups" have been undertaken but are not reported here because the nature of the known groups was such that it was impossible to make inferences about individual behaviors as corresponding to individual attitudes.[8] In addition many other investigations have used certain kinds of attitude measures as predictors within specific substantive contexts. Such studies permit little direct inference about the general relationship of concern here. The research selected for inclusion deals specifically with attitudes and corresponding individual behavior. These studies are those most frequently cited in connection with the argument and to our knowledge are considered to be the crucial investigations of the problem.

It is apparent from Table 1 that the degree of correspondence between measured attitude and other behaviors varies not only with the measure of attitude used, but also with the criterion which is taken as an indicator of behavior. Of the four studies that most nearly fulfill the methodological requirements set forth above, three show attitude measures to be highly associated with behavioral patterns. Considering all fifteen studies with no regard for their limitations, six report little relationship, three report moderate (or low-to-moderate) relationship, and six report high relationship. In view of these results, Campbell's conclusion is apparent

TABLE 1

SUMMARY OF STUDIES OF CORRESPONDENCE
BETWEEN MEASURED ATTITUDE AND BEHAVIORAL PATTERNS

Study	Attitude Measure	Criterion	Circumstances	
LaPiere	Hypothetical single question	Single act	Unusual	Low
Kutner	Single question	Single act	Unusual	Low
LaPiere	Stereotypical single question	Patterned behavior	Normal	Low
Bray	Summated rating scale	Single set of acts	Unusual	Low
Corey	Thurstone-Likert scale	Patterned behavior	Normal	Low
Zunich	Summated rating scale	Single set of acts	Unusual	Low
DeFleur	Summated differences scale	Single act	Unusual	Moderate
Linn	Intuitive scale	Single act	Unusual	Moderate
Pace	No indication	Patterned behavior	Normal	Low to Moderate
Rogers	Battery of single questions	Patterned behavior	Normal	High
Murphy (1)	Thurstone scale	Patterned behavior	Normal	High
Murphy (2)	No indication	Patterned behavior	Normal	High
Murphy (3)	No indication	Patterned behavior	Normal	High
Nettler	Thurstone scale	Patterned behavior	Normal	High
Poppleton	Thurstone, scored 4 ways	Patterned behavior	Normal	High

ly inescapable: "The degree of correspondence is, for the most part, yet to be discovered."[9] The above reconsideration suggests that the degree of correspondence observed is at least a function of (1) the measurement techniques employed, (2) the degree to which the criterion behavior constitutes action within the individuals' common range of experience, and (3) the degree to which the criterion behavior represents a repetitive behavioral configuration.

The investigation reported below had two purposes. The first concern was to determine the degree of correspondence between measured attitude and other behavior which would be observed when (1) the technique employed to measure attitude consisted of a multi-item instrument constructed according to replicable procedures which result at least in the objective ordering of respondents, (2) the criterion behaviors occurred within the common behavioral context of the individual, and (3) the behavioral situation occurred repetitively in the life experience of the individual.

The second purpose was the evaluation of the relative predictive efficiency of four frequently used measurement techniques in terms of the degree to which these techniques result in the ability to predict behavioral configurations.

DEVELOPMENT OF ATTITUDE MEASURES

It was suggested above that adequate investigation of the first problem required utilization of multi-item instruments. But since several measuring techniques are in vogue, it seemed desirable to employ more than one of them. The techniques evaluated were: (1) Thurstone successive-interval technique, (2) a semantic differential procedure, (3) a summated-rating (Likert) technique, and (4) a Guttman type scale. In addition, a simple self rating of attitude was examined. The efficiency of each of the five measures was assessed in terms of its correspondence with five criteria of behavior. The assessment was made under the conditions discussed above. These conditions were expected to maximize the relationship between measured attitudes and criterion behaviors.

Others have argued that if one wishes to predict a particular set of behaviors he should attempt to measure an attitude that is specific for a given individual as he relates to that class of behavior.[10] Given this argument, maximizing the credibility of the present study required an attempt to measure a specific rather than a general attitude. One would not expect to predict an individual's personal behavior with respect to his own marriage from a measure of his attitude toward marriage as a social institution. In the present instance, attitude toward personal participation in student political activity was taken as an appropriate measurement objective.

One hundred forty-five statements thought to reflect such an attitude were placed on a successive interval continuum by 213 student judges. The statements were formulated by the authors and several graduate students, using the literature on political participation in the larger society for suggestive outlines. These items were oriented around eight possible channels of individual political activity: (1) voting in student elections, (2) belonging to student political groups, (3) taking part in student political party activities, (4) taking part in student campaign activities, (5) keeping informed about student politics, (6) contact with student government officials, (7) interpersonal discussion of student politics, and (8) personal office holding or seeking.

The panel of judges consisted of entire classes of students, selected to give a broad representation of the student population. The statements were printed in eight-page booklets with the pages arranged randomly, and were submitted for judging with the customary instructions.[11] Following the procedures discussed by Edwards, successive-interval scale and Q values for the statements were calculated.[12] Fifteen statements were selected so that the scale values were approximately evenly spaced on the continuum and Q values were minimal.[13] For the test sample, the median scoring technique was used.[14]

The summated rating scale was built from the same basic 145 statements. Four editors independently classified the statements as to their favorable or unfavorable content. Those statements about which all four agreed were submitted to a separate sample of 213 students. The subjects were asked to respond to each statement on a five-point scale: strongly agree, agree, undecided, disagree, strongly disagree. Responses were weighted in the standard Likert fashion from zero to four. The fifteen items that discriminated best between the top fifty and the bottom fifty subjects were selected for this scale.

A semantic differential employing nine adjectival pairs was constructed for five concepts: (1) voting in student elections, (2) discussing student political issues, (3) holding student political office, (4) helping in a student political campaign, and (5) keeping informed about student politics. The nine adjectival pairs utilized were: good-bad, valuable-worthless, clean-dirty, pleasant-unpleasant, wise-foolish, fair-unfair, complex-simple, active-passive, and deep-shallow. The first six pairs represent the evaluative or attitude dimension. They were interspersed with the remaining three to obscure the purpose of the measurement (a procedure recommended by the originators of the semantic differential).[15] Pairs were selected using the criteria suggested by Osgood and his associates. Scores on all five concepts were summed and a mean taken as an ordinal measure of attitude toward personal participation in student political activity.

A set of items constituting a Guttman scale was derived using the same responses as those utilized for constructing the summated rating scale. A random sample of 95 questionnaires was selected from the 213 respondents. The statements were examined for scalability using the Cornell technique. Ten items, six dichotomous and four trichotomous, were found to form a scale with a coefficient of reproducibility of .928 and a minimal reproducibility of .635. All error appeared to be random.

These Guttman attitude items were retested for scalability after being administered to the test sample (N=301). The items met the criteria of scalability for this sample but only when used in dichotomous form. Accordingly the four trichotomous items were collapsed into dichotomies. The final scale had a coefficient of reproducibility of .930 and a minimal marginal reproducibility of .751. Menzel's coefficient of scalability for these data was .717,[16] and Schuessler's Test I resulted in a probability of less than .001.[17]

Once the instruments were constructed they were incorporated into a questionnaire including items about the student's background, participation in student political activity, and his group affiliations on the campus. In addition, the questionnaire included an item eliciting a self-rating of attitude toward student politics on a continuum from zero to eight. This questionnaire was administered to two large sections of a course in marriage and the family, which was composed of a widely variant student population. Freshmen were eliminated from consideration as were students who failed to provide complete data. The final set of subjects was composed of 301 upper-class students.

DEVELOPMENT OF CRITERION MEASURES

The criterion behavior was indexed in several ways. First, the voting behavior of each subject was determined by inspecting student-voting records in an election held one week prior to the administration of the questionnaire. Second, the respondent's report of his voting behavior for the previous four elections was taken as a behavioral indicator. Third, an index of behavioral patterns was constructed by combining responses to questions about frequency of engagement in various types of student political activity. Eight activities were found to form a Guttman scale for the 301 subjects. These activities included frequency of participation in meetings of a student assembly, frequency with which the individual had written to or talked with a student representative concerning an issue, frequency of voting over the past four elections, frequency of engagement in campaign activities on behalf of a particular candidate, frequency of reading the platforms of candidates for student political office, and frequency of discussion of student political issues in talking with friends. When the items were dichotomized, the scale was characterized by a coefficient of reproducibility of .907 and a minimal marginal reproducibility of .698. Again error appeared to be random. Menzel's coefficient of scalability was .675 and Schuessler's Test I yielded a probability of less than .001.

The fourth index of student political participation was devised by summing, in Likert fashion, the categories of response concerning frequency of engagement in ten types of student political activity. These activities included the eight previously mentioned as well as the frequency of personal office seeking and response to an item indicating whether the respondent had ever written a letter of protest to the student newspaper. A fifth measure of participation was an adaptation of the standard Woodward-Roper index of political participation involving a modified scoring of five of the activities already listed.[18]

The five criterion indexes were designed to represent alternate methods of measuring the same behavioral patterns. The degree of association between the criterion measures is reported in Table 2. In general the magnitude of association is relatively high. All measures of association are in the expected direction and are significantly non-zero at a probability level less than .001. These results suggest that the various indexes measured approximately the same aspects of the students' political involvement.

TABLE 2
INTERRELATIONSHIP AMONG CRITERION MEASURES

	Vote over time	Guttman index	Likert index	Woodward Roper index
Vote in last election	.778	.559	.636	.632
Vote over time	—	.577	.757	.789
Guttman index of political participation	—	—	.850	.721
Likert index of political participation	—	—	—	.869

The degree of interrelationship of the several attitude measures varied considerably (see Table 3). This points up the fact that various methods of measuring the same characteristic may result in the ordering of individuals quite differently. Presumably the variation is accounted for by error factors intrinsic to the measurement techniques. An assessment of the extent to which such factors affect the predictive power of the several instruments in this specific instance is presented below. Moreover, the present research design permitted certain inferences to be made about the nature of the error factors involved.

The behavioral indexes included one "objective" indicator and several "reported" indicators of activity. This raises questions with respect to the adequacy of such a design for making the assessment here proposed.

Specifically, it is known that reported behavior does not always correspond to actual behavior; and that the extent of error varies with kinds of information being reported.[19] In the present instance, it was possible to compare one report of a behavior with an independent record of that behavior. The subjects were asked if they had voted in the last student election. This report was compared with the voting records. In 11 per cent of the cases, the report and the record did not coincide. In 28 of the 33 instances of non-correspondence, subjects reported that they had voted when in fact they had not. In the remaining five cases, the subject's name was not included in the voting records. In these latter instances, it was not possible to determine whether the error resulted from inadequacies of the student government's record-keeping procedures or whether the subjects had falsified their names. The degree of error observed corresponds closely to that reported in the analysis of the political behavior of other populations.[20] Thus, the self-reported data in this instance appear to provide a fairly close approximation to the actual behavior of the subjects. This conclusion is reinforced by the findings reported in Table 2 which indicate relatively high association between recorded vote and four reported indexes of related behavior.

The present research design, then, permitted the assessment of the relative efficiency of scaling techniques by determining the correspondence of five measures of attitude to five measures of other behavior, including a single act and four indexes of reported configurations of behavior. All the criterion indexes were composed of, or referred to, behaviors occurring under normal social circumstances, and they represented referents for specific non-hypothetical attitude components.

FURTHER PROCEDURES

The attitude measures and criterion indexes used in this study were treated as ordinal data. A frequency distribution for each attitude scale was obtained, and the categories were then collapsed into six ordered classes, following the convention of equalization of marginals. The Guttman and Woodward-Roper indexes of participation also were collapsed into six categories. The seven categories of the summated index of participation were maintained to prevent a serious mal-distribution of category frequencies. The association between each scale and each index was measured by the Goodman-Kruskal gamma. Since gamma is somewhat sensitive to marginal distributions, and perhaps, the number of cells in a contingency table, care was taken to make comparisons across rows where tables with approximately equal cell numbers and marginal distributions were involved.

RESULTS

The results reported in Table 4 indicate that only a moderate degree of correspondence between measured attitude and other behavior can be observed when (1) scaling techniques are employed to measure attitude (2) the behavioral criterion is based upon a consideration of a series of acts occurring under normal circumstances. On the other hand, the data do show that the degree of correspondence observed is at least in part a function of the methodological conditions which maintain.

TABLE 3

INTERRELATIONSHIP AMONG ATTITUDE MEASURES

	Guttman	Thurstone	Sem Diff	Self-Rating
Likert	.796	.588	.619	.511
Guttman	—	.445	.523	.476
Thurstone	—	—	.432	.337
Sem Diff	—	—	—	.387

The data support the argument that greater correspondence between measured attitude and other behavior can be found when the behavioral criterion incorporates a wide range of activity with respect to the attitude object under consideration. Although the findings are not decisive, they do reveal that in five of six instances greatest association was found between the attitude measures and the Likert-type index which was derived from ten distinct kinds of behavior. The data also show that, in general, lower association was found for the voting indexes than for the Guttman and Woodward-Roper indexes based respectively on eight and five kinds of activity. Such results support the contention that the appropriate criterion measure to use in evaluating the predictive efficacy of attitude measure is one that includes sets of acts indicative of consistent or patterned behavior.

With respect to the assessment of the alternative measurement strategies, the results indicate that there is wide variation in the predictive power of the various instruments. In this instance, the Likert scale was clearly the best predictor of behavior. It was most highly associated with every one of the five behavioral indexes. The Thurstone scale showed the poorest correspondence—in only one case did it produce better prediction than any of the other measures. In fact, in four of five instances a simple self rating of attitude provided better results than the elaborate Thurstone procedure.

DISCUSSION

On the basis of a reconsideration of the relevant literature, it was maintained that multi-item attitude instruments would have considerable utility as predictors of behavior when such behavior represents a normal configuration of repetitive actions. The findings provide only modest support for this contention.

It could be argued that these findings strengthen the indictment against attitude measures as predictive tools. It is clear that attitude measurement alone, as examined herein, is not totally adequate as a predictor of behavior. However, when it is possible to obtain an average association of .543 using a Likert scale in its crude form, it seems entirely possible that technical refinements and additional methodological considerations could increase predictive efficiency. Investigation of the performance of the various measuring instruments suggests certain refinements and considerations meriting further exploration.

Analysis of the present data indicates that the differential predictive power of the various measurement approaches may be at least partially attributable to differences in reliability. Split-half reliability coefficients based upon the Spearman-Brown correction formula[21] were as follows: the Likert scale—.95; the semantic differential measure—.87; the Guttman scale—.80; and the Thurstone scale—.67. While the order in terms of reliability does not correspond perfectly with the predictive ordering, it does place the Likert and Thurstone measures in the same relative positions. The Likert scale was found to be the best predictor and to exhibit the greatest reliability, while the Thurstone scale is the poorest predictor and the least reliable. The findings with respect to the range of reliability are similar to those reported in other studies using Likert and Thurstone procedures. In addition, the available evidence suggests that in cases where the two types of scales are of equal length, one can expect the Likert scale to exhibit higher reliability.[22]

Differential reliability, however, does not seem to be a complete explanation for the findings. The Guttman scale exhibits lower observed reliability than the semantic differential, yet it performs considerably better as a predictor. In like manner the single-item self-rating of attitude would reasonably be expected to be less reliable than the multiple-item semantic differential and Thurstone scales, yet it is found to be a better predictor than either of these two scales.

It might also be argued that the superiority of the Likert over the Guttman technique can be accounted for by the fact that the original Likert scale was composed of 15 items while the Guttman scale contained only ten items. Since in general the greater the length of a test, the higher is its reliability,[23] it seemed desirable to rescore the Likert scale using the ten "best" items rather than the 15 "best" items. The data in Table 4 show that this procedure had little effect on the results. The ten-item Likert scale was still superior to the ten-item Guttman scale as well as to each of the other attitude measures.

A second factor appears to be the differential extent to which the various scaling procedures result in the derivation of scales incorporating a specificity dimension. Although each scale was designed to measure the same specific attitude relating to personal participation in student

TABLE 4

ASSOCIATIONS[1] BETWEEN ATTITUDE MEASURES AND BEHAVIORAL INDEXES

	Attitude Measure					
Behavior Index	15-item Likert	10-item Likert	Guttman	Self	Sem Diff	Thurstone
Record vote	.504	.459	.391	.285	.350	.318
Vote over time	.493	.423	.329	.365	.309	.213
Guttman index	.553	.559	.421	.410	.335	.248
Likert index	.619	.612	.535	.495	.364	.257
W-R index	.548	.535	.419	.425	.335	.238
Mean association	.543	.518	.419	.396	.339	.255

[1]Gamma.

political activity, the various scales do differ substantially with respect to the content specificity of the actual items incorporated. This observation is based on the assumption that response to an item is likely to be more specific for an individual if the item contains some self-reference. Thus, the larger the number of self-referent items included in a scale, the more specific is response likely to be. Comparison of the Likert, Guttman, and Thurstone scales in terms of the proportion of self-referent items derived for the final measuring instrument revealed a ranking corresponding exactly to the predictive ranking. For this comparison, items containing the personal pronouns "I" or "me," were considered to be self-referent in content. The Likert scale is found to rank first with 87 per cent of the items self-referent, the Guttman scale is second with 60 per cent and the Thurstone scale is ordered last with only 20 per cent of the items including a reference to self.

There are other technical differences between the different measuring procedures which may have some bearing on the findings. In addition to the advantage of greater reliability and specificity, the Likert technique also seems to have the particular advantage of providing for the operation of an intensity factor. Because scoring is influenced by the degree as well as direction of response to each item, intense judgments weight the final score assigned to an individual. Hence, an ordering of subjects by the summated rating procedure is not only a ranking on a favorable-unfavorable dimension, but a ranking influenced by how strongly the subject feels. A respondent who holds a favorable attitude but who does not feel intensely about it will consequently be ranked lower than one who holds a favorable attitude and supports that attitude with intense feelings.

Development of efficient means for handling such components as intensity and specificity may offer recognizable advantages for improving the predictive efficiency of attitude scales. The Guttman procedure for intensity analysis represents one technique for handling an additional dimension. But as ordinarily practiced, it lacks the advantage of permitting individual scores to be "corrected" for intensity (other than in a gross dichotomous sense). There is nothing, however, to prevent some combination of content score and intensity score to derive a "total" score. Certainly such possibilities deserve more exploration.

The semantic differential as a measure of attitude appears to suffer a serious disadvantage. Subjects tend to respond in a set. They observe that "desirable" things appear on one side of a continuum and "undesirable" things appear on the other. The discriminal process then apparently becomes a matter of self-evaluating overall attitude and marking the scale accordingly, with little distinction between the various adjectival pairs. Interspersing reversed continua probably only serves to make the respondent's task more difficult without fundamentally altering the problem. In this instance, the tendency for subjects to adopt a response set probably accounts for the fact that the semantic differential procedure resulted in a measure having high reliability but low predictive validity.

The findings in regard to the Thurstone technique are somewhat contrary to general methodological thinking with respect to attitude measurement. The Thurstone scale has been considered by some as the standard against which other attitude measures are to be compared. In addition to the factors of reliability and item-specificity, the poor showing of the Thurstone scale might also be influenced by the existence of a hiatus between the scaling of items and the process of measuring attitudes once the items are scaled. The judging procedure itself introduces a number of perceptual variables, the total effect of which has not been fully explored. Moreover, the nature of the typical response to Thurstone scales raises questions about the general adequacy of the Thurstone procedure. It is a common observation that respondents do not always endorse contiguous items. Indeed, subjects often endorse a wide range of items.[24] This does not make sense in light of the rationale of the procedure, and it may be largely responsible for some degree of unreliability and unpredictability.

The data presented here and the results of previous research with attitude measures strongly suggest that the error factors accounting for the differential predictability are to some extent intrinsic to the several measurement procedures. This conclusion, of course, cannot be advanced as compelling since any particular instance of the application of a given measuring technique or instrument represents only one of many possible applications. As such it is subject to various random errors. The crucial questions concerning these measurement procedures can only be answered convincingly when the results of numerous applications are available.

NOTES

We wish to acknowledge the helpful criticisms and suggestions we have received from Alexander L. Clark and Gary I. Schulman.

[1] Two more recent and noteworthy studies are: Pamela K. Poppleton and G. W. Pilkington, "A Comparison of Four Methods of Scoring an Attitude Scale in Relation to Its Reliability and Validity," *British Journal of Social and Clinical Psychology,* 3 (February, 1964), pp. 36-39; and Lawrence S. Linn, "Verbal Attitudes and Overt Behavior: A Study of Racial Discrimination," *Social Forces,* 43 (March, 1965), pp. 353-364. For general discussions of the issue see: Donald T. Campbell, "Social Attitudes and Other Acquired Behavioral Dispositions," in Sigmund Koch, editor, *Psychology: A Study of a Science,* Vol. 6, New York: McGraw-Hill, 1963; and Melvin L. DeFleur and Frank R. Westie, "Attitude as a Scientific Concept," *Social Forces,* 42 (October, 1963), pp. 17-31.

[2] Bert F. Green, "Attitude Measurement," in Gardner Lindzey, editor, *Handbook of Social Psychology,* Cambridge: Addison-Wesley, 1954, p. 340.

[3] Irwin Deutscher, "Words and Deeds: Social Science and Social Policy," *Social Problems,* 13 (Winter, 1966), pp. 235-254.

[4] Cf. Clyde H. Coombs, "Theory and Methods of Social Measurement," in Leon Festinger and Daniel Katz, *Research Methods in the Behavioral Sciences,* Chicago: Holt, Rinehart and Winston, 1953 and Lee J. Cronbach, *Essentials of Psychological Testing* (2nd edition), New York: Harper and Row, Publishers, 1960, pp. 130-131.

[5] Daniel Katz and Ezra Stotland, "A Preliminary Statement to a Theory of Attitude Structure and Change," in Sigmund Koch, editor, *Psychology: A Study of a Science,* Vol. 3, New York: McGraw-Hill, 1959.

[6] Campbell, *op. cit.*

[7] These studies include: Richard T. LaPiere, "Attitudes vs. Actions," *Social Forces,* 13 (December, 1934), pp. 230-237; Bernard Kutner, Carol Wilkins, and Penny Rechtman Yarrow, "Verbal Attitudes and Overt Behavior Involving Racial Prejudice," *Journal of Abnormal and Social Psychology,* 47 (July, 1952), pp. 649-652; Richard T. LaPiere, "Type-Rationalizations of Group Antipathy," *Social Forces,* 15 (December, 1936), pp. 232-237; Douglas W. Bray, "The Prediction of Behavior from Two Attitude Scales," *Journal of Abnormal and Social Psychology,* 45 (January, 1950), pp. 64-84; Stephen M. Corey, "Professed Attitudes and Actual Behavior," *Journal of Educational Psychology,* 38 (April, 1937), pp. 271-280; Michael Zunich; "A Study of the Relationship Between Child Rearing Attitudes and Maternal Behavior," *Journal of Experimental Education,* 30 (December, 1961), pp. 231-241; Melvin L. DeFleur and Frank R. Westie, "Verbal Attitudes and Overt Acts: An Experiment on the Salience of Attitudes," *American Sociological Review,* 23 (December, 1958), pp. 667-673; Linn, *op. cit.*; C. Robert Pace, "Opinion and Action: A Study of Invalidity of Attitude Measurement," *American Psychologist,* 4 (July, 1949), p. 242; Herbert W. Rogers, "Some Attitudes of Students in the R.O.T.C.," *Journal of Educational Psychology,* 26 (April, 1935), pp. 291-306; Gardner Murphy, Lois Barclay Murphy, and Theodore M. Newcomb, *Experimental Social Psychology,* New York: Harper and Brothers, 1937, pp. 894-912 (three studies are reviewed); Gwynne Nettler and Elizabeth Havely Golding, "The Measurement of Attitudes Toward the Japanese in America," *American Journal of Sociology,* 52 (July, 1946), pp. 31-39; and Poppleton and Pilkington, *op. cit.*

[8] See Corey, *op. cit.* for a review of some of these studies.

[9] Campbell, *op. cit.,* p. 162.

[10] Linn, *op. cit.* and DeFleur and Westie, "Attitude as a Scientific Concept," *op. cit.,* p. 30.

[11] The Seashore and Hevner method of rating items was used. See Robert H. Seashore and Kate Hevner, "A Time-Saving Device for the Construction of Attitude Scales," *Journal of Social Psychology,* 4 (August, 1933), pp. 366-372.

[12] Allen L. Edwards, *Techniques of Attitude Scale Construction,* New York: Appleton, Century, Crofts, 1957, pp. 123-138. An internal consistency test yielded an Absolute Average Deviation of .034, a value slightly higher than usually reported when the method of successive intervals is used to scale stimuli.

[13] This was not entirely possible, since only a few statements were found to have scale values near the middle of the continuum.

[14] Edwards, *op. cit.*, p. 145.

[15] Charles E. Osgood, George S. Suci, and Percy H. Tannenbaum, *The Measurement of Meaning,* Urbana: The University of Illinois Press, 1957. The same six evaluative pairs were used by Osgood and his associates in comparing the semantic differential with other measures of attitude. See pp. 192-195.

[16] Menzel suggests the level of acceptance for scales at somewhere between .60 and .65. Cf. Herbert Menzel, "A New Coefficient for Scalogram Analysis," *Public Opinion Quarterly,* 17 (Summer, 1953), pp. 268-280.

[17] Karl F. Schuessler, "A Note on the Statistical Significance of the Scalogram," *Sociometry,* 24 (September, 1961), pp. 312-318.

[18] See Julian L. Woodward and Elmo Roper, "Political Activity of American Citizens," *American Political Science Review,* 44 (December, 1950), pp. 872-885.

[19] Hugh J. Parry and Helen M. Crossley, "Validity of Responses to Survey Questions," *Public Opinion Quarterly,* 14 (Spring, 1950), pp. 61-80.

[20] See Charles R. Tittle and Richard J. Hill, "A Note on the Accuracy of Self-Reported Data and Prediction of Political Activity," *Public Opinion Quarterly,* forthcoming.

[21] To this point, the data have been treated as ordinal. The use of the Spearman-Brown procedure makes interval assumptions. However, to the authors' knowledge there exists no ordinally-based procedure which provides a reasonable alternative to the Spearman-Brown approach.

[22] Edwards, *op. cit.*, pp. 159-169.

[23] Harold Gulliksen, *Theory of Mental Tests,* New York: John Wiley and Sons, 1950, pp. 74-86.

[24] George J. Dudycha, "A Critical Examination of the Measurement of Attitude Toward War," *Journal of Social Psychology,* 18 (November, 1943), pp. 383-392; Selltiz, *et al., op. cit.,* pp. 359-365; and Otis Monroe Walter, Jr., "The Improvement of Attitude Research," *Journal of Social Psychology,* 33 (February, 1951), pp. 143-146.

7

THE RELATIONSHIP BETWEEN ATTITUDES AND BEHAVIOR AS A FUNCTION OF SPECIFICITY OF ATTITUDE OBJECT AND PRESENCE OF A SIGNIFICANT PERSON DURING ASSESSMENT CONDITIONS

Allan W. Wicker
and
Richard J. Pomazal

In a recent review of the literature on the relationship between verbally expressed attitudes and overt behaviors, Wicker (1969) listed a number of situational variables which, in addition to attitudes, may influence overt behavior. These include the specificity of the attitude objects; the actual or considered presence of certain people; normative prescriptions of proper behavior; the number and kind of alternative behaviors available; unforeseen, extraneous events; and expected and/or actual consequences of various acts. Wicker postulated that the attitude-behavior relationship is stronger, the more similar the situations in which verbal and overt behavioral responses are obtained, and he suggested that the above factors are dimensions along which the assessment situations could differ in similarity.

Thus one might expect a stronger attitude-behavior relationship when both the attitude object being rated and the overt behavior being observed are highly specific. For example, Fishbein (1966) has noted that researchers have often measured attitudes toward broad classes of people (e.g., Negroes) and related them to specific behaviors (e.g., cooperating with a particular Negro on a given task), generally finding little or no relationship between the two kinds of responses. He has suggested that the relationship between attitudes and behaviors should be stronger when investigators measure attitudes toward the specific overt behavior of interest (Fishbein, 1967). The specificity of attitude objects rated can be increased in other ways, such as employing specific persons as stimuli rather than classes of persons, and using specific events, rules, or policies which are related to the behavior of interest.

Reprinted from *Representative Research in Social Psychology* (Vol. 2, July, 1971, pp. 26-31) by permission of the editors.

Another dimension along which the attitude and behavioral assessment conditions can vary is the actual or considered presence of significant persons. For example, it would not be surprising if subjects showed an inconsistency between their anonymous responses on an attitude questionnaire and their overt behaviors in everyday life situations in which they might have to justify their actions to others (cf. Fendrich, 1967; Hyman, 1949, Warner & DeFleur, 1969). And assuming some pressure toward consistency (cf. Insko & Schopler, 1967), one might expect that if a significant person such as an experimenter were present both when the attitudes and overt behaviors were assessed, the attitude-behavior relationship should be stronger than if different investigators were employed for the two measures.

The present study attempts to examine the influence of the two variables mentioned above on the attitude-behavior relationship by examining college students' attitudes toward psychological research and their actual levels of participation as subjects. Specificity of attitude object was varied by asking the students to rate four concepts ranging from very general (scientific research) to very specific (the Psychology Department's policy regarding participation in psychological experiments by students enrolled in a particular course). The considered presence of a significant other person was manipulated by leading subjects to believe that the experiment for which their participation was requested was sponsored by the same or a different investigator than the one who had obtained the attitude responses.

METHOD

In the attitude measurement phase of the experiment, an attitude questionnaire was administered by the senior author to students in two different introduction to personality classes at the University of Wisconsin-Milwaukee. In each class, after being introduced by the instructor, he stated that he was a member of the Psychology Department's Human Subjects Committee, and thus was interested in students' attitudes toward various aspects of psychological research. He then read a brief statement of the Department's policy concerning students' participation in psychology experiments. The statement, which had been distributed to the students earlier in the semester, indicated that students in the introduction to personality course were expected to participate in experiments for which they would receive credit toward their final grade. It also outlined the rights and responsibilities of subjects, mentioning for example, that subjects could withdraw from any experiment at any time, and that they should not discuss experiments when requested not to do so by an experimenter. After the statement was read, the attitude questionnaire was distributed and students were informed they would receive one-half unit credit if they completed it. Students were asked to put their names on the questionnaire so that credit could be given.

The questionnaire, which was completed during the class period, was in the standard semantic differential format (Osgood, Suci and Tannenbaum, 1957). Four concepts appeared on separate pages: [a] scientific research, [b] psychological research, [c] participating as a subject in psychological experiments, and [d] Psychology Department's policy regarding participation in psychological experiments. The order of the concepts in the test booklet was randomly determined, and varied from one booklet to another. The concepts were rated on ten bipolar adjective scales, including the following five evaluative scales: useful-useless, desirable-undesirable, good-bad, pleasant-unpleasant, and meaningful-meaningless. A subject's attitude score was the sum of his responses on the five scales.

In the second phase of the experiment, students' availability to participate in a psychology experiment was determined. Students in the two classes were given different information regarding who was sponsoring an experiment in which they were asked to participate. The senior author returned to one class (Similar condition) one week after the attitude assessment and asked students to complete a form indicating their availability to participate in a 30-minute experiment he was conducting for which they would receive one-half unit credit. All persons present were asked to complete the form whether or not they were available to participate. The form asked subjects to indicate times during the day they would be available and to list their phone numbers so they could be contacted. Since any half-hour period between 8 a.m. and 6 p.m. for any weekday could be listed, it seems reasonable to construe expressed unavailability as an unwillingness to participate. The procedure in the other class (Dissimilar condition) was the same except participation was sought by a graduate student who identified the project as his own.

In the week following the administration of the availability to participate form, attempts were made to telephone all students who had expressed an availability to participate and who had completed an attitude questionnaire. The telephoning was done by 21 student experimenters enrolled in an experimental social psychology class. Students in the Similar condition were told they were being called in regard to Dr. Wicker's (the senior author's) experiment, while those in the Dissimilar condition were told that the call had to do with Mr. Altman's (the graduate student's) research. The callers gave each subject a choice among four alternative half-hour periods in which to participate; all of the times were ones the subject had previously listed as periods he would be available. If a subject agreed to participate at one of the four times, an appointment was scheduled and if he appeared, he participated in a verbal conditioning experiment. Persons who were available to participate but did not list a telephone number and those who could not be reached by telephone were dropped from the experiment. There were 121 students in the Similar condition for whom both attitudinal and behavioral data were available, i.e., who completed both the attitude questionnaire and the willingness to participate form, and who were also contacted by phone (if they were willing to participate). The *n* for the Dissimilar condition was 136.

The present behavioral measure of participation in a psychological experiment thus had four levels corresponding to steps in the recruitment process: [a] unavailable to participate (n=45), [b] available to participate, but not during one of the four times mentioned by the caller (n=29), [c] available to participate and to schedule an appointment, but failing to appear at the scheduled time (n=26), and [d] appearing at the scheduled time to participate in the experiment (n=157).

RESULTS

The four concepts rated on the attitude questionnaire were selected to represent four steps of increasing specificity of attitude object, from the general concept of scientific research to the specific concept of Psychology Department's policy regarding participation in psychological research. Intercorrelation of the responses of all subjects to the four concepts provided some support for this assumption: Attitudes toward scientific research were most closely related to attitudes toward psychological research (r=.69), and less closely related to the concepts of participation in psychological research as a subject (r=.39) and the Psychology Department's policy (r=.39). The latter two concepts were highly related to one another (r=.74), less closely to the concept, psychological research (r's=.52, .47), and least closely related to the concept, scientific research (both r's=.39). All coefficients are significant beyond the .01 probability level.

TABLE 1

Product-Moment Correlation Coefficients Relating Level of Behavior and Attitude Scale Responses

	Attitude Object			
Condition	Scientific research	Psychological research	Participating as a subject	Department's Policy
Similar[1]	.08	.12	.18*	.15
Dissimilar[2]	-.18*	.00	.18*	.23**
Combined	-.04	.06	.17**	.19**

[1]n=121 *$p \leq .05$
[2]n=136 **$p \leq .01$

The attitude-behavior relationship was examined by correlating the four-step behavioral scale with ratings of each of the four attitude concepts. Results of those analyses for the two groups are shown in Table 1. Although the coefficients are quite small, their pattern supports the hypothesis that increasing specificity of attitude objects increases the strength of the attitude-behavior relationship. However, the data do not consistently support the hypothesis that the actual or considered presence of a significant person at both the attitude and behavioral assessments will increase the strength of the attitude-behavior relationship: the attitude-behavior coefficient is larger in the Similar condition for only two of the four concepts.

A possible objection to the above analysis is that an interval scale is assumed for the four steps in the behavioral measure when product-moment correlation coefficients are calculated. To avoid this problem, the behavioral scale was dichotomized at three different points and point-biserial attitude-behavior correlation coefficients computed for each. The three behavioral dichotomies were: [a] stated availability to participate vs. stated unavailability, [b] stated availability and appointment scheduled vs. appointment not scheduled, and [c] stated availability, appointment scheduled and appeared vs. did not appear. These analyses revealed essentially the same pattern as the product-moment analysis: For each of the dichotomies, increasing specificity of the attitude object resulted in higher coefficients, while the Similar-Dissimilar manipulations did not have a consistent effect. The dichotomy yielding the highest coefficients was the stated availability vs. stated unavailability breakdown, for which the point-biserial coefficients were very similar to those in Table 1.

Another breakdown of the data involved the comparison of mean attitude scale scores for the subjects at each of the four behavioral levels, i.e., those who were unavailable, were available but not scheduled, were scheduled but did not appear, and appeared. The groups differed in mean attitude scores only for the concepts, participating as a subject in psychological research ($F = 3.49$; $df = 3/253$; $p < .05$), and Psychology Department's policy regarding participation in psychological experiments ($F = 4.09$; $df = 3/253$; $p < .01$). The mean attitude score for the two concepts, on a scale of +3 to -3, were as follows (attitude toward participation is listed first): unavailable, .8, .8; available but not scheduled, 1.3, 1.2; scheduled but did not appear, 1.3, 1.5; appeared, 1.3, 1.4. Thus there was a tendency for persons who had stated they were not available to participate to have less favorable attitudes toward participating as subjects and toward the Department's policy than persons who were available. Examination of the means suggests that there was little difference among the three groups of subjects who indicated they were available to participate, a fact consistent with the finding reported earlier that the dichotomy yielding the highest point-biserial coefficients was the available vs. unavailable breakdown.

DISCUSSION

The present results provide some confirmatory evidence that increasing the specificity of the attitude object increases the attitude-behavior relationship when the behavior of interest is also specific. However, the increase in predictability of behavior is quite small: the percentage of variance in the behavioral measure which can be accounted for by attitudinal responses ranged from 0.2% for ratings of scientific research to 3.6% for ratings of the Department's policy regarding students' participation in psychological research. Obviously, a great deal of behavior variance remains unaccounted for, even when specific attitude objects are employed.

Although the attitude-behavior coefficients in the present study are in the same range as most others in the literature (Wicker, 1969), the question can be raised as to whether stronger relationships might be obtained using more adequate measures of specific attitude concepts. For example, Fishbein (1967) has suggested measuring subjects' beliefs about the consequences of a given behavior and their evaluations of those consequences. Another approach was employed by Wicker (1970), who asked church members to evaluate each of a number of different levels of church behavior, such as attendance and contributions. That is, instead of asking subjects to rate "attending church regularly," they were asked to rate their degree of approval or disapproval of attending church every Sunday, of missing once or twice a year, and so on. The correlation coefficients relating this measure to actual church behaviors ranged from .06 to .37, with a mean r of .26.

The present results did not support the hypothesis that a stronger attitude-behavior relationship is obtained when a significant person is present at both the attitudinal and behavioral assessments than when he is present at only one of the assessments. The failure to support the hypothesis may be due to the relative weakness of the present manipulation, however. A faculty member who is conducting research may not be a very significant other from the subjects' perspective, especially when the assessment conditions involve group testing rather than a one-to-one experimenter-to-subject relationship. Moreover, the faculty experimenter was present only symbolically in the later stages of the behavioral assessment, i.e., when telephone calls were made to subjects in the Similar condition.

The data on mean attitude scale scores for subjects at different stages of the recruitment process are relevant to the concern of Rosenthal and Rosnow (1969) that subjects who volunteer to participate in psychological research may be different from those who do not volunteer. In the present study, volunteers had more favorable attitudes toward participating and toward a psychology department's policy regarding participation than did non-volunteers, but the two groups did not differ in their mean attitudes toward scientific research and psychological research.

Hopefully, future research on the attitude-behavior relationship will not merely relate the two kinds of response, but will attempt to test the contributions of other factors which have been postulated to influence the relationship (cf. Fishbein, 1967; Wicker, 1969).

REFERENCES

Fendrich, J. M. A study of the association among verbal attitudes, commitment, and overt behavior in different experimental situations. *Social Forces,* 1967, *45*, 347-355.

Fishbein, M. The relationships between beliefs, attitudes, and behavior. In S. Feldman (Ed.), *Cognitive consistency,* New York: Academic, 1966.

Fishbein, M. Attitude and the prediction of behavior. In M. Fishbein (Ed.), *Readings in attitude theory and measurement.* New York: Wiley, 1967.

Hyman, H. Inconsistencies as a problem in attitude measurement. *Journal of Social Issues,* 1949, *5* (3), 38-42.

Insko, C. A. & Schopler, J. Triadic consistency: A statement of affective-cognitive-conative consistency. *Psychological Review,* 1967, *74*, 361-376.

Osgood, C. E., Suci, G. J., & Tannenbaum, P. H. *The measurement of meaning.* Urbana: University of Illinois Press, 1957.

Rosenthal, R., & Rosnow, R. L. The volunteer subject. In R. Rosenthal & R. L. Rosnow (Eds.), *Artifact in behavioral research.* New York: Academic, 1969.

Warner, L. G. & DeFleur, M. L. Attitude as an interactional concept: social constraint and social distance as intervening variables between attitudes and action. *American Sociological Review*, 1969, *34*, 153-169.

Wicker, A. W. Attitudes versus actions: The relationship of verbal and overt behavioral responses to attitude objects. *Journal of Social Issues,* 1969, *25*, (4), 41-78.

Wicker, A. W. An examination of the "other variables" explanation of attitude-behavior inconsistency. Unpublished manuscript, Department of Psychology, University of Illinois, 1970.

IV

THEORETICAL REEXAMINATION

8

ATTITUDES, BEHAVIOR, AND THE INTERVENING VARIABLES

Howard J. Ehrlich

Studies on the relation of attitudes and behavior have almost consistently resulted in the conclusion that attitudes are a poor predictor of behavior. The majority of these studies have taken ethnic attitudes as the predictor and some mode of intergroup behavior as the predictand. The summary statement here has usually been of the form that prejudice is a poor predictor of discrimination (Bray, 1950; Brookover and Holland, 1952; DeFleur and Westie, 1958; Fishman, 1961; Killian, 1953; Kutner *et al.*, 1952; LaPiere, 1934, 1936; Linn, 1965; Lohman and Reitzes, 1952; Malof and Lott, 1962; Minard, 1952; Nettler and Golding, 1946; Saenger and Gilbert, 1950).

It is clear that many social scientists concerned with the study of prejudice and intergroup behavior have taken the prevailing interpretations of the evidence of attitude-behavior inconsistency as a premise toward the conclusion that attitude theory has proven inadequate. In his presidential address to the Society for the Study of Social Problems, Deutscher (1966:247) asserts that "no matter what one's theoretical orientation may be, he has no reason to expect to find congruence between attitudes and actions and every reason to expect to find discrepancies between them." DeFleur and Westie (1963:28), for another example, declare a *necessary* inconsistency between verbal scale scores and other overt actions, pointing to "social constraints" or situational norms as the crucial determinants of behavior. Consistency between attitudes and behavior occurs, they argue, "if the normative processes of the groups within which [people] are interacting are consistent."

Reprinted from *American Sociologist* (Vol. 4, February, 1969, pp. 35-41) by permission of the author and the American Sociological Association.

It is the thesis of this paper that the evidence for inconsistency may be rejected on both methodological and conceptual grounds, and that there is no necessary incompatibility between a theory of attitudes and theories of interpersonal or intergroup behavior. It is my intent, first, to present briefly the major arguments against interpretations of inconsistency, and then to provide a paradigm for the analysis of the attitude-behavior relation. I shall limit my examples to the study of prejudice and intergroup behavior.

METHODOLOGICAL ARGUMENTS

From a methodological standpoint it can be argued that attitude measurement, particularly in the domain of prejudice, has been demonstrated to be seriously imprecise and unreliable. Rosenthal (1966), in his review of experimenter error, summarized the effects of the real and perceived ethnicity of experimenters on test and questionnaire performance. From this evidence, it is apparent that the ethnic identity of the researcher significantly biases respondent behavior. Ehrlich (1964) and Ehrlich and Rinehart (1965) have demonstrated that forced-response formats in prejudice scales overstate the degree of prejudice and distort the manifest content of ethnic-group imagery. Fendrich (1967:355) provides a direct test of the effects of the measurement process on predicting intergroup behavior, concluding: "Verbal attitudes can be either consistent or inconsistent with overt behavior, depending upon the way respondents define the attitude measurement situation."

Measurement errors may also be examined in the operations through which the behaviors to be predicted and explained in the attitude-behavior paradigm are measured or assessed. While the operations for attitude-scale construction are relatively well standardized, the operations for observing and recording behavior, particularly in natural settings, are generally unstandardized and problem-specific. Further, while the items of attitude scales are presumably a representative set of statements from the attitude domain studied, most behavioral units selected for study have been chosen on a nonsystematic or *ad hoc* basis. It would seem plausible, therefore, to attribute some degree of recorded inconsistency to these less rigorous measures of overt actions in intergroup situations.

It may be, further, that our basic strategy has been wrong. We have generally measured attitudes toward a class of people, but made predictions about a person's behavior toward a specific member of that class (cf. Fishbein, 1966). Certainly a low order of correct predictions may be taken as a special case of the fallacy of ecological correlation (i.e., predicting unit behavior from a knowledge of aggregate relations). Perhaps, more appropriately, we should consider the alternatives: either we measure an attitude toward a specific person and then predict a subject's behavior toward that person, or we measure attitudes toward a class of people and predict a subject's behavior to some (perhaps phenomenologically) representative sample of that class.

On the basis of even these brief and limited methodological arguments, the evidence from past research must be re-examined. The conclusion that verbal attitude expressions are inconsistent with other overt behaviors must be suspended. In reviewing the conceptual arguments, I shall try to show that the conclusion is untenable.

CONCEPTUAL ARGUMENTS

The conceptual arguments that may be adduced to invalidate interpretations of inconsistency need not be tied to a specific theory of attitudes. The strategy of this presentation is based on the assumption that the most cogent arguments are those which can be easily stated in the language of the current, prevailing attitude theories.

In almost all current theories, attitudes are construed as having a componential structure. Not all the components of an attitude imply behavior. It follows from this that without a direct assessment of the "action potential" of an attitude component, the researcher's inference about the subject's behavior, or intentions, may be phenomenologically naive. This possibility is illustrated in a study by Kay (1947), who demonstrated that 36 per cent of a sample of presumably anti-Jewish items, drawn from the Levinson-Sanford scale of anti-Semitism, were judged by naive subjects as friendly or directionally unclear. Predictions of anti-Jewish behavior from these items would probably have displayed high error.

To adopt the argument that not all attitude components imply behavior, it is not necessary to endorse a multi-dimensional strategy of attitude-theory construction. The argument, from the standpoint of a unidimensional theory, simply becomes: not all attitudes imply behavior. Whatever the other outcomes of these theoretical strategies, they agree in their fundamental statements concerning the relation of attitudes and behavior. Fishbein (1966:213), a leading unidimensional theorist, states his position clearly:

> Because attitude is a hypothetical variable abstracted from the *totality* of an individual's beliefs, behavioral intentions, and actions, toward a given object . . . any given belief, behavioral intention, or behavior, therefore, may be uncorrelated or even negatively correlated with his attitude. Thus, rather than viewing specific beliefs or classes of beliefs and specific behavioral intentions as part of attitude, these phenomena must be studied as variables in their own right, that, like attitudes, may or may not function as determinants of a specific behavior.

Different scaling models and measurement procedures differentially assess the behaviorally directive components of attitudes. The current major scaling models focus primarily on two attitude components, usually direction and intensity; only the procedure of summated ratings considers both dimensions simultaneously. Where an attitude scale is focused on a single component and where that component has a low action potential, successful prediction should be highly unlikely. Tittle and Hill (1967) provide some confirming evidence. Aside from formal scaling, the two major procedures for measuring prejudice—the stereotype check list and the social-distance questionnaire—similarly tap only a single attitude component. The check list assesses only the salience (typicality) of a stereotype, and that usually in a categorical manner, while social-distance measures provide a report solely of behavioral intentions, usually abstracted from situational reference. Only where these components entail a high directiveness for behavior should a high congruence with behavior be expected.

It may be argued further that the determination of the structure of an attitude at any point in time requires the determination of the interrelations of the components that constitute the attitude. An attitude can be defined as well formed when all of its components achieve some balance and that balanced state persists over time. If this conceptualization is adequate, it follows that reliable predictions of behavior can occur only from well-formed attitudes, or, in the absence of a well-formed attitude, only when the predicted behavior is close in time to the attitude measurement. Even then, it may be the case that the measurement process per se can change the state of a poorly balanced attitude.

Not only does a single attitude comprise several components, but a single attitude object may implicate many attitudes. Predictions of behavior that do not account for all (or at least the major) attitudes evoked by an object will probably be wrong. In a variation on this argument, Rokeach (1967:530) has contended that at least two attitudes are required to make a correct prediction of behavior.

> . . . an attitude may be focused either on an object or on a situation. In the first instance we have in mind an attitude-object, which may be concrete or abstract, involving a person, a group, an institution, or an issue. In the second instance the attitude is focused on a specific situation, an event, or an activity. To say that a person has an enduring attitude toward a given object is to say that this attitude will, when activated, somehow determine his behavior toward the attitude-object across situations; conversely, to say that a person has an enduring attitude toward a given situation is to say that this attitude will, when activated, determine his behavior toward the situation, across attitude-objects.

It may be that the reported inconsistency between attitude and behavior is a partial result of our naivete in phenomenological analysis, i.e., our inability to ascertain the intentional meaning of an actor's verbal and nonverbal acts. Without denying the crudities of phenomenological analysis in contemporary social psychology, the fundamental problem may be that our presumed observations of inconsistencies derive from our failure to specify the criteria for judging a consistent or inconsistent response. Campbell (1961:160) provides a graphic illustration of the problem of assessing consistency:

> On an arithmetic test of four items, the child who gets only two items correct is not necessarily regarded as less consistent than the child who gets all right or all wrong. If he gets the two easiest right and the two hardest wrong, he is equally consistent. On intelligence we today think in terms of a continuum, and can conceive of consistent mediocrity. . . . we can regard honesty as something people have in degree, rather than an all-or-none trait. A person of intermediate degree can be just as consistent as a person of extreme position, and his attitude can be determined from his behavior just as well. . . . For intelligence and honesty, we have achieved dimensionality in our thinking. For more emotion-laden topics, such as standing up for civil rights, we have not. If a university president protects a pacifist professor but fires an atheist, we call him inconsistent. If he protects a pacifist and an atheist, but fires a Communist, we accuse him of backing down under pressure. Conceptually, we have the notion of a total non-defendant of professors' rights and a total defender of professors' rights, and lack any concept of genuine mediocrity which would *in consistency* produce defense in a situation of low threshold and firing in another situation with a higher threshold value.

The assessment of consistency is initially contingent on the conditions of adequate measurement and the stability of an attitude. Assuming these conditions, it is then necessary to enumerate the set of obligatory and optional behaviors that comprise the attitude domain. Presumably, this is a highly limited set of behaviors, or at least the obligatory behaviors form a highly limited subset. The number of observations required for a sample of this set or subset of behaviors will doubtless be fixed by the degree to which these behaviors are scalar. The extent to which an individual's verbal and nonverbal behaviors may achieve some level of consistency will then depend upon quasi-logical (probably social-psychological) criteria of contradiction. Such criteria, implicit in everyday behavior, have yet to be made explicit.

STRATEGY FOR RESEARCH: THE INTERVENING VARIABLES

The search for a more appropriate research strategy must begin with the understanding that the simple question of the consistency of attitudes and behavior is misleading. The correct representation of the problem should take the form: Under what conditions, and to what degree, are attitudes of a given type related to behaviors of a given type? My intent in this section, then, is to identify the social and psychological conditions that intervene between attitudes and behavior. As a matter of intellectual strategy, I shall limit myself here to those variables most directly related to attitude theory. Elsewhere I have attempted to identify the relevant variables of social structure in considering the analogous problem of the relation of role expectations to role behavior (Preiss and Ehrlich, 1966:Chap. 9). Current alternatives may be reviewed in Fishbein (1966) and Himmelstrand (1960).

Clarity. For consistency to occur there has to be a clear way for an attitude to be expressed in behavior. For some attitudes and for some behaviors, the relationship may not be clear. This indeterminacy could appear under a number of possible conditions, the importance of which we shall probably have to ferret out through intensive descriptive research. Williams (1964:329), in discussing the characteristics of behavior in unclear interracial situations, provides a prospectus for research:

> The unfamiliar situation is, by definition, initially one of uncertainty, which is another way of saying that it induces some degree of insecurity. Past experience does not suffice as a guide, and old norms may not lead to the usual results. New situations are likely, therefore, to instigate heightened alertness—including a generalized vigilance toward cues that may indicate what action will lead to what consequences. Under the circumstances of uncertainty and sharpened attentiveness, the individual who first acts with an appearance of decisiveness and confidence is likely to have marked influence. It can and does often happen that the people in leadership positions are themselves confused; for them the situation is not even structured enough to suggest where to turn for clarification. We saw that, in consequence, action on the part of any other participant became disproportionately important in determining their definitions. Confused participants sought indices of how others defined the situation. Since the crucial question in many of these situations was whether or not membership in a particular racial category (Negro) precluded membership in other groups or categories, the first action to be taken by a white was often interpreted by all as an index of acceptance or rejection.

Expressibility. Some attitudes may be clearly expressible only in verbal behavior. Extremely radical, highly unconventional, or strongly antisocial attitudes may in fact have their primary expression in verbal behaviors or in fantasy. Some attitudes may have their expression in sublimated behavior. Attitudes about matters which a person defines, or which are socially defined, as highly intimate may also have their primary expressions in verbal and fantasy behavior. Other expressions may be deliberately concealed from observation.

Disclosure. Related to expressibility is the willingness of a person to disclose his attitude. Under many circumstances, the failure to disclose one's attitude may be neither an attitude-consistent nor an attitude-inconsistent act. In the case of attitudes toward oneself, their disclosure or concealment has indicated such a regular pattern of occurrence that the conditions of disclosure could represent an important class of variables for more general consideration. The research stimulated by Jourard (1964) has confirmed that people vary in their characteristic level of disclosure of self-attitudes. It has also been established, particularly from the work of Altman and Haythorn (1965), that these individual differences are responsive to controlled situational variation both for the number of self-attitude statements disclosed and for their depth of intimacy. Following from this, Graeven (1967) has demonstrated that for thirteen different categories of self-attitude statements and for levels of intimacy associated with each of these categories, all subjects—regardless of their characteristic level of disclosure—reciprocated by category and intimacy the disclosures made by another person. This limited research suggests that reciprocity in the verbal and nonverbal expression of attitudes may be a standard interpersonal tactic as well as a more generalized norm of interpersonal behavior. Thus, it may be hypothesized that attitudes expressible in interpersonal situations may not be disclosed either because others do not express their attitudes or because the actor fails to perceive them. Further, the "race-belief" and the "attitude similarity" hypotheses of Rokeach (1960) and Byrne (1961) suggest an obverse to the disclosure hypothesis: Attitudes expressible in interpersonal situations may not be disclosed when the actor perceives his attitudes as contrary to the attitudes of others in the situation. These disclosure hypotheses will no doubt have to be qualified by considerations of the duration of the situation, among other situational properties.

Perspective and the Definition of the Act. The indeterminate status of the attitude-behavior relation may also be a consequence of perspective. An act consistent from the standpoint of the actor may appear to the observer to be inconsistent. This becomes particularly problematic when an actor deliberately chooses not to act, or when the outcome of an act is contrary to what the actor intended.

Perhaps the most confounding problem of the matter of intent as related to the outcome of an act is that of the social definition of an act. Regardless of the actor's intent, both the scientist as an observer and the actor as an observer of himself must cope with the prevailing social definition. Where the disparity between a personal and social construction of an act is very great, it seems likely that over time an actor may come to question or even redefine his own behavior. The presumed seriousness of this problem has led some social scientists to take the position that a motivational theory must necessarily be a theory of rationalization of behavior (Mills, 1940:906-907):

> The aspect of motive which this conception grasps is its intrinsically social character. A satisfactory or adequate motive is one that satisfied the questioners of an act or program, whether it be the other's or the actor's. As a word, a motive tends to be one which is to the actor and to the other mem-

bers of a situation an unquestioned answer to questions concerning social and lingual conduct. A stable motive is an ultimate in justificatory conversation. The words which in a type situation will fulfill this function are circumscribed by the vocabulary of motives acceptable for such situations. Motives are accepted justifications for present, future, or past programs or acts.

As a theory of motivation, the conspectus of Mills is seriously defective. Nevertheless, the systematic study of vocabularies of motives should lead to a more sophisticated understanding of intentional behavior and self-report. This uniquely sociological perspective furthermore points to three parameters of self-report requiring serious consideration: the strength of prevailing definitions of social acts, the disparity between personal and social definitions of social acts, and the time between an act and the actor's report of his intent, or vice versa.

The sociology of motivational analysis leads us to still another consideration. The same act over time and in different social contexts changes its meaning, i.e., its social definition. Attitude-consistent behavior at one time may be perceived as inconsistent at another time. Yesterday's radical may be today's impediment to progress, though neither his attitudes nor behavior have changed in consistency. Morton Deutsch (1949:49), who calls this the problem of "unrecognized locomotion," describes it:

> To the extent that we do not take cognizance of how changes beyond our control affect our positions in relation to our goals, we are likely to behave in ways which are either inconsistent or irrelevant to our purposes. The incorrect assessment of present position is likely to lead to a faulty perception of the direction to one's goal.

Finally, informal evidence indicates that people sometimes intentionally act in an attitude-inconsistent manner. Such behavior, which may be an important condition for attitude change, may have its basis in either personal curiosity or an attempt to achieve novelty in an unstimulating environment. Inconsistent behavior may also be a primary means by which individuals test themselves and others.

Learning. The discussion so far has focused on the condition of clarity in the relation of attitudes to behavior, where the strategic problems become the determination of an attitude's expressibility and the nexus of intention to act. It is now appropriate to introduce the three assumptions hidden in this discussion. The first of these is the learning assumption. Even where a clear and expressible relation exists between an attitude and behavior, it is not necessary to assume that an actor knows how to behave in a consistent manner. The major determinant of attitude-discrepant behavior may be that an actor has not learned how to express his attitude in action competently. One determinant of the adequacy of such learning may be the level of direct or vicarious experience of the actor, if any, in such behavior situations. Under this condition of no or poor learning, inaction, inappropriate behavior, and sometimes ineffective behavior are defined by the observer as inconsistent acts. Certainly, learning how to behave in a manner consistent with one's attitudes is a primary objective of socialization at all stages of the life cycle.

Accessibility. The second of the assumptions implicit in discussions of attitude-consistent behavior is the assumption of opportunity and access. Knowing how to behave in an appropriate manner is insufficient if the opportunity, access, or perceived access to the opportunity is nonexistent. For example, the study of ethnic intermarriage reveals that the best predictor of intermarriage is the opportunity to intermarry. For Negro-white marriages, for instance, opportunity is partly defined by the proportion of eligible mates, the degree of residential segregation, and the degree of status congruence (Heer, 1966).

Competence. Even knowing what is consistent and having the opportunity to engage in attitude-consistent behavior is only one necessary condition for such behavior. Not only must an actor learn what comprises appropriate behavior, but he must learn how to use his skills and muster his personal resources in order for his actions to be effective. Thus, the third assumption implicit in most past discussions has been an assumption of skill and resource. Patently, individuals vary in the skills they have developed and in the resources they can mobilize for behavior in any given situation. Inferences about behavior, therefore, must take into account such individual differences. An ostensibly inconsistent act may indicate only the actor's deficient skill, his lack of resources, or his inability to organize his resources for effective behavior. It is possible that inferences about behavior and consistency may be biased in the direction of more skillful individuals by the fact that they may emit more behaviors, and/or perform them more confidently and more effectively.

The research strategies indicated so far are of substantial consequence in establishing the attitude-behavior relation. Two widely discussed problems of crucial importance remain: the problem of situational analysis and the problem of multiple-attitude analysis.

Situational Analysis. In the absence of any well-established guidelines for such analysis, it seems reasonable to consider as separate problems those concerned with the structural, primarily physical, characteristics of situations and those concerned with the social dimensions. The focus of structural analysis is, first, the study of the properties of situations and their interrelationships, and second, the study of the relation of these properties to behavior. Barker and his associates (1955, 1963) have developed an extensive language and research operations for structural analysis, but these have not yet had application to the kinds of problems that concern us here. Hall (1963, 1966) has provided systematic procedures for assessing the effects of space on interpersonal behavior, and Sommer (1967) has recently reviewed this developing literature. For the social dimensions of situations, the most well-developed schemes now exist for the analysis of role behavior (e.g., Biddle and Thomas, 1966; Preiss and Ehrlich, 1966) and for the analysis of interaction processes (Borgatta and Crowther, 1965). Although the significance of role playing and role enactment for attitude change has been clearly demonstrated (Sarbin, 1964), attitude theorists have generally ignored role and related theories (and role theorists have generally ignored attitude variables).

Situational characteristics are often given theoretical consideration only if they are *perceived* by the actor, and sometimes they are considered only in terms of the actor's *attitudes* toward them. This strategy may be misleading. It remains to be demonstrated that the actor does, in fact, perceive and have an attitude toward situational properties and that such attitudes are of meaningful behavioral relevance. While many situational variables are invariably perceived, other situational variables of behavioral importance, particularly the structural characteristics, are probably seldom perceived. Whatever the strategy of situational analysis in attitude research, the warrant for its priority should be clear. In the classic formulation of Lewin: behavior is a function of the person and his environment.

Multiple Attitudes. A strategy for research on multiple attitudes is based on the assumptions that for some situations and objects more than one attitude will be evoked and that the behavioral strength of a set of attitudes may be formally determined. The research of Bayton, McAllister, and Hamer (1956), for example, has indicated that attitudes toward social class appear almost as important as race attitudes in determining the stereotypes assigned to Negroes. Triandis (1967) has demonstrated that the expression of behavioral intentions varies across the class, sex, ethnicity, occupation, and belief similarity of the attitude object. For example, behavior toward a Negro female physician may be primarily directed by one's attitudes toward Negroes, toward females, toward physicians, toward any two of these characteristics, or toward all three simultaneously. The development of a calculus of attitudes across attitude objects and situations should seriously be considered as an item of high research priority.

CONCLUDING REMARKS

The intervening variables presented here were specifically limited to those directly related to current attitude theories. I began by indicating that not all attitudes are behaviorally expressible, or at least clearly expressible, in interpersonal behavior. Some attitudes are deliberately not expressed in behavior, and I suggested that we examine the interpersonal conditions under which people are willing or unwilling to disclose their attitudes.

The exact behavior that complements a specific attitude is not always clear, and the presumed clarity of an act is itself a consequence of the perspective from which it is evaluated as well as the time that intervenes between act and evaluation. Knowledge of how to act consistently has to be learned, and not all actors will be able to use their knowledge with equal competence. Beyond these conditions, it still remains to be demonstrated that the actor has the opportunity to act appropriately. Finally, I indicated that the actor's failure to act in a manner consistent with a given attitude could be a direct result of other situational constraints or a result of conflict with other relevant attitudes that are more important to the behaviors under analysis.

The specific effects that each of these intervening variables has on behavior remains to be determined. There should be no doubt, however, that the study of these variables and the relation of attitudes to behavior is of strategic significance in the development of social psychology. The question I raised about this relation, in beginning our examination of the intervening variables, is a major instance of the classic problem of social psychology. Under what conditions, how, and to what degree do aspects of social structure and aspects of personality determine interpersonal behavior?

REFERENCES

Altman, I., and W. W. Haythorn
1965 "Interpersonal exchange in isolation." Sociometry 28:411–426.
Barker, R. G., and H. F. Wright
1955 Midwest and Its Children. New York: Harper & Row.
Barker, R. G. (ed.)
1963 The Stream of Behavior. New York: Appleton-Century-Crofts.
Bayton, J. A., *et al.*
1956 "Race-class stereotypes." Journal of Negro Education 25 (Winter): 75–78.
Biddle, B. J., and E. J. Thomas (eds.)
1966 Role Theory: Concepts and Research. New York: Wiley.
Borgatta, E. F., and B. Crowther
1965 A Workbook for the Study of Social Interaction Processes. Chicago: Rand-McNally.
Bray, D. W.
1950 "The prediction of behavior from two attitude scales." Journal of Abnormal and Social Psychology 45:64–84.
Brookover, W., and J. Holland
1952 "An inquiry into the meaning of minority group attitude expressions." American Sociological Review 17:196–202.
Byrne, D.
1961 "Interpersonal attraction and attitude similarity." Journal of Abnormal and Social Psychology 62:713–715.
Campbell, D. T.
1961 "Social attitudes and other acquired behavioral dispositions," in S. Koch (ed.), Psychology: A Study of a Science, v. 6. New York: McGraw-Hill.
DeFleur, M. L., and F. R. Westie
1963 "Attitude as a Scientific Concept." Social Forces 42:17–31.
1958 "Verbal Attitudes and Overt Acts: An Experiment on the Salience of Attitudes." American Sociological Review 23:667–673.

Deutsch, M.
1949 "The Directions of Behavior: A Field-Theoretical Approach to the Understanding of Inconsistencies." Journal of Social Issues 5:43–51.

Deutscher, I.
1966 "Words and deeds: social science and social policy." Social Problems 13 (Winter): 235-254.

Ehrlich, H. J.
1964 "Instrument error and the study of prejudice." Social Forces 43:197–206.

Ehrlich, H. J., and J. W. Rinehart
1965 "A brief report on the methodology of stereotype research." Social Forces 43:564–575.

Fendrich, J. M.
1967 "A study of the association among verbal attitudes, commitment and overt behavior in different experimental situations." Social Forces 45:347-355.

Fishbein, M.
1966 "The relationships between beliefs, attitudes, and behavior," in S. Feldman (ed.), Cognitive Consistency. New York: Academic Press.

Fishman, J.
1961 "Some social and psychological determinants of intergroup relations in changing neighborhoods: an introduction to the Bridgeview study." Social Forces 40:42–51.

Graeven, D. B.
1967 Reciprocal Self-Disclosure in a Dyadic Situation. M. A. Thesis, University of Iowa.

Hall, E. T.
1966 The Hidden Dimension. New York: Doubleday.
1963 "A system of notation of proxemic behavior." American Anthropologist 65:1003–1026.

Heer, D. M.
1966 "Negro-white marriage in the United States." Journal of Marriage and the Family 28:262–273.

Himmelstrand, U.
1960 "Verbal attitudes and behavior: a paradigm for the study of message transmissions and transformations. Public Opinion Quarterly 24:224-250.

Jourard, S. M.
1964 The Transparent Self. Princeton, N.J.: Van Nostrand.

Kay, L. W.
1947 "Frame of reference in 'pro' and 'anti' evaluation of test items." Journal of Social Psychology 25:63–68.

Killian, L. M.
1953 "The adjustment of Southern white migrants to Northern urban norms." Social Forces 32:66–69.

Kutner, B., C. Wilkins, and P. Yarrow
1952 "Verbal attitudes and overt behavior involving racial prejudice." Journal of Abnormal and Social Psychology 47:649–652.

LaPiere, R. T.
1936 "Type-rationalizations of group antipathy." Social Forces 15:232–237.
1934 "Attitudes vs. actions." Social Forces 13:230–237.

Linn, L. S.
1965 "Verbal attitudes and overt behavior: a study of racial discrimination." Social Forces 43:353–364.

Lohman, J. P., and D. C. Reitzes
1952 "Note on race relations in mass society." American Journal of Sociology 58:240–246.

Malof, M., and A. Lott
1962 "Ethnocentrism and the acceptance of Negro support in a group situation." Journal of Abnormal and Social Psychology 65:254–258.

Mills, C. W.
1940 "Situated actions and vocabularies of motive." American Sociological Review 5:904–913.

Minard, R. D.
1952 "Race relationships in the Pocahontas coal field." Journal of Social Issues 8:29-44.
Nettler, G., and E. H. Golding
1946 "The measurement of attitudes toward the Japanese in America." American Journal of Sociology 52:31–39.
Preiss, J. J., and H. J. Ehrlich
1966 An Examination of Role Theory. Lincoln: University of Nebraska Press.
Rokeach, M.
1967 "Attitude change and behavioral change." Public Opinion Quarterly 30:529–550.
1960 The Open and the Closed Mind. New York: Basic Books.
Rosenthal, R.
1966 Experimenter Effects in Behavorial Research. New York: Appleton–Century–Crofts.
Saenger, G. H., and E. Gilbert
1950 "Customer reactions to the integration of Negro sales personnel." Public Opinion Quarterly 4:57–76.
Sarbin, T. R.
1964 "Role theoretical interpretation of psychological change." Pp. 176–219 in P. Worchel and D. Byrne (eds.), Personality Change. New York: Wiley.
Sommer, R.
1967 "Small group ecology." Psychological Bulletin 67:145–152.
Tittle, C. R., and R. J. Hill
1967 "Attitude measurement and prediction of behavior: an evaluation of conditions and measurement techniques." Sociometry 30:199–213.
Triandis, H. C.
1967 "Toward an analysis of the components of interpersonal attitudes." Pp. 227–270 in C. W. Sherif and M. Sherif (eds.), Attitude, Ego-Involvement, and Change. New York: Wiley.
Williams, R. M.
1964 Strangers Next Door. Englewood Cliffs, N.J.: Prentice-Hall.

9

WORDS, DEEDS, AND THE PERCEPTION OF CONSEQUENCES AND RESPONSIBILITY IN ACTION SITUATIONS

Shalom H. Schwartz

The question of how verbalizations concerning attitudes, opinions, and norms are related to overt behaviors is of continuing concern in social science. Deutscher (1966a) has compiled a bibliography of several hundred sources dealing with aspects of this question. Yet the conclusions drawn by reviewers of this literature are widely divergent. DeFleur and Westie (1963), for example, labeled the idea that there should be consistency between verbal behavior and actions "the fallacy of expected correspondence," arguing that verbalizations and overt actions constitute separate universes of response. Yet Campbell (1963, pp. 157-162) asserted that true inconsistency is rarely found, and called what is reported in the social attitude literature "pseudoinconsistency." He cited failure to recognize that verbal behavior and overt behavior have different situational thresholds as the basis for many inconsistency interpretations.

The springboard for the research reported here is the often noted fact that verbalizations are commonly elicited or measured in one setting, while the actions which they presumably might govern are observed in another (cf. Campbell, 1963; DeFleur & Westie, 1958; Deutscher 1966b; Fendrich, 1967; Himmelstrand, 1960; Hyman, 1959; Linn, 1965; Tittle & Hill, 1967). Thus, while a scientist or some other observer may think that a particular norm or attitude he has measured or inferred is pertinent, the actor himself may not define the situation of action as one in which this norm or attitude applies. This suggests that some of the apparent inconsistency between words and deeds occurs because potentially pertinent norms or attitudes are not activated when people face choices of

Reprinted from *Journal of Personality and Social Psychology* (Vol. 10, November, 1968, pp. 232-242).

behavior. To determine when consistency is to be expected, it is important to identify conditions that influence how people define action situations and thereby influence which of their attitudes, opinions, or norms, if any, they perceive to be applicable.

In the present research, interest was directed to the broad class of interpersonal behavior governed by moral norms. From an analysis of literature devoted to the delineation of moral behavior, two conditions were derived which are necessary before people define interpersonal action situations in ways that activate moral norms. It was noted that actors are evaluated morally only when their actions are seen as resulting from decisions over which they have some control, that is, for which they are responsible. Moreover, moral norms are applied only to those actions that have consequences for the welfare of persons or other social actors. The necessary conditions for the activation of moral norms that follow from this analysis are: (*a*) the person must have some awareness that his potential acts may have consequences for the welfare of others, and (*b*) he must ascribe some degree of responsibility for these acts and their consequences to himself.

It is proposed here that when these conditions are fulfilled a person's moral norms are activated, and they may then influence his overt behavior. Counternorms, threats, and self-interest may deflect the impact of these norms on action, of course, so that strong associations are not guaranteed. When the conditions are *not* fulfilled, however, there is no expectation that the person's moral norms will be activated or, therefore, that they will influence action. A man who opposes killing, for example, may not be influenced by this norm in his actions as a soldier on the battlefield (*a*) if he is unaware that the consequences of his shooting may be to kill, or if he denies awareness of this fact, and (*b*) if he holds the enemy, his sergeant, or some other source outside himself responsible for what he is doing. If he perceives the situation as an encounter with people who may be killed by acts for which he is responsible, however, the proscription against killing *is* likely to exert pressure on his actions.

Since much of social interaction consists of responsible behavior with consequences for the welfare of others, testing of hypotheses generated from this view of the activation of moral norms can contribute to understanding of the general relationship between words and deeds. This paper first examines how variations in ascription of responsibility to the self affect the relationships of norms to behavior in natural settings, in the domains of considerateness, reliability, and helpfulness. It then examines the joint effects of ascription of responsibility and awareness of consequences for the welfare of others upon these relationships. The general hypothesis tested is that the correspondence between personal norms and overt interpersonal behavior increases with an increase in the probability that people view themselves, in action situations, as the responsible originators of action and are aware that their potential acts may have consequences for the welfare of others.

Variations in how people perceive responsibility and consequences can be produced experimentally. Alternatively, if people show stable tendencies to ascribe responsibility to the self and to become aware of consequences, these tendencies can be taken as indexes of how likely they are to define action situations in a manner leading to the activation of appropriate moral norms. The present research adopts the latter approach. Findings of studies in which experimental variation of situational cues may have influenced the perception of responsibility are examined in the discussion.

As Heider and others have noted (Heider, 1958; Pepitone, 1958), perceiving persons as the absolute causal origins of events is a common simplifying device. Most interpersonal situations are so complex that they provide a wide variety of sources to which a person may ascribe responsibility for his acts and their outcomes. Ascribing responsibility away from the self may occur in two ways: first, as part of the person's initial perception of the action situation, or second, as a defensive response to disturbing emotions aroused in anticipation of violating a norm he feels is applicable. Defensive denial of responsibility permits a redefinition of the situation as one in which that norm is no longer an appropriate basis for evaluating the self (cf. the technique of "denial of responsibility" [Sykes & Matza, 1957]).

The conception of Ascription of Responsibility (AR) as a personal tendency can be clarified by contrasting it with other individual dispositions to which it may be related empirically or conceptually. Like *internal-external control* (Rotter, 1966), which refers to people's beliefs about how reinforcement is controlled, AR is addressed to how people view the causal relations between actions and their outcomes. Regardless of where a person locates control over the reinforcements he receives from an act, however, he may ascribe responsibility for the act and its consequences toward or away from himself.

AR shares with *avoidant interpretation* (Schroder & Hunt, 1957; cf. Rosenzweig, 1954) both an emphasis on attribution of responsibility as crucial in the definition of action situations and the idea that avoiding loss of self-esteem can motivate denial of personal responsibility for anticipated or performed behavior. It differs in its focus on moral responsibility (i.e., for the interpersonal consequences of acts) rather than responsibility for performance on a task. AR may also appear similar to the continuum implied in Riesman's description of character structure as *inner-directed* or *other-directed* (Riesman, Glazer & Denney, 1950). Note, however, that Riesman is interested in the location of the norms that direct action, while the present concept refers to the source to which the actor ascribes responsibility, irrespective of the actual source of normative influence.

Hypotheses

It has been proposed that the activation of a particular moral norm in a person facing an action situation requires that he ascribe to himself some degree of responsibility for the actions governed by the norm and for their consequences. Assuming that activation of a norm is necessary in order for it to influence behavior in an action situation, it is hypothesized that:

1. The correspondence between personal norms and overt behavior is stronger among those high in the tendency to ascribe responsibility to the self than among those low in this tendency.

According to this analysis, a second prerequisite for the activation of moral norms, in addition to accepting responsibility, is that the person have some awareness that his potential acts may have consequences for the welfare of others. Evidence that Awareness of Consequences (AC) does moderate the correspondence between norms and behavior is presented elsewhere (Schwartz, 1968). Since the indexes of AC and of AR were found to be unrelated ($r = -.07$, $p. > .45$), it is reasonable to consider each variable separately, as is done in Hypothesis 1. The theoretical analysis of moral decision making suggests, however, that these two variables interact. It is only when there is *both* awareness of interpersonal consequences and acceptance of responsibility for them that norms governing these consequences are likely to be experienced as applicable and to influence behavior, except insofar as other pressures supporting them are brought to bear (e.g., they are invoked by someone else in the situation).

Viewing AR and AC as personal tendencies, it is among those people high in both that the prerequisites for defining action situations as moral encounters are most likely to be met. Those high in one tendency alone are only slightly more likely to experience activation of appropriate moral norms than are those low in both, since one barrier to activation is still liable to operate. This leads to the following hypothesis regarding the interaction between AR and AC in their effect upon the correspondence between norms and behavior:

2. The correspondence between personal norms and overt behavior is smallest among those low in both AR and AC, greater among those high in one tendency but low in the other (mixed), and greatest among those high in both AR and AC. Furthermore, the interaction between AR and AC is expressed by a greater increase in the correspondence from the mixed to the high group than from the low to the mixed group.

An indirect test of the assertion that AR functions to activate moral norms can be made by examining the direct relationship between AR scores and interpersonal behavior, given certain characteristics of the data in the current research. The behavior studied was considerateness, reliability, and helpfulness among college men, as rated by peers. While variation in the strength of personal norms endorsed permitted study of the correspondence between norms and behavior, the preponderance of norms favored some degree of action promoting the welfare of others. Viewing AR to the self as an index of the probability that personal norms will be activated in an action situation, AR is expected to be related to the behavior predominantly encouraged by the norms available for activation. It is therefore hypothesized that:

3. The greater the tendency of people to ascribe responsibility toward rather than away from the self, the more considerate, reliable, and helpful they are in relations with their peers.

It should be noted that in theory AR activates moral norms whether they are prosocial or antisocial. This is assumed in the framing of Hypotheses 1 and 2, though the activation of prosocial norms alone might still lead to confirmation of these hypotheses, given that only 20% of the norms that were expressed opposed peer welfare. To the extent that the latter norms were activated, the direct relationship predicted in Hypothesis 3 would be attenuated.

METHOD

The sample consisted of 118 male undergraduates, members of nine self-contained residential groups. The groups, whose members had been living together for at least 4 months prior to the research, ranged in size from 12 to 14. Diversity of background, outlook, and life style were sought by studying four groups of students at a Lutheran junior college, and four fraternity groups (two Gentile, two Jewish) and a cooperative housing unit at a large state university. The former were primarily sons of blue collar and clerical workers who were preparing for careers in the ministry or parochial education. The latter were mainly liberal arts students, sons of professionals and businessmen. Data were gathered over a 2- or 3-week period in three sessions of approximately 1 hour each, held in the houses of each group. AR and AC were measured during the first session, personal norms during the second, and peer ratings of interpersonal behavior were obtained during the final session.

Instruments

Ascription of Responsibility

A set of 24 opinion and self-descriptive items was used to tap AR. The items allude to actions with interpersonal consequences and provide an explicit or implicit rationale for ascribing responsibility for these actions away from the actor. Responses accepting the rationale, thereby removing at least some of the actor's responsibility, are interpreted as signs of a tendency to ascribe responsibility away from the self. Responses that reject the rationale are taken to reflect a tendency to ascribe responsibility to the self. One point was given for each response indicating ascription to the self, with items balanced for agreement (A) and disagreement (D). Responses ranging from strongly agree to strongly disagree were dichotomized for agreement.

Among the rationales for ignoring or denying the actor's responsibility built into the items were role requirements, conforming, extreme provocation, absence of intentionality, illness, legality, and preoccupation. The AR was expressed in terms of blame, fault, forgiveness, guilt, justifiability, excusing, holding responsible, etc. The following are three illustrative items marked with the response receiving a score:

D You can't blame basically good people who are forced by their environment to be inconsiderate of others.

A Being very upset or preoccupied does not excuse a person for doing anything he would ordinarily avoid.

D If a person is nasty to me, I feel very little responsibility to treat him well.

Reliability. Various indexes suggested that the internal consistency of the AR scale was moderately high, considering that the items sample a broadly generalized orientation over a number of different situations. The Kuder-Richardson coefficient of reliability was .67; and the mean biserial correlations of the items with the total score *minus each item itself* was .23. A test-retest reliability coefficient of .63 was obtained for a sample of 109 subjects (92% of the original group) who returned a copy of the questionnaire mailed to them 7-10 months after the group administration. Mean total scores for the two administrations of the AR scale were 15.6 and 16.2, with standard deviations of 3.30 and 3.34, respectively.

Validity. In addition to the aforementioned content criteria, findings in two studies suggest that the AR scale taps the construct it was designed to measure. Assuming that most adults hold norms supporting reciprocity for cooperation and opposing exploitation, the following hypothesis regarding behavior in a "Prisoner's Dilemma" game was generated: Subjects who score high in AR are more likely to behave cooperatively than subjects low in AR following trials in which they have gained at their partners' expense by competing, while the partners cooperated. This hypothesis presupposed that those high in AR are likely to define the situation as one in which they are responsible to abide by norms of reciprocity, while those who score low are more likely to interpret the situation as "merely a game" or to hold the experimenter or luck responsible for their partners' losses. The hypothesis was confirmed ($p < .025$, $N = 50$).

A second study examined the relationship between AR and socioeconomic status. Based on differences in objective living conditions and in socialization experiences (e.g., Bronfenbrenner, 1965; Pearlin & Kohn, 1966), it was hypothesized that middle-class women score higher in AR than working-class women. A 10-item AR scale was administered to 44 housewives in a door-to-door survey, and this sample was split at the median on AR. The hypothesis was confirmed when the women were assigned to middle- and working-class subsamples according to both their husbands' occupations (gamma = .87, $p. < .001$) and their subjective class identification (gamma = .77, $p. < .005$).

Consideration of the AR construct and of the scale items might suggest that it reflects tendencies other than AR. Low correlations of an earlier 26-item version of the AR scale with sets of items purported to measure concern with self (r=.14, N=71), self-esteem (r=.04, N=71), and authoritarianism (r=.10, N=50) cast doubt on three possible alternative interpretations. Moreover, a correlation of —.01 between AR and Social Desirability (Crowne & Marlowe, 1964) was obtained in the present research.

Awareness of Consequences

A projective test, in which subjects describe the thoughts and feelings that might run through the minds of people facing a series of decisions with interpersonal consequences, was used to index AC. Responses were scored blindly by two coders who attained 93% agreement within 1 point on a 5-point scale measuring "the extent to which the actor is aware of the potential consequences of his behavior for the welfare of others as part of his decision-making process [see Schwartz, 1968]."

Personal Norms

Each subject read nine hypothetical incidents and was instructed to imagine that he himself or a peer was faced with the decision to act in each. The incidents were intended to tap considerateness (1-3), reliability (4-6), and helpfulness (7-9). The first incident, for example, was: "The girl he was going with has just broken off with one of the fellows in your house. He seems rather hurt and upset. Another fellow starts to rib him. You are tempted to rib him too. Should you?" Following each incident, subjects were asked: "How would you feel he (you) ought to act?" An alternative of action favorable to peer welfare was considered by the protagonist in five incidents, an unfavorable alternative in four.

Subjects indicated their norms in each incident by endorsing one of seven statements that specified with varying strength whether or not one (you) ought to do what the central figure in the incident was considering. The statements ranged from 1 (really ought to . . . clear and strong obligation . . .) to 7 (really ought *not* . . . clear and strong obligation *not* to do it). Instructions stressed personal feelings, regardless of peer opinions, and asked for what one would actually expect of himself, not for ideals. A majority of subjects reported that they had been involved personally in incidents similar to seven of the nine.

Interpersonal Behavior

The same nine incidents, phrased to permit introducing each peer in turn as the person facing a decision, were presented. For each member of their residential group, subjects were asked: "How likely is it that the person you are describing would do what is suggested in the incident . . . ?" Responses ranged from 1 (definitely yes) to 7 (definitely no). The index of a subject's interpersonal behavior for each incident was the average of his ratings by all his peers. Subjects also rated each other on the general traits of considerateness, reliability, and helpfulness.

A factor analysis of these 12 peer ratings of behavior was performed to determine whether subjects responded to the incidents as though they represented the three domains intended in their construction. A normalized varimax rotation of the principal axes solution yielded three orthogonal dimensions, corresponding quite closely to the three moral domains and accounting for 79% of the total variance. Incident 3 loaded heavily on helpfulness, rather than on considerateness as originally presumed, and is treated accordingly. All 12 items were positively intercorrelated, had large positive loadings on the primary dimension of the unrotated factor matrix ($>.53$), and showed about the same variability. It therefore seemed legitimate and desirable to derive more reliable indexes of behavior by combining individual scores on the items within each domain, and by combining scores on all 12 items into a summary index of behavior.

RESULTS

Hypothesis 1. This hypothesis is based on the theoretical assertion that AR to the self is needed to activate appropriate norms in an action situation. It was tested by comparing the association between the norms people endorsed for the various incidents and peer ratings of their behavior in these incidents, within subsamples showing different levels of AR. The total sample was divided as evenly as possible into subjects at four levels of AR. The hypothesis implies that correlations between norms and peer ratings of behavior are near 0, or even negative among those lowest in AR, depending upon whether this variable indexes tendencies for initial perception or subsequent defense. The hypothesis further implies that the correlations are increasingly positive among subsamples showing progressively higher levels of AR.

In the first column of Table 1, it is observed that the correlations between personal norms and behavior for the total sample were significantly positive in only three incidents. Correlations of the more reliable indexes of behavior based on combining peer-rating items with indexes of norms based on the corresponding incidents were all significant, though still fairly weak. The absence of stronger relationships is traceable, according to the theory proposed here, to the failure of some subjects to experience activation of the appropriate norms in the action situations for which peer ratings were obtained. Support for this explanation is found in the near-zero correlations in the lowest AR subsample, shown in the second column.

The trend of correlations across the levels of AR provides general confirmation for Hypothesis 1. This trend can be expressed in several ways. The correlations become more positive as one moves to each higher level of AR for six of the nine incidents and for the summary behavior index. For eight of nine incidents, and for all of the indexes, the correlations are higher in Level IV than in Level I. For the summary index, the difference in correlations between Level IV and Level I reaches the .10 significance level.

Note that the results for the considerateness index do not confirm the hypothesis. Although the predicted trend is observed for Incident 2 and for considerateness as a trait, the trend reversal found in Incident 1 dominates in the index. The consistent findings in Table 1 might be attributed to artifact, if the range of variation in norms or behavior increased systematically across levels of AR. The variances for norms and behavior ratings, however, did not show such a pattern of increase.

TABLE 1

CORRELATIONS BETWEEN PERSONAL NORMS AND PEER RATINGS OF BEHAVIOR FOR SUBSAMPLES SHOWING FOUR LEVELS OF ASCRIPTION OF RESPONSIBILITY

Item		Levels of ascription of responsibility			
	All *Ss* *n*=118	I (Low) *n*=27	II *n*=30	III *n*=33	IV (High) *n*=28
Indexes					
Summary	.22**	.02	.15	.20	.37*
Considerateness	.18*	.14	.18	.07	.21
Reliability	.16*	–.07	.07	.16	.29
Helpfulness	.20**	–.01	.10	.22	.33*
Incidents					
1	.10	.15	.22	–.04	.10
2	.14	.03	.12	.13	.22
3	.20**	.10	.12	.19	.30
4	–.12	–.30	–.07	–.07	.10
5	.10	.03	.10	.01	.15
6	.20**	.04	.13	.28	.32*
7	.26**	–.08	.25	.30*	.41*
8	.08	.00	.01	.03	.21
9	–.07	–.07	–.13	.07	.09

*$p < .05$ (one-tailed).
**$p < .01$ (one-tailed).

In the above test of Hypothesis 1, subjects from the various residential groups were combined into one sample which was then subdivided on

AR. This presents a problem if peer ratings of behavior reflect rating biases unique to the residential groups. Testing the hypothesis within groups eliminates this possible source of bias. While the correlations compared are then based on very small samples, trends found in such a test can reinforce or cast doubt on the conclusions drawn with the combined sample. Accordingly, members of each residential group were assigned to subgroups above and below the median AR score for their group, and correlations between norms and peer ratings of behavior within each subgroup were compared.

Results of these comparisons also support the hypothesis. For the summary index, the correlation was more positive in the high than in the low AR subgroup in eight of the nine groups ($p<.02$). Considering incidents separately, the correlation was more positive in at least six of nine groups for every incident except the first, the same incident in which there was a trend reversal for the combined sample. These findings suggest that rating biases unique to residential groups were not important determinants of the results reported in Table 1.

Hypothesis 2. Data examined thus far pertain to the impact of AR alone on the likelihood that appropriate moral norms are activated in action situations. The second hypothesis was based on reasoning that awareness of consequences for the welfare of others and ascription of responsibility to the self interact. That is, both must be present if situations are to be defined so as to produce an impact of norms on interpersonal behavior. To test this hypothesis, the total sample was divided into those above the median in AR and AC (high), those above the median in one tendency but below it in the other (mixed), and those below the median in both (low). Correlations between personal norms and peer ratings of behavior within these three subsamples are shown in Table 2.

As predicted, the correlations become more positive when moving from the low through the mixed to the high subsample for every incident and index. As the theory implies, moreover, within the subsample low in both tendencies there was no relationship between norms and behavior. Since the absence of either tendency may prevent the spontaneous activation of appropriate moral norms, the weakness of the associations in the mixed subsample was also expected. Among those most likely to define action situations as moral encounters, however (i.e., the high subsample), the relationships were significantly positive and of sufficient strength in several instances to suggest that these people were indeed influenced in their actions by the norms they had verbalized.

The hypothesized interaction between AR and AC in the activation of moral norms was expected to express itself by a greater increase in the correlation between norms and behavior when comparing the mixed with the high subsample, than when comparing the mixed with the low subsample. As is evident in Table 2, this was the case for eight of the nine

TABLE 2

CORRELATIONS BETWEEN PERSONAL NORMS AND PEER RATINGS OF BEHAVIOR FOR SUBSAMPLES SHOWING THREE COMBINATIONS OF ASCRIPTION OF RESPONSIBILITY AND AWARENESS OF CONSEQUENCES

	Ascription of responsibility and awareness of consequences		
Item	Low n=29	Mixed n=54	High n=35
Indexes			
Summary	.01	.17	.47**
Considerateness	.06	.13	.41**
Reliability	–.04	.09	.34*
Helpfulness	.00	.16	.42**
Incidents			
1	.02	.11	.27
2	.04	.09	.29*
3	.07	.15	.32*
4	–.21	–.11	.10
5	.03	.09	.17
6	.06	.18	.46**
7	.06	.21	.39*
8	.01	.09	.15
9	–.12	–.06	.08

*$p < .05$ (one-tailed).
**$p < .01$ (one-tailed).

incidents and for all the indexes. The former increases averaged about twice the size of the latter. For the summary index, the differences between the correlations in the high and mixed subsamples almost attained significance ($p < .07$).

To examine further the interaction between AR and AC, comparisons of correlations between the summary indexes of norms and of behavior were carried out for more refined subsamples. In Table 3, correlations are presented for four levels of each tendency within subsamples divided at the median on the other. The analysis took this form, rather than a 4 × 4 table, because almost half the cells in the latter would contain six or fewer cases on which to compute correlations. The findings in Table 3 suggest that differences in Awareness of Consequences may be slightly more important than differences in Ascription of Responsibility for activating moral norms. Note that in almost every instance the increases in correlations observed across levels of AC within a single level of AR are greater than the increases across levels of AR within the equivalent levels of AC.

Because the correlations between norms and behavior are based on aggregate rather than individual data, evidence that AR and AC interact in activating norms rather than simply having an additive effect cannot be conclusive. The findings in Table 3 are consistent with an interaction

TABLE 3

CORRELATIONS BETWEEN SUMMARY INDEXES OF PERSONAL NORMS AND PEER RATINGS OF BEHAVIOR FOR SUBSAMPLES SPLIT ON ASCRIPTION OF RESPONSIBILITY AND AWARENESS OF CONSEQUENCES

	Level			
Ascription of responsibility	I (Low)	II	III	IV (High)
Awareness of consequences				
Low	−.03 (14)[1]	.05 (15)	.09 (14)	.14 (12)
High	.11 (13)	.20 (15)	.37 (19)	.54 (16)
	Awareness of consequences			
Ascription of responsibility				
Low	−.02 (14)	.03 (15)	.10 (19)	.22 (9)
High	.03 (13)	.10 (13)	.32 (21)	.58 (14)

[1]Parentheses indicate number of subjects upon whom the correlation is based.

TABLE 4

CORRELATIONS OF AR AND AC WITH PEER RATINGS OF BEHAVIOR ACROSS THE TOTAL SAMPLE

Item	Ascription of responsibility (AR)	Awareness of Consequences (AC)	Multiple *R* AR & AC
Summary index	.22**	.27**	.36**
Considerateness index	.21**	.22**	.32**
Incident 1	.16*	.13*	.21*
Incident 2	.22*	.21**	.32**
Trait	.19*	.25**	.33**
Reliability index	.10	.24**	.27**
Incident 4	.05	.22**	.22*
Incident 5	.07	.20**	.22*
Incident 6	.18*	.20**	.28**
Trait	.13*	.22**	.26**
Helpfulness index	.28**	.27**	.40**
Incident 3	.19*	.26**	.33**
Incident 7	.25**	.24**	.36**
Incident 8	.29**	.21**	.37**
Incident 9	.25**	.26**	.37**
Trait	.24**	.24**	.35**

Note.—$N = 118$.
*$p < .05$ (one-tailed).
**$p < .01$ (one-tailed).

model, however. Thus, among those low in AC, the impact of increasing AR upon the correspondence between norms and behavior is small; and among those low in AR the impact of AC upon this correspondence is only slight. Among those high in AC, on the other hand, the impact of increasing AR is quite strong; and among those high in AR, the impact of AC is striking. It is probably reasonable to estimate that the summary index of personal norms accounts for between 35% and 40% of the variance in peer ratings of behavior among individuals who are most strongly predisposed both to be aware of consequences for others in action situations and to ascribe responsibility for these consequences to themselves.

Hypothesis 3. In this hypothesis, a direct positive relationship of AR to considerateness, reliability, and helpfulness was predicted. This was based on the fact that the norms held by most subjects encouraged behavior promoting peer welfare, coupled with the assumption that AR scores are an index of the probability that these norms will be activated. The correlations between AR and peer ratings of behavior across the total sample, arranged according to the three domains, are reported in the first column of Table 4. The hypothesis was clearly confirmed for behavior in the domains of considerateness and helpfulness, but not reliability.

The results of testing Hypothesis 3 within residential groups were essentially the same. As shown in Table 5, the correlations between AR

TABLE 5

CORRELATIONS BETWEEN ASCRIPTION OF RESPONSIBILITY AND PEER RATINGS OF BEHAVIOR WITHIN RESIDENTIAL GROUPS

Residential group	*N*	Domains: Considerateness	Domains: Reliability	Domains: Helpfulness	Summary index
1	12	−.06	−.18	.05	−.06
2	14	−.21	−.20	−.30	−.24
3	13	.32	.48*	.14	.38
4	13	.62*	.47	.46	.67**
5	12	.44	.29	.58*	.48
6	14	−.07	.15	.12	.09
7	14	.47*	.42	.42	.49*
8	13	.07	−.52	−.30	−.31
9	13	.41	.39	.48*	.48*
M for all groups[1]	118	.24**	.15	.19*	.24**

[1]Based on *r* to s transformations, weighted for group size.
*$p<.05$ (one-tailed).
**$p<.01$ (one-tailed).

and the behavior indexes were positive within six or seven of the nine groups in each of the domains. The mean within-group correlations were significantly positive for considerateness, helpfulness, and the summary index. A comparison of the mean correlations with the correlations for these indexes across ths total sample (Table 4) suggests that the latter do not reflect important rating biases be residential groups. Both within and across groups the findings for reliability were least in keeping with the hypothesis.

DISCUSSION

If AR scores were highly related to holding norms favorable to the welfare of others, the findings might be interpreted as evidence that AR is itself an index of personal norms, rather than a variable that moderates the impact of norms upon behavior. That this was not the case is attested to by correlations between AR and norms ranging from –.06 to .28, with 1% or less of the variance shared in seven of the nine incidents. It therefore seems more legitimate to interpret the correlations between AR and behavior as evidence that ascribing responsibility to the self contributes to the activation of moral norms.

What can be learned about the way AR functions from its failure to correlate significantly with peer ratings of reliability? The main difference between incidents in this domain and in the others was that here the actor had already incurred a specific obligation to people who were virtually certain to notice and censure a failure to fulfill it. Thus other people would probably impose responsibility upon the actor regardless of his own views, preventing him from denying responsibility either in his initial definition of the action situation or subsequently as a defense. This suggests that AR has its theorized effects only when the actor has an opportunity to ignore or reject his responsibility without others forcibly imposing upon him and threatening sanctions. This interpretation of the functioning of AR is supported by the findings reported in Tables 1 and 4 for the one reliability incident in which denial of responsibility was quite possible, Incident 6.

Given the absence of association between AR and AC, it is interesting to note the multiple correlations obtained by combining the two tendencies. The pertinent data are found in Table 4. AR and AC were correlated approximately equally with considerateness and helpfulness, with the latter correlations higher for both tendencies. Combining the tendencies for multiple prediction yielded significant correlations in every instance, though the increase in variance accounted for over Awareness of Consequences alone was only slight in the domain of reliability.

The correlational results of this research support the proposition that awareness that one's potential acts have consequences for the welfare of others, and ascription of responsibility for these acts and their consequences to the self are necessary conditions for the activation of moral norms and their influence upon behavior in action situations. The simplifying assumption was made here that scores on the AR and AC instruments indicated whether subjects in fact became aware of consequences and accepted responsibility in action situations on which their peers' judgments of them were based. This, together with the limited reliability of the instruments themselves, may partially explain why the correlations between norms and behavior, even in subsamples high in both tendencies, were not always substantial.

Direct confirmation of the theoretical contention of the current investigation requires experimental research in which the subjects' definitions of the situation—their perceptions of consequences, of responsibility, and of what norms are applicable—are manipulated, and their interpersonal behavior observed. Interpretations of results of a few experimental studies in which ascription of responsibility may have been manipulated and affected the activation of widely held norms supporting the welfare of others will indicate the directions such research might take.

Milgram (1965) observed that the closer the experimenter and the more prestigious the research organization, the greater the proportion of subjects who inflicted serious pain upon a supposed victim. Self-reports by the subjects and speculation by Milgram imply that under these conditions one difference was that subjects tended to ascribe responsibility for their actions away from themselves and to the experimenter.

Schopler and Matthews (1965) found that powerful subjects were less helpful to dependent partners when they believed the latter had volunteered to be dependent than when they believed the dependency had been imposed on them. Here, in facing the decision of whether to give help, it was probably easier for subjects to ascribe responsibility for helping away from the self when the other could be defined as responsible for his own predicament.

Subjects in an experiment by Lerner and Matthews (1967) described peers as less attractive in a condition where they perceived themselves to be responsible for their peer's assignment to an anxiety-provoking task than in a condition where peers were seen as responsible for choosing their own fate. Despite the lesser attractiveness of peers in the former condition, however, more subjects offered to comfort them in this condition. Thus, comfort was offered more readily in the condition in which ascription of responsibility away from the self for what might happen to peers was more difficult.

It would be interesting to examine how variations in the two personal tendencies interact with variations in the salience of responsibility and interpersonal consequences in the situation to moderate the correspondence between norms and behavior. It is also important to investigate whether the processes studied here are general to interpersonal behavior when strong proscriptive norms are at stake, when the consequences of action are very serious or have career implications, or when the people involved differ in status and power. Moreover, one might ask whether there are preconditions for the activation of moral norms other than the two identified here.

In this report, the correspondence between single personal norms and behavior has been discussed. When faced with decisions to act, however, people are seldom subject exclusively to unambiguous personal directives. They may hold various norms that are brought into conflict when applied to a single decision; they are often aware of the expectations of significant others whose views may affect their behavior. Hence, perfect correlations of behavior with specifically measured personal norms are not to be expected. In situations where people's own clearly held norms contradict the norms they attribute to significant others, there is some reason to think that AR may differentiate between those who adhere to their own norms and those whose actions follow the expectations of others. This, too, is a topic for the future.

REFERENCES

Bronfenbrenner, U. Socialization and social class through time and space. In H. Proshansky & B. Seidenberg (Eds.), *Basic studies in social psychology*. New York: Holt, Rinehart & Winston, 1965.

Campbell, D. T. Social attitudes and acquired behavioral dispositions. In S. Koch (Ed.), *Psychology: A study of a science*. Vol. 6. New York: McGraw-Hill, 1963.

Crowne, D. P., & Marlowe, D. *The approval motive: Studies in evaluative dependence*. New York: Wiley, 1964.

DeFleur, M. L., & Westie, F. A. Verbal attitudes and overt acts: An experiment in the salience of attitudes. *American Sociological Review*, 1958, 23, 667-673.

DeFleur, M. L., & Westie, F. A. Attitudes as a scientific concept. *Social Forces*, 1963, 42, 17-31.

Deutscher, I. Bibliography on the relation between sentiments and acts. Syracuse, N.Y.: Syracuse University Youth Development Center, 1966. (a)

Deutscher, I. Words and deeds: Social science and social policy. *Social Problems*, 1966, 13, 235-254. (b)

Fendrich, J. M. A study of the association among verbal attitudes, commitment and overt behavior in different experimental situations. *Social Forces*, 1967, 45, 347-355.

Heider, F. Social perception and phenomenal causality. In R. Tagiuri & L. Petrullo (Eds.), *Person perception and interpersonal behavior*. Stanford: Stanford University Press, 1958.

Himmelstrand, U. Verbal attitudes and behavior: A paradigm for the study of message transmissions and transformations. *Public Opinion Quarterly*, 1960, 24, 224-250.

Hyman, H. H. Inconsistencies as a problem of attitude measurement. *Journal of Social Issues, 1959, 5, 38-42.*

Lerner, M. J., & Mathews, G. Reactions to suffering of others under conditions of indirect responsibility. *Journal of Personality and Social Psychology*, 1967, 5, 319-325.

Linn, L. S. Verbal attitudes and overt behavior: A study of racial discrimination. *Social Forces*, 1965, 43, 353-364.

Milgram, S. Some conditions of obedience and disobedience to authority. *Human Relations,* 1965, 18, 57-75.

Pearlin, L. I., & Kohn, M. L. Social class, occupation and parental values: A cross-national study. *American Sociological Review,* 1966, 31, 466-479.

Pepitone, A. Attributions of causality, social attitudes and cognitive matching processes. In R. Tagiuri & L. Petrullo (Eds.), *Person perception and interpersonal behavior.* Stanford: Stanford University Press, 1958.

Riesman, D., Glazer, N., & Denney, R. *The lonely crowd.* New Haven: Yale University Press, 1950.

Rosenzweig, S. An outline of frustration theory. In J. M. Hunt (Ed.), *Personality and the behavior disorders.* Vol. 1. New York: Ronald Press, 1954.

Rotter, J. B. Generalized expectancies for internal versus external control of reinforcement. *Psychological Monographs,* 1966, 80(1, Whole No. 609).

Schopler, J., & Matthews, M. W. The influence of the perceived locus of partner's dependence on the use of interpersonal power. *Journal of Personality and Social Psychology,* 1965, 2, 609-612.

Schroder, H. M., & Hunt, D. E. Failure-avoidance in situational interpretation and problem solving. *Psychological Monographs,* 1957, 71(3, Whole No. 432).

Schwartz, S. H. *Moral orientations and interpersonal conduct in moral encounters.* (Doctoral dissertation, University of Michigan) Ann Arbor, Mich.: University Microfilms, 1967, No. 67-15,690.

Schwartz, S. H. Awareness of consequences and the influence of moral norms on interpersonal behavior. *Sociometry,* 1968, 31.

Sykes, G. M., & Matza, D. Techniques of neutralization: A theory of delinquency. *American Sociological Review,* 1957, 22, 664-670.

Tittle, C. R., & Hill, R. J. Attitude measurement and prediction of behavior: An evaluation of conditions and measurement techniques. *Sociometry,* 1967, 30, 199-213.

10

IDEOLOGY, SOCIAL STRUCTURE, AND THE YORTY-BRADLEY MAYORALTY ELECTION

Vincent Jeffries
and
H. Edward Ransford

There can be little doubt that the last decade has been one of extreme turmoil and conflict in the United States. These years have been dominated by the continuing and intensified revolt of powerless groups (blacks, Mexican-Americans, students, women), an unpopular war, campus disruptions, numerous riots in cities across the country, political assassinations, increasing crime, and a severe testing of the society's tolerance for dissent. All these events have been accompanied by intensified ideological consciousness and conflict, by a growing concern for "law and order," and by strong efforts to maintain social stability and the status quo.

The Los Angeles mayoral election between the incumbent mayor, Sam Yorty, and a black candidate, Thomas Bradley, displayed in microcosm many of the tensions and polar outlooks present in the society of the United States today. The primary campaign was calm and non-ideological, with almost no campaign activity on the part of the incumbent. The primary results showed Bradley leading Yorty by 16 percentage points. The tenor and ideological level of the campaign changed drastically in the runoff. Bradley continued to campaign on the issues of Mayor Yorty's administration of city government and on his own ability to form a new "coalition of conscience" between the ages and the races if elected mayor. Opposite to this plea, the mayor's campaign seemed to elicit issues which divide the populace. One observer described Mayor Yorty's campaign in the following manner:

> Playing on voter fear of racial violence, he predicted openly that Mr. Bradley, if elected, would turn the city over to the black and left-wing extremists

Reprinted from *Social Problems* (Vol. 19, No. 3, 1972, pp. 358-372) by permission of the authors and The Society for the Study of Social Problems.

and militants. He even unleashed a charge of Communist influence in the Bradley campaign. He said if Mr. Bradley were elected the police department would virtually be dismantled and the city left easy prey for violence. No observer in city politics remembers a more starkly brutal campaign (Waugh, 1969).

The Mayor won. The final runoff showed 53 percent of the vote for Yorty, 47 percent for Bradley.

THEORETICAL PERSPECTIVE AND HYPOTHESES

A basic thesis of this paper is that societal protest and disruption have produced a new ideology based on order at all cost and a reaffirmation of traditional American values. We developed an ideological measure that tapped some of these concerns: concern for law and order, fear of a left wing threat, and a desire for more patriotism.[1] The total score from these components was titled the Troubled American Beliefs (hereafter frequently referred to as TAB).[2] Our immediate research question is: to what extent did this belief system affect voting behavior in the Yorty-Bradley election? The implications of this study are, however, far more general. They extend to the subject of understanding contemporary political events and to the theoretical problem of the influence of ideological factors upon the political process. Troubled American Beliefs are certainly not limited to this election. Several political observers have spoken of the increased importance of the "social issue" in many recent elections (Scammon and Wattenberg, 1970:35-44). Similarly, the influence of ideological factors upon reactions to political campaigns and voting behavior is one of fundamental importance to theories of political life.

Theories of personality, supported by empirical studies, generally agree that personality is to some degree integrated; i.e., there is a consistency and organization of its component parts (see, for example, Allport, 1955:88-93; Krech and Crutchfield, 1948:60-70; Festinger, 1957: Rokeach, 1968; Smith, 1969:97-116). This integration involves a hierarchical structure in which the more fundamental and general ideological elements provide focal points for the organization of the more specific and less stable. Similarly, the existing ideological structure is one of the major factors influencing how new events and ideologies will be interpreted and accepted or rejected. Despite the obvious applicability of these findings, Rokeach (1968-69) has appropriately observed that an examination of the current state of public opinion research reveals that very little attention has been directed toward examining the underlying ideological basis of opinions pertaining to specific issues. Most studies of ideological factors and voting behavior have emphasized that voters do not ordinarily think along ideological lines. For example, data from The American Voter (Campbell, *et al.,* 1960) indicate that only about one-tenth of the electorate have well thought out political belief systems. However, recent evidence from the Goldwater campaign (Field and Anderson, 1969:380-398) suggests that when the voting public is aroused to think along ideological lines, ideologies do become very important. Additional evidence shows that large proportions of the electorate have been ideologically aroused by social issues in the last decade (Scammon and Wattenberg, 1970:35-44; Sears and Kinder, 1970). We posit that these issues of crime, violence, protest, and threats to traditional values have been so stark and visible that a high degree of intellectual sophistication is not a prerequisite for ideological consciousness. Our measure of Troubled American Beliefs represents some of these concerns.

We shall investigate the influence of ideological factors upon voting behavior by examining a number of research questions and hypotheses:

1. Given the fact that the election highlighted Yorty as a champion of law and order, patriotism, and anti-communism, we predict that those scoring high on the Troubled American Beliefs will be more likely to vote for Yorty than those scoring low.

2. In this election and in others involving black candidates, a frequent question is whether social issues such as law and order are separate from prejudice toward blacks. We will explore the relative effects of TAB and prejudice on the vote.

3. Throughout the campaign, extremely emotional and seemingly potent issues developed, such as the question of Yorty's incompetence as leader of the city or the belief that city hall would be taken over by black militants if Bradley were to be elected. What was the effect of these campaign issues and how did they interact with TAB and prejudice as determiners of the vote?

4. Drawing from the theoretical view that generalized ideological elements serve as focal points for the organization of more specific issues, we hypothesize that those scoring high on the Troubled American Beliefs will tend to accept the campaign issues in support of Yorty and reject campaign issues favoring Bradley.

5. Finally, we investigate the interplay of TAB with two structural variables, age and class. Following Lipset's (1963:87-126) thesis of working class social conservatism, we hypothesize that blue-collar workers will be more likely than those higher in the class structure to vote for Yorty and score high on the Troubled American Beliefs. Similarly, the political generation thesis (Heberle, 1951:118-127) suggests to us that young voters will more likely favor Bradley.

SAMPLE AND METHODOLOGY

Data were obtained from a probability sample of 461 Caucasian adults who report having voted in the Yorty-Bradley runoff election. The sample was drawn from predominantly white areas of Los Angeles, primarily in the San Fernando Valley. This section of the Los Angeles Metropolitan area contains a population of approximately one million, constitutes about one-half of the white electorate in city elections, and is undoubtedly typical of many suburban areas across the country. Although subjects were selected by a probability model (involving random areas, blocks, and block corners as interviewer starting points), the sample should be classified as "disproportional stratified," since blue-collar areas were oversampled to provide sufficient cases for testing the hypotheses. Additionally, there was a careful control over the sex of the respondent so that an approximately equal number of males and females (one respondent per household) were interviewed.

The index of Troubled American Beliefs is composed of three measures: law and order, threat from extreme left wingers and Communists, and patriotism.[3] The three measures are equally weighted in the index of Troubled American Beliefs.[4] While these three components of TAB are somewhat distinct conceptually, we consider that each contains the common element of a sense of threat from internal or external forces and the necessity to reaffirm social stability. From this point of view we felt justified in combining the three into a single index. Empirical support for this decision was shown by a strong intercorrelation among the three components of TAB.[5]

The measure of general prejudice toward blacks is composed of items pertaining to stereotypes, social distance, trust, and blacks in positions of superordination over whites.[6]

The probability for chi-square is included in all tables presented in this paper, and Cramer's V is reported as a measure of strength of association.

TROUBLED AMERICAN BELIEFS, PREJUDICE TOWARD BLACKS, AND THE VOTE

Both Mayor Yorty's previous reputation and the campaign issues he initiated were such that they would be expected to attract voters high on Troubled American Beliefs. Similarly, it was highly reasonable to believe that Bradley, as a black man, would become a symbol and focal point for the racial fears and hostility of the prejudiced person. This was particularly true given the concerted attempt during the campaign to link Bradley with "black militants" and "black power" ideology.[7] Table 1 confirms these common sense and popular explanations of why voters made the choices they did between Bradley and Yorty.[8]

Many magazine and newspaper accounts referred to prejudice toward blacks as the principal force in the election. Accordingly, it is an interesting question whether Troubled American Beliefs will continue to predict the vote with prejudice held constant. As Table 2 shows, TAB

TABLE 1

PERCENT VOTING FOR YORTY BY TROUBLED AMERICAN BELIEFS AND BY PREJUDICE TOWARD BLACKS

	Yorty %	
A. Troubled American Beliefs		
Low	26	(115)
Medium	65	(146)
High	86	(175)
	P=.001	V=.50
B. Prejudice		
Low	39	(173)
Medium	61	(93)
High	87	(159)
	P=.001	V=.44

does remain a strong predictor of the vote for the "lows" and "moderates" in prejudice, but for the "highs" in prejudice it has much less predictive power. In other words, for those in our sample who are tolerant or only slightly prejudiced in attitude (about 70 percent of the sample) the Troubled American concerns (law and order, patriotism, leftwing threat) are crucial to the vote. The relationship can also be read in the other direction: prejudice has a strong effect on the vote for Yorty when TAB is low or medium, but much less effect when TAB is high. Thus, the two factors seem to be somewhat independent sources of the vote, and they interact with each other.[9] The cumulative effect of TAB and prejudice is indeed striking. When both are low, there is a 90:10 vote for Bradley; when both are high, there is a 90:10 vote for Yorty.

TABLE 2

TROUBLED AMERICAN BELIEFS, PREJUDICE, AND THE VOTE

	Prejudice		
	Low	Medium	High
	Yorty	Yorty	Yorty
TAB	%	%	%
Low	10 (70)	31 (26)	73 (15)
Medium	46 (54)	68 (28)	83 (50)
High	72 (40)	85 (34)	90 (84)
	P=.001	P=.001	P=NS(.20)
	V=.53	V=.47	V=.16

BELIEF SYSTEMS, CAMPAIGN ISSUES AND THE VOTE

In addition to Troubled American Beliefs and prejudice toward blacks a number of highly emotional campaign issues were introduced that appeared to have a substantial effect on voter choice. We shall examine the effect of these issues taken singly, and in combination with TAB and prejudice, as determiners of the vote.

Five major issues of the campaign were included in the research instrument.[10] Despite the fact that Bradley was a former member of the Los Angeles Police Department and had no previous reputation as an extreme liberal or radical, Yorty backers spoke increasingly of a decline in police morale and effectiveness if Bradley were to win. To capture the impact of this issue an index of "Police Fears" was constructed.[11] The Yorty forces also made a concerted effort to portray Bradley as sympathetic to and unduly influenced by "black militants" and "black power" ideology. (Item: "Black militants would have had too much influence in city government if Bradley had been elected.") Mayor Yorty's competence was another major issue in the campaign. Three statements, reflecting the main charges made against the mayor, were combined into a "Yorty Incompetent" index.[12] Another charge made against Yorty was that he ran a racist campaign. (Item: "Mayor Yorty ran a racist campaign.") In addition to the aforementioned criticisms of Yorty, Bradley's major appeal to the electorate was that he could form a "coalition of conscience" between the ages and the races and in so doing reduce divisiveness in the city. (Item: "The election of Bradley would have served to unite people of different ages and races in our city.")

All of the campaign issues show a significance level (chi-square) of .001 or less when related to the vote. Correlations (Cramer's V) are .55 for the police fear issue, .52 for the black militant issue, .54 for the issue of Yorty's incompetence, .58 for the racist campaign issue, and .59 for Bradley's appeal of social unity. Zero-order relationships show that the campaign issues were far more effective for Yorty than they were for Bradley. Among respondents taking a position favorable to Yorty, between 89 and 95 percent voted for him. On the other hand, among those taking a position favorable to Bradley only 57 to 69 percent actually voted for him. Put another way, between 31 and 43 percent of those taking a position favorable to Bradley still vote for Yorty.

The data presented in Table 3 show the combined effects of TAB, prejudice, and the campaign issues upon the vote. Several interesting findings are evident. First, it appears that the independent effects of generalized beliefs (TAB, prejudice) and the campaign issues are overall about the same. The most striking differences in voting behavior are found under the combined effect of both generalized beliefs and the campaign issues (e.g., 17 percent vote for Yorty when TAB is low and

TABLE 3

PERCENT VOTING FOR YORTY BY TROUBLED AMERICAN BELIEFS AND BY PREJUDICE TOWARD BLACKS WITH "YORTY INCOMPETENCE," "BRADLEY WILL UNITE," "YORTY RAN RACIST CAMPAIGN," "BLACK MILITANTS," AND "POLICE FEARS" CONTROLLED

	Yorty Incompetent %	Yorty Competent %	Yorty Ran Racist Campaign %	Yorty Did Not Run Racist Campaign %	Bradley Will Unite %	Bradley Will Not Unite %
1. Troubled American Beliefs						
Low	16 (87)	58 (19)	15 (93)	65 (20)	12 (84)	61 (28)
Medium	41 (70)	90 (68)	37 (65)	89 (75)	39 (57)	83 (87)
High	67 (55)	95 (108)	65 (63)	97 (109)	54 (50)	99 (117)
	P=.001	P=.001	P=.001	P=.001	P=.001	P=.001
	V=.42	V=.36	V=.43	V=.33	V=.38	V=.40
2. Prejudice						
Low	14 (107)	81 (59)	16 (115)	86 (56)	18 (104)	71 (66)
Medium	43 (46)	87 (39)	43 (49)	81 (40)	27 (40)	88 (50)
High	72 (58)	98 (87)	67 (55)	98 (91)	63 (46)	97 (106)
	P=.001	P=.01	P=.001	P=.01	P=.001	P=.001
	V=.52	V=.25	V=.46	V=.26	V=.40	V=.33

TABLE 3 (*Continued*)

	Reject Black Militant Issue %	Accept Black Militant Issue %	Low Police Fears %	High Police Fears %
1. Troubled American Beliefs				
Low	17 (99)	71 (14)	20 (100)	67 (12)
Medium	47 (90)	94 (53)	45 (75)	91 (54)
High	68 (76)	99 (94)	65 (60)	99 (94)
	P=.001	P=.001	P=.001	P=.001
	V=.42	V=.35	V=.38	V=.36
2. Prejudice				
Low	27 (140)	86 (29)	22 (124)	94 (35)
Medium	44 (63)	96 (27)	39 (49)	91 (35)
High	70 (61)	97 (96)	71 (56)	95 (83)
	P=.001	P=.07	P=.001	P=NS(.75)
	V=.36	V=.19	V=.42	V=.06

the black militant issue is rejected vs. a 99 percent vote for Yorty when TAB is high and this issue is accepted). There are two other patterns which show a striking regularity across the five campaign issues. First, generalized belief systems (TAB, prejudice) have their strongest effect upon the vote for Yorty when the respondent takes a position unfavorable to Yorty on the campaign issues.[13] This pattern is particularly strong in the case of prejudice (e.g., a 49 percent vs. a one percent difference in the case of the police fear issue). A second pattern emerges in the effect of the campaign issues upon the vote at different levels of TAB and prejudice. With one exception (TAB and Bradley unite) the effect of the campaign issues is smallest when generalized beliefs are highest in their intensity (e.g., a 70 percent vs. a 31 percent difference in the case of prejudice and the racist campaign issue). Putting these two findings together it appears that there was a dynamic interaction between generalized beliefs and campaign issues in their effect upon the vote. That is, when persons were not particularly prejudiced or "Troubled" (low or moderate score) the campaign issues were important stimuli convincing many to vote for Yorty. But as TAB and prejudice increase in intensity, they tend to be more powerful influences on the vote and the person no longer needs the added stimulus of the campaign issue to vote for Yorty. Thus a majority (54 percent to 72 percent) of voters who are high on TAB or prejudice will endorse Yorty even if they take a position on the campaign issues which is unfavorable to him.

One further finding contained in Table 3 is worthy of attention. It is reasonable to assume that both the competency of candidates and a degree of social unity greater than that evident at the time of the election are crucial conditions to the maintenance of a viable democratic society. From this perspective, it is important to note that among respondents who are high on TAB, 67 percent still vote for Yorty even when they consider him to be incompetent, while 54 percent who believe that Bradley could have helped to bring age and racial groups closer together still voted for Yorty. Among those high in prejudice toward blacks, the comparable numbers voting for Yorty are 72 and 63 percent. Troubled American Beliefs and racial prejudice are indeed social forces to be reckoned with and ones which will influence voters to relegate to a position of secondary importance both the qualifications of their leaders and the possibility of a unified society.

BELIEF SYSTEMS AND THE ACCEPTANCE OR REJECTION OF CAMPAIGN ISSUES

The preceding analysis may have given the impression that belief systems and campaign issues are completely independent predictors of the vote. But the relationships presented in Table 3 still allow for the possibility that generalized beliefs (TAB and prejudice) and campaign issues have a lot to do with each other. We propose to show that for many persons prior generalized beliefs influenced acceptance or rejection of the campaign issues.

We have previously noted that past theory and research show that generalized ideologies influence the organization of more specific attitudes and opinions, and provide the frame of reference for interpreting new events. We consider that both Troubled American Beliefs and prejudice toward blacks are more general and prior in time to the campaign issues and perceptions of the candidates. As such, they should form the nuclei around which the campaign issues were evaluated and accepted or rejected. The data support this view. For example, people high on TAB were not only more likely to accept the fear issues (police fears, black militants), where one would expect a relationship due to the obvious logical link, but also the other three issues (Yorty incompetent, Bradley unite, Yorty racist campaign), where the connection is much less obvious. Respondents high on prejudice also interpret all of the issues in a manner favorable to Yorty.

Table 4 presents the relationship between TAB and the campaign issues with prejudice controlled. High Troubled American Beliefs is linked with a pro-Yorty position on all of the campaign issues, though the relationship diminishes somewhat when prejudice is high. Reading the table to assess the effect of prejudice shows that prejudice still predicts the campaign issues among those low or medium in TAB, except in the case of the Yorty incompetent issue. When TAB is high, prejudice has a noteworthy effect only in the case of the police and black militant issues. Troubled American Beliefs thus appears to have been a more important ideological nucleus than was prejudice in this election. Apparently, for many voters, the position on TAB and prejudice influenced them to interpret the campaign issues to match these more generalized and prior ideologies, even when there was not a clear logical link between the general orientation and a particular campaign issue. In a sense, the voter assembles the campaign issues to match his more basic ideological out look. Ideological cross pressures are minimized. A strain toward consistency is operative.[14]

SOCIAL STRUCTURE, IDEOLOGY, AND THE VOTE

It has been shown that the Troubled American Beliefs were extremely important for a Yorty victory. In this final part of the analysis, two structural variables are introduced: age and social class. These structural variables will be viewed both independently and in combination with TAB as predictors of the vote.

In the case of social class, many studies of political behavior have shown that blue-collar workers support left-wing parties and candidates when the issues are strictly economic in nature. However, when it comes to issues of civil liberties, working class persons appear to be more mo-

TABLE 4

CAMPAIGN ISSUES BY TROUBLED AMERICAN BELIEFS WITH PREJUDICE TOWARD BLACKS CONTROLLED

TAB	Yorty Incompetent "No" %	Bradley Unite "No" %	Racist Campaign "No" %	Police Fears "Yes" %	Black Militant Influence "Yes" %
			Prejudice Low		
Low	14 (69)	16 (69)	10 (70)	1 (69)	3 (69)
Medium	38 (52)	52 (54)	44 (52)	33 (49)	23 (53)
High	71 (38)	59 (39)	55 (40)	47 (36)	38 (39)
	P=.001	P=.001	P=.001	P=.001	P=.001
	V=.46	V=.40	V=.42	V=.47	V=.37
			Prejudice Medium		
Low	26 (23)	28 (25)	28 (25)	21 (24)	16 (25)
Medium	41 (27)	64 (28)	46 (28)	46 (26)	33 (27)
High	69 (32)	70 (33)	62 (32)	57 (30)	39 (33)
	P=.01	P=.01	P=.05	P=.05	P=NS(.20)
	V=.36	V=.36	V=.28	V=.30	V=.21
			Prejudice High		
Low	25 (12)	50 (14)	36 (14)	33 (15)	47 (15)
Medium	68 (47)	71 (49)	69 (48)	49 (43)	50 (50)
High	59 (78)	71 (79)	65 (83)	69 (75)	70 (83)
	P=.05	P=NS(.30)	P=.10	P=.01	P=.05
	V=.23	V=.13	V=.19	V=.26	V=.21

tivated by a conservative outlook to reaffirm the social order than by a social change orientation (Lipset, 1963:87-126, 230-278). Since the Yorty-Bradley election was highlighted by issues of extremism and law and order while lacking any clear economic issues, we expected that blue-collar workers would be more likely to support Yorty. Additionally, we expected blue-collar workers to score high on Troubled American Beliefs.

Table 5 presents the relationship between two measures of socioeconomic status (occupation and education) and the vote. Our predictions are definitely confirmed, though the relationships are not as strong as expected. For example, it is true that 77 percent of the blue collar workers voted for Yorty but so also did 64 percent of the clerical, managerial, and sales group and 51 percent of the upper-white-collar professionals. The correlations between class variables and TAB (not shown) produced similar moderate relationships.[15] In sum, the blue-collar environment does not seem to be a massive source of Troubled American Beliefs or support for Yorty.

Turning to the second structural variable, age, we expected the young voter would be more likely to support Bradley. A great deal has been written about the youth counterculture and the fact that young people

TABLE 5

PERCENT VOTING FOR YORTY BY OCCUPATION, EDUCATION, AND AGE

	Yorty %	
Occupation		
Blue Collar	77	(165)
Clerical, Sales, Managerial	64	(154)
Professional	51	(136)
		P=.001
		V=.18
Education		
High School Grad or Less	75	(208)
Some College	59	(149)
College Grad or More	48	(103)
		P=.001
		V=.23
Age		
21-25	32	(38)
26-45	63	(243)
45 and over	71	(178)
		P=.001
		V=.21

are carriers of an entirely different set of values and life experiences (Roszak, 1969). Drawing from the theoretical perspective that different generations have been exposed to different values, issues, and events that shape their political outlook (Heberle, 1951:118-127), we were especially interested in the age category from 21-25. This is the group that was gaining political consciousness at the time the campus revolution was beginning (Free Speech Movement, 1964) and blacks were rebelling in the ghettos.

To be nurtured on dissent and cries for social justice for the oppressed rather than patriotism and order should result in a far more libertarian outlook for these young voters. Thus Yorty's statements linking Bradley with a decline in law and order should have far less potency among the young. Further, we reasoned that young voters would be attracted to Bradley because he is black and was depicted as progressive and capable of uniting various age and racial groups in the city. Table 5 supports these expectations, with 21-25-year-olds showing far more support for Bradley than older age groups.[16]

We turn now to the joint effect of structure (class and age) and TAB on the vote. Our most basic question was whether occupation, education, and age would continue to predict the vote with TAB held constant. At a more theoretical level, we were interested in the relative predictive power of ideology and social structure in the context of this election.

TABLE 6

PERCENT VOTING FOR YORTY BY OCCUPATION, EDUCATION AND AGE, WITH TROUBLED AMERICAN BELIEFS CONTROLLED

	Low TAB Yorty %		Medium TAB Yorty %		High TAB Yorty %	
Occupation						
Blue Collar	32	(25)	71	(51)	86	(80)
Clerical, Sales and Managerial	33	(39)	69	(58)	82	(49)
Professional	16	(50)	53	(34)	91	(44)
	P=NS(.20)		P=NS(.20)		P=NS(.50)	
	V=.19		V=.15		V=.10	
Education						
High School Grad or Less	31	(29)	73	(67)	86	(101)
Some College	23	(39)	66	(56)	83	(46)
College Grad or More	24	(46)	39	(23)	89	(28)
	P=NS(.70)		P=.02		P=NS(.75)	
	V=.08		V=.24		V=.06	
Age						
21-25	15	(13)	29	(14)	60	(10)
26-45	24	(68)	69	(80)	90	(81)
45 and over	30	(33)	71	(51)	84	(84)
	P=NS(.70)		P=.01		P=.05	
	V=.10		V=.25		V=.20	

Table 6 provides some answers to these questions. Looking first at the joint effect of social class and TAB, we see that when people are high on TAB, occupation and education no longer predict the vote, i.e., practically everyone votes for Yorty. For these highly Troubled Americans, ideological factors thus clearly override class position. Among those moderately "troubled," however, the story is a little different, with education having a sizable impact upon the vote. For example, only 39 percent of college graduates who are medium in TAB voted for Yorty as compared to 73 percent of the high school who are medium in this belief system. In other words, those moderately "troubled" by and large vote for Yorty, but not the college graduates. A high degree of education seems to partially offset the connection between ideology and the vote. Perhaps these moderately "troubled" college graduates did not convert their societal concerns into a Yorty vote because they were less likely to accept the fear campaign issues. That is, high education was acting as a buffer against ready acceptance that Bradley was an extremist and would produce a collapse in law and order. Exploration of the fear issues (not shown) supports this interpretation. The college graduates were less likely to accept the fear issues even with TAB controlled.[17]

In the case of age, there are similar results except that age continues to predict for both the "moderates" and the "highs" in Troubled American Beliefs. For every level of TAB, the 21-25-year-olds are noticeably different from the two older age groups. Thus there is a definite structural effect, with younger voters being much less likely to convert TAB into a vote for Yorty. Again we postulate that the explanation may be in the campaign appeals, with younger voters more likely to reject the fear appeals and to accept the view that Bradley could have united the ages and races. Exploration of these issues supports this view. Age is consistently related to acceptance of Bradley's appeal to unite the ages and races and to rejection of the police fear issue. These relationships between age and the campaign issues persist with TAB held constant.

SUMMARY AND CONCLUSIONS

This study began with a basic premise: the protest and dissent in our society is producing an angry backlash ideology in the white majority based on law and order, patriotism, and leftwing threat. Our expectations that these Troubled American Beliefs would have some effect on political behavior were strongly confirmed. Both TAB and prejudice toward blacks were of overwhelming importance to Sam Yorty's mayoral victory. Since there promises to be a great deal more protest in coming years (i.e., as youth, blacks, Chicanos, and other liberation groups continue to press for massive change), TAB should continue to be highly relevant for predicting political behavior. Indeed a provocative question is whether or not Troubled American Beliefs has become such a strong factor in elections that it is overwhelming the traditional economic liberal-conservative ideology. Unfortunately, in the Yorty-Bradley election, issues of governmental control vs. individualism and *laissez faire* were not at stake and both candidates were Democrats. Results of the recent 1970 elections suggest that both the economic and social issues are extremely important in explaining voting patterns and that it is difficult to assign primacy to one or the other.

A secondary goal of this paper was to study the interaction between two structural variables (socioeconomic status, age) and TAB in predicting voting behavior. In recent years there has been a great deal of attention given to the blue-collar man as uniquely angry about such events as campus violence, compensatory job opportunities for blacks, and the emergence of long-haired hippies with a hedonistic life style (Greely, 1969:1-2). Given the nature of the issues in the Yorty-Bradley election, we expected that class position would be a strong determiner of the vote. Instead, we find that for those who score high on TAB, class differences wash out completely. Further, the blue-collar environment appears to be only a moderate source of the Troubled American Beliefs. It is, of course, possible that the "troubled" blue-collar man is more prone to physical force and violence than those higher in the class structure (as exemplified by an assault on students in one recent "hard hat march"). But in terms of normative behavior like voting, those who are highly "troubled" vote their fears, be they white-collar professionals or blue-collar men. The age generation variable proved to be a more formidable factor in the vote than social class. The 21-25-year-old group was unique in its strong support for Bradley. With TAB held constant the relationship was only slightly altered. Our data thus provide indirect support for the political generation thesis (Heberle, 1951:118-127) and suggest that the young voter constitutes a new force that must be taken into account in studies of political behavior. The study indicates the need for more systematic and direct investigations, within the framework of political generations, of the societal and world events which have shaped the political ideologies of the young. What, precisely, has been the impact of such events as the black liberation, student, and anti-war movements, upon the political mentality and voting behavior of youth?

The major focus of voting studies to date has been upon the influence of social structures, situational cross-pressures, family background, and opinion leaders upon political party choice and voting behavior. The findings of this study regarding ideological factors and the vote indicate the need to concentrate added effort toward the systematic investigation of both generalized belief systems and campaign issues as other basic dimensions of political behavior.

REFERENCES

Allport, Gordon W.
1955 Becoming. New Haven: Yale University Press, pp. 88-93.

Becker, J. T. and E. Heaton, Jr.
1967 "The election of Senator Edward R. Brooke." Public Opinion Quarterly 31:346-358.

Berelson, Bernard and Gary A. Steiner
1964 Human Behavior. New York: Harcourt, Brace and World, Inc., pp. 574-580.

Campbell, A., P. E. Converse, W. E. Miller, D. E. Stokes
1960 The American Voter. New York: John Wiley and Sons.

Festinger, Leon
1957 A Theory of Cognitive Dissonance. Evanston, Illinois: Row, Peterson and Company.

Field, J. O. and E. Anderson
1969 "Ideology in the public's conceptualization of the 1964 election." Public Opinion Quarterly 33:380-398.

Greely, A. M.
1969 "America's not so silent minority," Los Angeles Times, Opinion. (Dec. 7): 1-2.

Heberle, Rudolph
1951 Social Movements. New York: Appleton-Century-Crofts Inc., pp. 118-127.

Krech, David and Richard S. Crutchfield
1948 Theory and Problems of Social Psychology. New York: McGraw-Hill, pp. 60-70.

Lipset, Seymour Martin
1963 Political Man. New York: Anchor, pp. 87-126.

Lipset, Seymour Martin, P. F. Lazarsfeld, A. H. Barton, and J. Linz
1954 "The psychology of voting: An analysis of political behavior," in G. Lindzey, ed., Handbook of Social Psychology, Reading, Massachusetts: Addison-Wesley Publishing Company, Inc., Vol. 2, pp. 1124-1175.

Newsweek
1969 "The troubled American: A special report on the white majority," Newsweek 71 (Oct. 6): 28-73.

Rokeach, Milton
1968 Beliefs, Attitudes and Values. San Francisco: Jossey-Bass Inc.
1968- "The role of values in public opinion research." Public Opinion Quarterly 32:547-559.

Roszak, T.
1969 The Making of a Counter Culture. New York: Anchor.

Scammon, R. M. and B. J. Wattenberg
1970 The Real Majority. New York: Coward-McCann, Inc., pp. 35-44.

Sears, David and D. R. Kinder
1970 "The good life, 'white racism,' and the Los Angeles voter." Unpublished paper delivered at Western Psychological Association Meetings, Los Angeles (April 15).

Smith, M. Brewster
1969 Social Psychology and Human Values. Chicago: Aldine, pp. 97-116.

Waugh, J. C.
1969 "Yorty wrests victory." The Christian Science Monitor (May 29).

NOTES

This paper is entirely a joint effort. The ordering of names does not in any way imply junior or senior authorship. This investigation was supported by Biomedical Sciences Support Grant FR-07012-03 from the General Research Support Branch, Division of Research Resources, Bureau of Health Professions, Education and Manpower Training, National Institutes of Health, and by a grant from the San Fernando Valley State College Foundation. Computer time was provided by the Computer Center at San Fernando Valley State College and by the University Computing Center at the University of Southern California. We are grateful to Melvin Seeman, Ralph Turner, and Clarence Tygart for constructive criticisms of earlier drafts of this paper.

[1] The terms "ideology" and "ideological factors" are used in this study to refer to ideas, as contrasted to social structure (occupation, education, age). The ideological factors investigated in this study are Troubled American Beliefs, prejudice toward blacks, and the campaign issues raised during the election. Such ideologies may vary from specific (an opinion about a particular person) to general (a belief in the innate goodness of all human beings). Further, they may vary from unorganized opinions (such as the topic headings appearing on page one of the daily newspaper) to highly organized systems (the Constitution of the United States). Both TAB and prejudice are considered to be intermediate between the extremes of either of these continuums. They are fairly generalized beliefs whose component parts are compatible, but are not, for most individuals, highly organized systems of beliefs that can be readily articulated and justified. They are thus not ideologies in the sense that this term is usually used in sociological literature. The campaign issues are far more specific than are TAB or prejudice, and are probably less organized.

[2] This designation was derived from a recent issue of Newsweek entitled "The Troubled American: A Special Report on the White Majority," Newsweek 71 (Oct. 6, 1969):28-73.

[3] Endorsement of a law and order ideology was indicated by responses to the following three items: There is too much concern with law and order in our country today (Agree 19 percent, Disagree 81 percent); The most important task facing our society today is to maintain law and order (Agree 74 percent, Disagree 26 percent); People should be more concerned with solving our social problems and less concerned about law and order (Agree 42 percent, Disagree 58 percent). Left-wing threat was measured by the following two items: The Communist conspiracy is a real threat to our country (Agree 79 percent, Disagree 21 percent); Extreme left wingers are trying to destroy the American way of life (Agree 80 percent, Disagree 20 percent). Patriotism was measured by the following item: What we need in this country is more patriotism (Agree 84 percent, Disagree 16 percent).

[4] Separate indices of law and order and left-wing threat were constructed, and dichotomized as closely as possible to the median. Combined with patriotism, the TAB index thus

ranges from 0-3, and is trichotomized according to the distribution. Excluding NA's 41 percent of the sample scored high on all three components of TAB, 33 percent scored high on two, while 26 percent scored high on one or none of the TAB components. There are 25 NA's.

[5] Correlations (Gamma) between the components of TAB range from .64 to .89 averaging .79.

[6] The measure of general prejudice toward blacks is composed of three stereotype items ("less native intelligence," "violent," "lazy and ignorant"), three social distance items ("dance," "live next door," "marry"), one item pertaining to degree of trust of blacks ("most," "some," and "none") and three items pertaining to blacks in positions of superordination over whites ("President of U.S.," "supervisor on job," "children taught by black teacher"). Each type of prejudice was equally weighted in the index by constructing a dichotomous score for each, thus giving the index a range of zero to four. With NA's excluded, 42 percent of the sample score zero, rejecting all four measures of prejudice, 23 percent score one, 14 percent two, nine percent three, and 12 percent score four, being high on prejudice for all four measures. For purposes of analysis, the index is trichotomized. There are 36 respondents excluded from the analysis due to no answers.

[7] A recent study indicated that when a black candidate is not linked to extremism, the influence of prejudice may be diminished (Becker and Heaton, 1967).

[8] The reader will note that there are an unusually high number of cases missing in the tables, particularly those which contain prejudice as a variable. There are a total of 36 NA's on the prejudice measure, most falling in this category due to a failure to respond to the social distance measure. To assess the effect of these missing cases, the runs shown in the tables were repeated with a measure of prejudice excluding the social distance component (NA = 17). Since none of the findings changed to any significant degree, we are reporting the results which include the social distance measure on the rationale that from a conceptual standpoint this is a more adequate measure of prejudice. The unusually high number of NA's (60) in Table 2 is due to the fact that the NA's on TAB and prejudice are in no instance the same respondents.

[9] Another matter concerned us. To what extent is TAB empirically distinct from the authoritarian outlook? We were gratified to find that TAB persisted as a strong predictor of the vote with authoritarianism controlled. When authoritarianism is low, there is a 71 percent difference in the vote according to TAB (P = .001, V = .51). With authoritarianism medium, there is a 52 percent difference (P = .001, V = .44); while with authoritarianism high, the vote shows a 47 percent difference according to TAB (P = .001, V = .30).

[10] All questions pertaining to campaign issues were formulated after a careful study of local and national reports of the election.

[11] "If Bradley won the election many police officers would have resigned." "Mayor Yorty was the man needed to keep our streets safe." "If Bradley won the election the police would have found it more difficult to do a good job."

[12] "Mayor Yorty neglected the city by his constant traveling." "There was a great deal of corruption in Yorty's administration." "Yorty has not provided adequate leadership to the city."

[13] E.g., Yorty incompetent, Yorty ran racist campaign, Bradley will unite, reject black militant issue, reject police fear issue.

[14] This pattern has been observed in many other studies of voting behavior. See, for example, Berelson and Steiner, 1964: 574-580; Lipset, *et al.,* 1954: 1124-1175.

[15] The V between occupation and TAB is .17 (P = .001). The V between education and TAB is .22 (P = .001).

[16] The 26-30 age group is different from the 21-25 group but highly similar to the 31-45 group in voting behavior.

[17] The V between education and the black extremism issue is .24 (P = .001). With TAB held constant the V's range from .13 to .35. The V between education and the police fear issue is .23 (P = .001). With TAB held constant the V's range from .08 to .23.

ATTITUDE AS AN INTERACTIONAL CONCEPT: SOCIAL CONSTRAINT AND SOCIAL DISTANCE AS INTERVENING VARIABLES BETWEEN ATTITUDES AND ACTION

Lyle G. Warner
and
Melvin L. DeFleur

The issue of how much correspondence exists between attitudes and action has been widely debated. At present, there appear to be three rather distinct views. For convenience, these can be called (1) the postulate of consistency, (2) the postulate of independent variation, and (3) the postulate of contingent consistency. The principal ideas represented in each of these views are summarized below:

The Postulate of Consistency: Each year numerous studies are designed to probe attitudes through the use of standardized scales. Such research is frequently premised upon the supposition that verbal attitude assessments provide reasonably valid guides for predicting what action people would take if they were confronted with the object of their attitude.[1] Turner has recently summarized critically the attitude-action relationship as seen within this perspective:

> "The commonsense meaning of attitude is some psychic unit which corresponds exactly with a category of behavior. Given opportunity, the absence of counter-vailing attitudes, and an appropriate situation, one predicts behavior from attitude on the basis that behavior is a direct reproduction of attitude." (Turner, 1968:3).

The Postulate of Independent Variation: Perhaps the best-known challenge to the postulate of consistency in the area of racial attitudes was that of Robert K. Merton (1949). In a theoretical analysis of the relationship between prejudice and discrimination, he noted the gap between creed and conduct which Myrdal called the "American Dilemma." Merton maintained that this gap was a function of three variables: (1) the cultural creed honored in cultural tradition and party enacted in

Reprinted from the *American Sociological Review* (Vol. 34, April, 1969, pp. 153-169) by permission of the authors and the American Sociological Association.

law; (2) the beliefs and attitudes of individuals regarding the principles of the creed; and (3) the actual practices of individuals with reference to it. Within this system of variables, he stated that there was no reason to assume that attitudes and behavior would be consistently related: "Stated in formal sociological terms, this asserts that attitudes and overt behavior vary independently. Prejudicial attitudes need not coincide with discriminatory behavior." (Merton, 1949: 102-103). Merton did note that in different regions of the country where distinctive normative climates prevailed, one might expect different probabilities of discrimination, depending upon initial attitude. Thus, he also suggested that attitudinal variables could be important.

The Postulate of Contingent Consistency: An impressive number of studies have accumulated which seriously challenge both the postulate of consistency and the postulate of independent variation. A clear cut conclusion from the data which have emerged from all of these studies seems inescapable: neither postulate adequately describes the ways in which attitudes and actions are linked. Fortunately, much of the research which has led to this conclusion has also been aimed at exploring various "situational" concepts and their influence on attitude-related behavior. The results strongly suggest that such interactional concepts as norms, roles, group memberships, reference groups, subcultures, etc., pose *contingent* conditions which can modify the relationship between attitudes and action.

The nature and extent of consistency and inconsistency between attitudes and action have been explored in empirical studies of differing degrees of sophistication. Perhaps the best known early work is the classic study by LaPiere (1934). During the early 1950's, papers such as those by Minard (1952), Lohman and Reitzes (1954) and Kutner et al. (1952), reported on a variety of social settings in which behavior presumed to be related to attitudes was observed. It was not possible to predict the directions of these actions from the information used as indicators of the participants' attitudes. Although these studies lacked precision and control (Campbell, 1963:159-162 and Rokeach, 1967), they raised serious doubts about the correspondence between attitudes and action.

The experimental approach of DeFleur and Westie (1958), Linn (1965), and Fendrich (1967) placed subjects, whose attitudes had been carefully assessed, into more rigorously controlled situations where they were afforded "behavioral opportunities" to act in accord with their known attitudes. It was clear from these studies that there was no simple way in which actions toward an object could be accurately predicted from knowledge of relevant attitudes alone.

Clearly, an adequate theory of attitude must take into account the intervening situational variables which modify the relationship between attitudes and action. As a step toward this in the area of ethnic relations, Yinger (1965) has developed a theoretical model of the relationship between prejudicial attitudes and overt discrimination which is based in part upon the earlier analysis by Merton (1949). In Yinger's view, discriminatory behavior for both the prejudiced and the nonprejudiced is contingent upon the surrounding subcultural system within which action takes place. This model is illustrated in Figure 1.

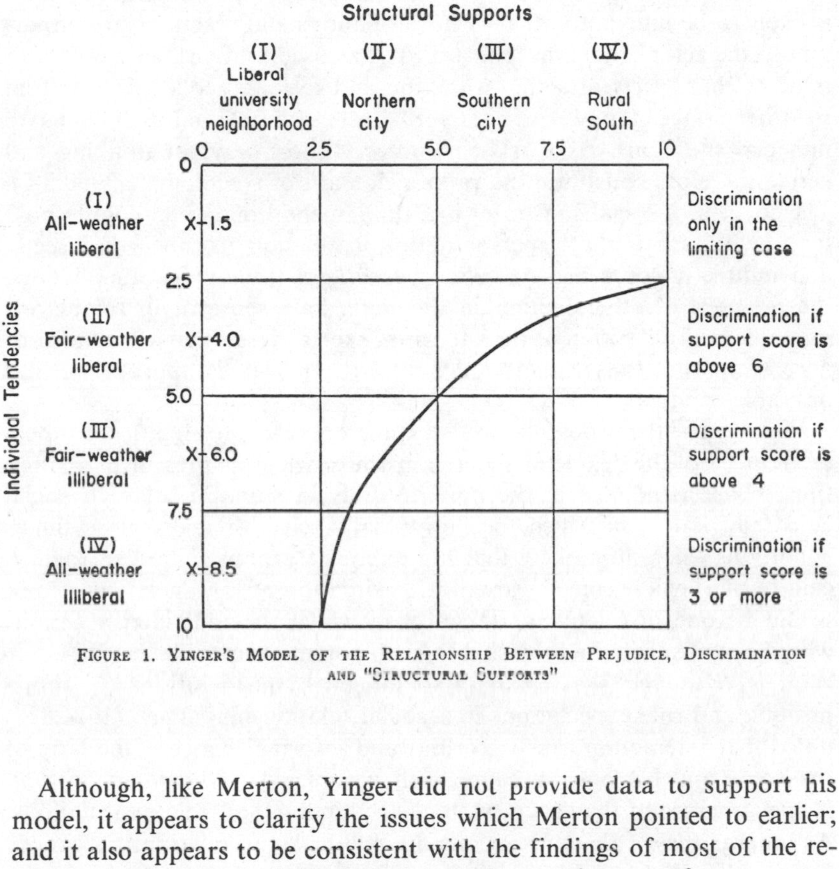

FIGURE 1. YINGER'S MODEL OF THE RELATIONSHIP BETWEEN PREJUDICE, DISCRIMINATION AND "STRUCTURAL SUPPORTS"

Although, like Merton, Yinger did not provide data to support his model, it appears to clarify the issues which Merton pointed to earlier; and it also appears to be consistent with the findings of most of the research which has accumulated during the intervening years.[2]

In summary, we may assume that the weight of evidence indicates that neither the postulate of consistency nor that of independent variation is tenable. A number of intervening variables operate to alter the contingencies of action for persons with given attitudes. Thus far, this set of situational variables and their influence on action has not been fully identified.

SOCIAL CONSTRAINT AND SOCIAL DISTANCE AS SITUATIONAL VARIABLES

It is toward a better understanding of the influence of two specific types of situational variables on the relationship between attitudes and behavior that the present paper is addressed—namely, "social constraint" and "social distance." The ways in which these two terms are actually being used are clarified below.

Social Constraint refers to potential influences on behavior which are introduced into a situation of action because the nature of that behavior is likely to be known to others whose opinions and reactions are important to the actor. The term "constraint" was used by Durkheim (1950) to indicate that "ways of acting, thinking and feeling," collectively shared by others, have a "power of coercion" over an individual as he behaves in social situations. As Durkheim notes, "These ways of thinking and acting therefore constitute the proper domain of sociology." (1950:3-4). The concept of social constraint is a fundamental one. Sociologists hold it to be axiomatic that a person acting in relation to others is directly and indirectly compelled to *behave as others expect.* In other words, the presence of others, either in the immediate sense or in the actor's psychological definition of the situation, exerts pressure to act in accordance with what those others are perceived to feel as appropriate and desirable conduct.

We may use the probability of exposing one's acts to significant others as an index of the degree of social constraint which is present in a situation. Thus, as defined in the present study, a situation of high social constraint is one in which the individual's behavior takes place under conditions where it is likely that his reference groups (or others significant to him) will become aware of it. A situation of low social constraint would be one of relative anonymity, in which the individual's actions would be unlikely to be subjected to such potential surveillance.

Social Distance is based upon sociological considerations of status-position and role expectations in a social relationship.[3] Park (1924:339) noted that interaction can be cordial and informal between the lady of the house and her cook because each occupies a *well-defined position* in the structure of the group, with clearly understood role expectations. As long as these role expectations are fulfilled, the relationship can be permitted to be personal and intimate. Beneath their pleasant exchanges, however, lie the realities of differential status positions. Even the most intimate type of relationship can be entered into while social distance is maintained.

If underlying considerations of ascribed positions are ignored by an actor in entering into a social relationship with another from a lower status category, he *reduces* social distance between himself and the other. A denial of social distance considerations which others hold to be important may result in the application of sanctions. It is for this reason that, in a situation which requires a decision concerning acceptance or rejection of a person in a lower status category as a partner in interaction, social distance, social constraint and attitude form a single system of interactional considerations, a *gestalt,* confronting the actor. That is, they are experienced by a subject as a single system of variables impinging upon his decisions concerning acceptance or rejection of the attitude object.

The importance of these variables in mediating attitude-linked behavior became apparent in prior research. Subjects have reported these considerations as meaningful gestalts at the moment of contemplation of an act of acceptance or rejection of Negroes within the framework of sociological experiments and studies (DeFleur and Westie, 1958; Linn, 1965; DeFriese and Ford, 1968). In spite of their complexity from a conceptual point of view, therefore, both social distance and social constraint are meaningful considerations within the perspectives of an ordinary person who must decide how to behave in an attitude-action situation.

OVERVIEW OF THE PROCEDURES

Verbal attitude data and information for controlled assignment of subjects to experimental conditions were collected from several hundred college students (mostly freshmen) in a border state university at the beginning of their spring semester 1967. The overt behavior data were collected toward the end of the same semester. The factors of social distance and social constraint were varied within a simple experimental design in such a way that several kinds of action situations were provided. Finally, fifty follow-up interviews were conducted by telephone with a sample of subjects in order to check on their perceptions of the "realism" of the study.

In the present field experiment, the attitude under study is prejudice toward Negroes.[4] Using this attitude topic permits the present research to build upon a tradition of prior studies in which this particular issue has been used in the investigation of attitude-action relationships (cf. Fendrich, 1967 for a discussion of these studies). The overt behavior under observation consists of responses to a *letter* which was received by each subject. This letter, which came in several different versions, requested the recipient to *sign a pledge* and to *mail this pledge* back to the sender. These pledges committed the subject to engage in one of several varieties of behavior involving Negroes. These behaviors ranged from dating a Negro to making an anonymous contribution to a Negro educational charity. The use of signatures as a form of overt behavior builds upon earlier studies of attitude-action correspondence (DeFleur and Westie, 1958; Linn, 1965; DeFriese and Ford, 1968). The details of these techniques, the instruments used, and the methods of control employed are discussed more fully in the sections which follow.

MEASURING THE VERBAL ATTITUDE

The verbal attitude data were collected by means of a standard Likert scale. This scale was constructed from items which had been used in previous research (Middleton, 1960; Westie, 1965; DeFriese and Ford, 1968). Data for a pretest of these items were collected from 60 students during the semester preceding the larger study. An item analysis was performed on the original 34 items in order to select those 16 items which best distinguished subjects who had prejudiced attitudes from subjects who had nonprejudiced attitudes (cf. Edwards, 1957; chap. 6).[5] A split-half reliability coefficient was then calculated (r=.84). Application of the Spearman-Brown Prophecy formula as a correction factor yielded a coefficient of .97.

The refined items were placed in an elaborate "Public Information Questionnaire," which was presented to 731 students enrolled in sections of Introductory Sociology during the first week of the spring semester. This questionnaire was portrayed as part of a routine study of public opinion concerning "topics which have been found to be of interest to college students like yourself." The topics covered in the twelve-page questionnaire ranged from the war in Viet Nam to questions about education, civil rights, the war on poverty, the draft, politics, and the American Negro. This device provided a context wherein the attitude scale "made sense" within the framework of opinion topics being probed.

After the completion of the gathering of questionnaire data, the subjects were divided into four groupings on the basis of their attitude scores. The first two quartiles constituted the "least-prejudiced" group, while the third and fourth quartiles constituted the "most-prejudiced" group. Further details will be presented in the section on the experimental design.

MEASURING OVERT BEHAVIOR AND CONTROLLING SITUATIONAL VARIABLES

A unique method was used for collecting data on overt behavior toward the attitude object. As has been indicated, a letter was sent through the mail to subjects who had filled out the "Public Information Questionnaire" earlier in the semester. There were eight different letters. These letters were designed to elicit behavioral responses under varying social distance considerations. While each subject received only one version, every letter requested the recipient to participate in some form of action involving Negroes. The subject was to sign a pledge that he would engage in the action at a later date. Or, if he chose, he could sign indicating that he disapproved of the action being solicited. In either case, he was to return the signed document to the sender in an enclosed, stamped and self-addressed envelope.

In order to establish some outside criteria for the selection of the social distance considerations to be used in the letters, preliminary testing was done on 83 students during the semester preceding the major study. Eight items which posed various kinds of acts that the subject could indicate he would or would not perform were selected for inclusion in the "Public Information Questionnaire."[6] The data collected in the questionnaire were used to obtain ratings on the items in order to evaluate their potential use in the letters. The intent was to obtain a set of items which would provide implications of either reducing or maintaining social distance for a person *performing the acts* described in the items.

After the collection of the study data, the responses of the main body of subjects were analyzed to determine if the items met the criteria established for a Guttman scale (Edwards, 1957: chap. 7). A good ranking was obtained with respect to the level of social distance implied in the items.[7] For simplicity, however, this ranking was dichotomized. In the items listed in Footnote 6, Items 1 through 4 represent forms of action in which lowering of social distance is implied. That is, they all require a dropping of informal barriers which are culturally established by admitting Negroes to equalities of status which are not widely accepted by whites. These items, in other words, pose situations of action in which a *reduction* of social distance is implied.

Items 5 through 8, on the other hand, portray situations of action in which a reduction of social distance is not implied to the same degree as that of the first four items. That is, these forms of action can be engaged in by whites without a lowering of informal barriers, or the abandonment of established status distinctions. Thus, these items pose situations of action in which social distance can be *maintained.*[8] It should be noted that all these latter items involve acting with respect to Negroes within an educational framework. Apparently, these subjects defined participating in actions involving Negroes as "acceptable" as long as the framework of action pertained to educational matters. This interpretation is consistent with the findings of Westie, who in a recent study noted that ". . . people tend to go along with intergroup arrangements that are *faits accomplis."* (Westie, 1965: 538).

In addition to the inclusion of social distance considerations, each letter was prepared in two forms: (1) a "private" form, which assured the subject of anonymity in the later action (and in the signed statement) and (2) a "public" form, which advised the subject that his pledged actions would be disclosed to others via the campus newspaper and other media. These two forms of the letters provided the high and low conditions of *social constraint.*

The letters were sent under the auspices of a fictitious campus student organization, the "Henry Clay Club," and signed by one of the authors as "President." The return envelope was addressed to a cooperating faculty member identified as "Faculty Advisor." There was, of course, no such club; it was strictly a creation of the research plan. The name of the club in our judgment has no significance concerning race relations. The name was widely known locally and provided a simple neutral cover. In spite of the elaborate prearrangements with the student newspaper, the campus office governing student organizations, and others, none of the subjects who received a letter questioned the club's authenticity or inquired about the nature and purposes of this fictitious organization.

APPLICATION OF CONTROLS IN THE SELECTIONS OF SUBJECTS

The initial "Public Information Questionnaire" included both the attitude scale described and information pertaining to social distance implications of various kinds of behavior, plus a number of background variables to be used as controls. The subjects were assigned to attitude quartiles, depending upon their score on the verbal attitude scale. The subjects in each quartile were then matched on the following control variables, using the technique of frequency distribution control:[9] age, sex, education of father, education of mother, education of subject, marital status, social class (based upon father's occupation), residential history and group membership. Residential history was composed of two indices: a regional index and a mobility index. The regional index was based upon the area of the country (Southeast, Northwest, Southwest, etc.) in which the subject had spent the greater part of his life. The mobility index was based upon the degree to which the subject had moved from one region to another. Group membership refers to an index based upon the number and type of campus groups to which the subject belonged.[10]

The application of these controls resulted in reducing the number of subjects participating in the experiment. The availability sample for the study was originally composed of 731 students. After the application of the controls, a total of 537 subjects remained. However, the procedure yielded reasonably homogeneous groupings of subjects for the purpose of experimental design.

THE EXPERIMENTAL DESIGN

The experimental design used in the present study brings together the several factors and variables which have been discussed in previous sections. These include: (1) the subject's verbal attitude, (2) the control variables,[11] (3) the implications of social distance reduction or maintenance in the behaviors requested of the subjects, and (4) the level of social constraint pertaining to the requested behaviors.

A schematic representation of the experimental design is shown in Figure 2. On the left side of the diagram it can be noted that the subjects were stratified into quartile groupings based upon their initial attitude.

Once this step was completed, the subjects in each quartile were *randomly* assigned to one of the two social constraint conditions (high or low). The resulting groupings within a given quartile received the different forms of the letter (public or private), according to their assigned cell. The factor of social distance was handled in a similar manner. Within each social constraint condition, and for every quartile, the reducing and maintaining implications of social distance were appropriately represented.

VERBAL ATTITUDE QUARTILE	SOCIAL CONSTRAINT			
	High (public condition)		Low (private condition)	
	SOCIAL DISTANCE IMPLICATIONS		SOCIAL DISTANCE IMPLICATIONS	
	Reducing	Maintaining	Reducing	Maintaining
Least Prejudiced Subjects				
Most Prejudiced Subjects				

FIGURE 2. GENERAL DESIGN FOR THE COLLECTION OF OVERT BEHAVIOR DATA

Each cell in the design was balanced by assigning to it a proportionate number of males and females. Equal numbers of those who had indicated on the initial questionnaire that they would or would not engage in the behaviors under study (see Footnote 6) were also assigned to each cell.

Obviously, a number of hypotheses could be generated from Figure 2, which has the general form of a factorial design. However, the data were organized around several general propositions rather than around a large number of specific hypotheses. There is, after all, no tightly articulated theory underlying the present research in the sense of an interrelated set of generalizations from which theorems can be derived with the aid of a logical calculus. The research is inductive rather than deductive. Therefore, the following three broad propositions can be stated as a framework within which to discuss the results.

First of all, our interest centers on the relationship between attitudes and action. A general proposition can be stated in the following terms:

Proposition 1: There will be a significant relationship between initial distance considerations and overt behavior. The proportion of explained variance will be low because of the impact of attitudes.

Secondly, the factor of social constraint should have a substantial influence on attitude-action consistency. There is no reason to assume, however, that this influence will be uniform under all conditions indicated within the experimental design. We may state the following general proposition:

Proposition 2: There will be a significant relationship between social constraint and overt behavior. The proportion of explained variance will be low because of the impact of attitudes.

Finally, the factor of social distance should influence attitude-behavior relationships. The following proposition can be used as a guide in interpreting the data.

Proposition 3: There will be a significant relationship between social attitude and overt behavior. However, the proportion of explained variance will be low because of the impact of situational variables.

In addition to these general propositions, each cell of the experimental design places several variables in interactive conjunction with each other. Hypotheses could be formulated for each of these. Since there is no rigorous basis for predicting the direction of these influences, these combinations will be discussed in an *ad hoc* manner.

RESULTS:

The results of the experiment are summarized in Tables 1, 2, and 3. Table 1 shows the percent of subjects in each of the major conditions who elected to *comply* with the request posed by the letter they received. That is, they signed the letter pledging that they would engage in the requested attitude-related act and they returned the letter to the sender. The rates of compliance differed greatly under the various experimental conditions. For example, for the most-prejudiced subjects under the combined conditions of "high" social constraint and an act requiring a "reducing" of social distance, the rate of return for a signed pledge of compliance was only 1.5% of the letters originally sent out to subjects in this experimental condition.

Table 2, on the other hand, shows the percent of subjects who refused to comply with the request in the letter they received. These subjcts signed the letter indicating refusal and returned it to the experimenters. Examination of Table 2 indicates that refusal rates also varied substantially among the several conditions of the experiment. For example, the cell which corresponds to the illustration above, with the "most-prejudiced" subjects under the combined conditions of "high" social constraint and an act requiring a "reducing" of social distance, the rate of signed refusal was 22.4% of the letters originally sent out within these conditions.

To interpret these findings within a probability framework, a third table was constructed. Table 3 is based upon only those who returned a signed letter, either agreeing to comply or refusing to comply. These letters were classified into the percent complying and the percent refusing. It must be noted that correspondence between attitude and action is indicated by compliance for the nonprejudiced and by refusal to comply for the prejudiced. If only chance factors were operating in a situation of this type, 50% of the returned letters should indicate compliance and the other 50%, refusal. Therefore, where the conditions imposed by the experiment had no influence on the results, subtracting the number of letters indicating refusal from those indicating compliance (in any given cell of the table) should yield results not significantly different from *zero*. On the other hand, if the conditions used in the experiment had some influence on the relative proportion of compliance and refusal, subtracting the percent who refused from the percent who complied should yield difference in percents which are significantly different from zero. Thus, the cells of Table 3 show plus and minus percentage values which were obtained by this procedure. A plus value indicates an excess of compliance over refusal. A minus value indicates the reverse, an excess of refusal over compliance. The probabilities for these differences were obtained by applying the (two-tailed) t-test for the significance of differences between proportions, where n's were greater than 20, or the (two-tailed) binomial distribution where n's were smaller than or equal to 20.

This analysis provides no interpretation of the impact of the experimental conditions for those subjects who did not return a letter. We may note that there was no expectation that the majority would return a letter. The interest was in the relative predictability for those who complied versus those who refused. The technique used should not be confused with the usual "mail-back" procedure for data-gathering, where the objective is to infer population parameters from mailed returns. The present research aims at inferences concerning the comparative importance of conditions within a specific experimental design. It does not attempt to estimate population parameters. In this respect, it is quite similar to a laboratory experiment. A separate study of those who did not return a letter would be important and would undoubtedly produce interesting results. Because of limitations of space, the present report does not pursue this task.[12]

Proposition 1 stated that there would be a significant relationship between initial attitude and the direction of overt behavior, but that it would be weak because of the influence of intervening situational conditions. From Table 3, the influence of attitude on behavior is apparent. For the

TABLE 1

NUMBERS OF LETTERS SENT UNDER EACH EXPERIMENTAL CONDITION AND PERCENT WHICH WERE SIGNED AND RETURNED TO COMPLY WITH REQUESTED BEHAVIOR

Verbal Attitude Quartile	Social Constraint: High Social Distance Implications: Reducing: n sent	Reducing: percent complied	Maintaining: n sent	Maintaining: percent complied	Low Social Distance Implications: Reducing: n sent	Reducing: percent complied	Maintaining: n sent	Maintaining: percent complied	Total: n sent	Total: percent complied
Least Prejudiced (Q_1+Q_2)	67	9.0	77	15.6	64	17.2	75	12.0	283	13.4
High social constraint:	........(n sent=144; 12.5%)									
Low social constraint:	....(n sent=139; 14.4%)									
Social distance reducing:	...........................(n sent=131; 13.0%)									
Social distance maintaining:	...........................(n sent=152; 13.8%)									
Most Prejudiced (Q_3+Q_4)	67	1.5	59	6.8	69	13.0	59	6.8	254	7.1
High social constraint:	.........(n sent=126; 4.0%)									
Low social constraint:	....(n sent=128; 10.2%)									
Social distance reducing:	............................(n sent=136; 7.4%)									
Social distance maintaining:	............................(n sent=118; 6.8%)									
Combined Quartiles	134	5.2	136	11.8	133	15.0	134	9.7		
High social constraint:	.........(n sent=270; 8.5%)									
Low social constraint:	....(n sent=267; 12.4%)									
Social distance reducing:	...........................(n sent=267; 10.1%)									
Social distance maintaining:	...........................(n sent=270; 10.7%)									

TABLE 2

NUMBERS OF LETTERS SENT UNDER EACH EXPERIMENTAL CONDITION AND PERCENT WHICH WERE SIGNED AND RETURNED REFUSING TO COMPLY WITH REQUESTED BEHAVIOR

Verbal Attitude Quartile	Social Constraint: High Social Distance Implications: Reducing: n sent	percent refused	Maintaining: n sent	percent refused	Low Social Distance Implications: Reducing: n sent	percent refused	Maintaining: n sent	percent refused	Total: n sent	percent refused
Least Prejudiced										
(Q_1+Q_2)	67	17.9	77	3.9	64	14.1	75	5.3	283	9.9
High social constraint:	(n sent=144; 10.4%)									
Low social constraint:	(n sent=139; 9.4%)									
Social distance reducing:	(n sent=131; 16.0%)									
Social distance maintaining:	(n sent=152; 4.6%)									
Most Prejudiced										
(Q_3+Q_4)	67	22.4	59	20.3	69	10.1	59	8.5	254	15.4
High social constraint:	(n sent=126; 21.4%)									
Low social constraint:	(n sent=128; 9.4%)									
Social distance reducing:	(n sent=136; 16.2%)									
Social distance maintaining:	(n sent=118; 14.4%)									
Combined Quartiles	134	20.1	136	11.0	133	12.0	134	6.7		
High social constraint:	(n sent=270; 15.6%)									
Low socia constraint:	(n sent=267; 9.4%)									
Social distance reducing:	(n sent=267; 16.1%)									
Social distance maintaining:	(n sent=270; 8.9%)									

TABLE 3

PERCENT COMPLYING MINUS PERCENT REFUSING, CONSIDERING ONLY THOSE WHO RETURNED THEIR LETTER

Verbal Attitude Quartile	Social Constraint: High Social Distance Implications: Reducing		High Social Distance Implications: Maintaining		Low Social Distance Implications: Reducing		Low Social Distance Implications: Maintaining	Total
Least Prejudiced								
(Q_1+Q_2)	−33.3		+60.0*		+10.0		+38.5	+15.2*
High social constraint:		(+9.1)						
Low social constraint:						(+21.2)*		
Social distance reducing:				(−10.5)				
Social distance maintaining:				(+50.0)*				
Most Prejudiced								
(Q_3+Q_4)	−87.5*		−50.0		+12.5		−11.1	−36.8*
High social constraint:	(−68.8)*							
Low social constraint:						(+4.0)		
Social distance reducing:				(−37.5)*				
Social distance maintaining:				(−36.0)*				
Combined Quartiles	−58.8*		+3.2		+11.1		+18.2	
High social constraint:		(−29.2)*						
Low social constraint:						(+13.8)*		
Social distance reducing:				(−22.9)*				
Social distance maintaining:				(+9.4)				

*Indicates p less than .05.

least prejudiced subjects, taken as a whole, the value in the right hand margin is +15.2 percentage points, indicating a significant excess of compliance over refusal. For the most prejudiced subjects, the marginal value of –36.8 indicates a significant excess of refusals over compliance. These findings lend some support to the idea that a person with a positive attitude will tend to act favorably toward the objects of that attitude while a person with a negative attitude will tend to refuse to engage in an act which is inconsistent with that attitude. These data may appear to support the postulate of consistency between attitudes and action. However, if this postulate were completely tenable, values of plus and minus 100 percent would be required in these marginal cells (assuming valid assessments of both attitudes and behavior). They are considerably less than that. Therefore a large amount of consistency is not present.

Since the postulates of consistency and of independent variation are not tenable, we may turn to the intervening variables of social constraint and social distance to assess their importance in the attitude-action relationship. Proposition 2 stated that there would be a significant relationship between social constraint and behavior. The impact of social constraint can be seen by examining the marginal values in the bottom of Table 3. The value of –29.2 percentage points, associated with high social constraint, indicates a significant excess of refusals over compliance. Thus, regardless of whether the subject was among the most or least prejudiced, the factor of high social constraint (disclosing his actions to others) tended to inhibit his willingness to comply with the requested behavior. For the condition of low social constraint, and regardless of initial attitude, the corresponding marginal in the table is +13.8. This indicates a significant excess of compliance over refusal. A condition of anonymity, in other words, led to increased probabilities of compliance with the attitude-related act. Subjects were more willing to pledge themselves to engage in the requested behaviors when they were assured their actions were not visible to others.

Finally, Proposition 3 stated that there would be a significant relationship between social distance considerations and overt behavior. The impact of social distance implications can be seen by examining the bottom marginals of Table 3. In situations which required a reduction of social distance, there was a significant excess of refusals over compliance. The difference is –22.9 percentage points. Thus, regardless of initial attitude, subjects tended to refuse to engage in the requested behavior in situations in which a reduction of social distances was implied; where social distance could be maintained, however, no clear relationship to behavior was noticed. That is, the +9.4 excess of compliance over refusal is not significantly different from zero. Thus Propositions 1, 2 and 3 were generally supported.

Proposition 2, however, suggests that the direction of one's attitude is an important factor. To assemble evidence on this issue, we may examine Table 4 (derived from Table 3) which shows the relevant data in convenient form.

TABLE 4

PERCENT COMPLYING MINUS PERCENT REFUSING, HIGH AND LOW SOCIAL CONSTRAINT ONLY

Verbal Attitude	Social Constraint: High	Social Constraint: Low
Least Prejudiced	+9.1	+21.2*
Most Prejudiced	–68.8*	+4.0

*Indicates p less than .05.

As can be seen, high social constraint had a substantial inhibiting effect upon the least prejudiced subjects. Since the requested act was one generally disapproved within relevant norms, the exposure to potential surveillance provided by the condition of high social constraint produced inconsistency between attitudes and action for the least prejudiced subjects. In fact, there was no clear relationship under these conditions between attitude and action as indicated by a nonsignificant value of +9.1 percentage points. For the most prejudiced subjects, on the other hand, a condition of high social constraint tended to produce substantial consistency between attitudes and action. The general norms surrounding the act, the potential surveillance resulting from high social constraint and the initial attitude all combined to produce a very high level of refusal over compliance (–68.8). This indicates consistency between the negative attitude and rejection of the attitude object.

Low social constraint had a somewhat opposite influence. Here, the protections of anonymity permitted the least-prejudiced subjects to act more favorably toward the attitude object. They tended toward consistency in their attitudes and actions, under the conditions provided by low social constraint. The most prejudiced subjects, on the other hand, showed no significant relationship between their attitude and actions, under the conditions provided by low social constraint. Thus, in a relatively constraint-free environment, the most prejudiced subjects did not uniformly reject the attitude-object.

Overall, Proposition 2 appears to be tenable. High and low social constraint did indeed have differential effects upon the most and least prejudiced. These were, however, rather complex. The direction of initial attitude was clearly important, but the social constraint factor operated rather differently under specific interactional conditions.

The third general proposition, concerning the influence of social distance implications, also suggests that the direction of one's attitude will modify the relationship between social distance consideration and behavior. Evidence on this broad hypothesis can be derived from Table 3. The relevant data are summarized in Table 5.

For the least-prejudiced subjects, under the condition where the act implied a reduction of social distance, only a change-like relationship is observed between attitudes and action (a –10.5 percentage points excess of refusal over compliance). Where social distance could be maintained while performing the requested act, however, there was a significant excess of compliance over refusal (+50.0), indicating substantial correspondence between attitude and behavior. For the most prejudiced subjects, where the act implied a reduction of social distance, the excess of refusal over compliance was –37.5. Under conditions in which the act did not imply a reduction of social distance, the most-prejudiced subjects still exhibited a significant excess of refusal over compliance (–36.0). This may be attributable to the confounding influence of high social constraint. Thus, social distance implications would seem to have substantial effects among both the least-prejudiced subjects and the most-prejudiced subjects. In particular, consistency between attitudes and action was sharply reduced for the least-prejudiced subjects when the act implied a reduction of social distance. Thus, the general idea expressed in Proposition 3 appears tenable.

TABLE 5

PERCENT COMPLYING MINUS PERCENT REFUSING, SOCIAL DISTANCE IMPLICATIONS ONLY

Verbal Attitude	Social Distance Implications: Reducing	Social Distance Implications: Maintaining
Least Prejudiced:	–10.5	+50.0*
Most Prejudiced:	–37.5*	36.0*

*Indicates p less than .05.

The three-way interactions between social constraint, social distance and initial attitude are presented in Table 6. We may first observe the relationship between situational variables and behavior for the least prejudiced subjects. Under conditions of high social constraint in which a reduction of social distance is implied, there is an excess of refusal over compliance (–33.3 percentage points). However, because of small n's, this relationship is not significantly different from zero (indicating no relationship between attitudes and behavior). Under conditions of high social constraint in which social distance can be maintained, there is a significant excess of compliance over refusal (+60.0), indicating a high degree of correspondence between attitudes and action. Under conditions of low social constraint, there is little or no relationship between attitudes and behavior (possibly due to the small n's in these cells). However, the trend appears to be in the same direction as that observed under conditions of high social constraint.

These interactional situations seem to have had a somewhat different effect for the most prejudiced subjects. Under conditions of high social constraint, where the act implied a reduction of social distance, there is a significant excess of refusal over compliance. Thus the figure –87.5 percentage points indicates a high degree of consistency between a negative attitude and rejection of the attitude object. Under the conditions of low social constraint, the relationship between attitudes and behavior does not appear to be significant.

TABLE 6

PERCENT COMPLYING MINUS PERCENT REFUSING, SOCIAL DISTANCE AND SOCIAL CONSTRAINT CONSIDERED JOINTLY

	Social Constraint			
	High Social Distance Implications		Low Social Distance Implications	
Verbal Attitude	Reducing	Maintaining	Reducing	Maintaining
Least Prejudiced:	–33.3	+60.0*	+10.0	+38.5
Most Prejudiced:	–87.5*	–50.0	+12.5	–11.1

*Indicates p less than .05.

In summary of the foregoing examination of the results of the experiment, the following empirical regularities were observed:

1. For the *most-prejudiced* subjects, taken as a whole, there is a significant relationship between attitudes and behavior (Table 3).

2. For the *least-prejudiced* subjects, taken as a whole, there is a significant relationship between attitudes and behavior (Table 3).

3. Regardless of initial attitude, the factor of *high social constraint* tends to inhibit the subjects' willingness to comply with the requested behavior (Table 3).

4. Regardless of initial attitude, the factor of *low social constraint* tends to promote the subjects' willingness to comply with the requested behavior (Table 3).

5. Regardless of initial attitude, a situation which implies reduction of social distance tends to inhibit the subjects' willingness to comply with the requested behavior (Table 3).

6. Under conditions of *low social constraint,* there is a significant correspondence between attitudes and behavior for the least-prejudiced subjects (Table 4).

7. Under conditions of *high social constraint,* there is a significant correspondence between attitudes and behavior for the most-prejudiced subjects (Table 4).

8. Under conditions which imply either a *reduction of social distance* or *maintenance of social distance,* there is a significant correspondence between attitudes and behavior for the most-prejudiced subjects (Table 5).

9. Under conditions which imply *maintenance of social distance* there is a significant correspondence between attitudes and behavior for the least-prejudiced subjects (Table 5).

10. Under conditions of *high social constraint* in which *social distance* can be *maintained,* there is a significant correspondence between attitudes and behavior for the least-prejudiced subjects (Table 6).

11. Under conditions of *high social constraint* in which *social distance* is *reduced,* there is a significant correspondence between attitudes and behavior for the most-prejudiced subjects (Table 6).

DISCUSSION:

The experimental conditions used in the present study are composed of various combinations of the social constraint and social distance dichotomies discussed previously. Both of these rather complex factors relate directly to norms in the following manner. First, disclosure of an act (high social constraint situation) makes it possible for others to administer external sanctions upon one's behavior. Presumably, when one's behavior is open to surveilance by others, the individual is subject to possible negative sanctions if his behavior deviates from the expectations that others hold or the norms to which they give approval.[13] Secondly, social distance considerations have implications for interaction. If one denies social distance considerations which others define as normative, he risks potential sanctions—provided these others discover the nature of his act. It is therefore necessary to make assertions as to whether norms are favorable or unfavorable toward certain types of interaction. As was pointed out earlier, an underlying assumption of the present study is that the normative environment is hostile toward integration (see Footnote 4). In view of these statements, the findings of the present research are reasonably consistent with what one might expect. Thus, the least-prejudiced subjects tend to be most consistent when they are not exposed to potential sanctions which support norms that are unfavorable toward integration. That is, their attitudes and actions tend to correspond under low social constraint (anonymity protected) and social distance maintaining situations. When, however, they are asked to behave favorably toward the attitude object in situations in which they would be violating norms (social distance reduction) and directly disclosing their acts to others (high social constraint), a great deal of inconsistency can be noted between their attitudes and behavior.

For the most-prejudiced subjects, on the other hand, norms which are hostile toward integration are *supportive* of their attitudes. Thus, for the most-prejudiced subjects, one would expect the greatest correspondence between attitudes and behavior under conditions of surveillance (high social constraint) and for those acts which are normatively prohibited (reduction of social distance and hence lowering of barriers to interaction). The results of the present study seem to support these interpretations quite clearly.

In general, the present data and the interpretations are consistent with a "field view of prejudice and discrimination." (Yinger, 1965:244-266). This viewpoint specifies the joint implications of individual tendencies (attitudes) and structural supports (norms) for behavior. Or, stated differently, these data support the postulate of contingent consistency.

In spite of this general support for the point of view represented by Yinger, it can be suggested that a more adequate formulation of the way in which behavior is linked with attitude in the area of ethnic relations would combine: (1) Merton's original types of discriminators, (2) Yinger's model of the differential probability of discriminatory acts which are contingent upon varying socio-cultural environments, and (3) the theoretical implications of the data assembled in the present paper.

Merton's categories, of course, are little more than locations of individuals on a dichotomous measurement of attitude, combined with a two-fold classification of conformity or non-conformity to official creeds (of non-discrimination). Although Merton maintained, as we noted earlier, that attitude and action vary independently, his verbal discussion did little to clarify the issue.

The strength of Yinger's formulation is that he attempted to specify for each of Merton's types the kind of socio-cultural system within which discrimination was or was not likely to occur. This clarified the relationship between attitudes and action by subsuming it under the postulate of contingent consistency rather than that of independent variation.

Unfortunately, Yinger's model is not satisfactory in all respects. For one thing, it was generated (as was Merton's original work) on the basis of hypothetical data. Furthermore, it makes certain logically inconsistent predictions. (For example, it provides a cell representing the "all-weather illiberal" who does *not* discriminate in a "liberal environment." Such a person would scarcely be an "all-weather" discriminator.) Finally, the model depicts rather specific socio-cultural environments which may not be in tune with the contemporary climate of ethnic relations. (For example, a "northern city" may now be a highly prejudiced cultural environment.)

For these reasons, a modified and somewhat more general model, suggested in part by our present data, has been formulated to describe ideal-typical relationships prevailing between types of discriminators (following Merton) and the situational variables within which discrimination is to be predicted. This formulation is portrayed graphically in Figure 3:

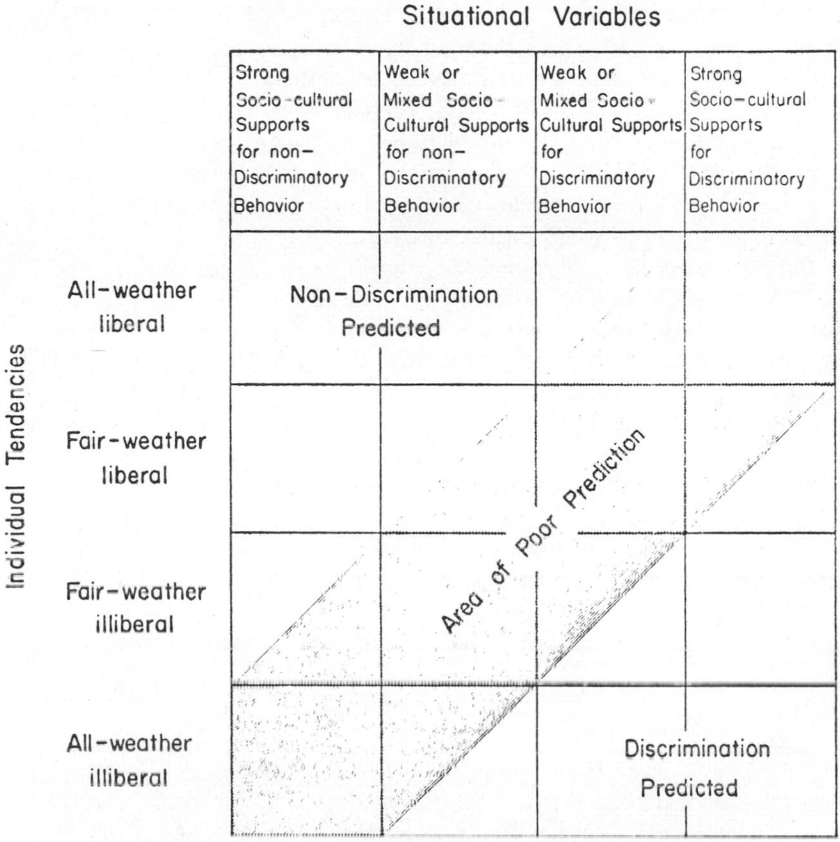

FIGURE 3. SCHEMATIC REPRESENTATION OF HYPOTHESIZED RELATIONSHIP BETWEEN ATTITUDES, SITUATIONAL VARIABLES, AND OVERT BEHAVIOR

The relationships suggested in Figure 3 constitute an oversimplified representation of the general shape which a more adequate theory of discrimination will eventually take. The Merton typology is still a simple twofold system which should be replaced with more sophisticated continua. There may be a number of "individual tendencies" in addition to attitudes which can be identified. Rokeach, for example, suggests that beliefs and values play an important part in the attitudinal behavior of the individual (Rokeach 1967). Numerous other individual variables can be suggested (inner and other directedness, need for approval, alienation, status anxiety, etc.). The situational variables, which are lumped together into a simple four-fold system, can obviously be broken down into a multiplicity of interactional and cultural concepts. These may alter the probabilities that a person with given individual tendencies will engage in an act of discrimination. The present research has indicated in empirical terms the way in which two such variables can be important (social distance and social constraint, as defined). Numerous other potential situational variables have been or can be suggested (reference groups, significant others, voluntary organizations, peers, roles, subcultures, etc.). As research accumulates, these factors can be placed in multivariate systems which should provide causal models explaining and predicting the probability of discrimination under a wide variety of personal, social and cultural situations. Hopefully, the oversimplified scheme suggested in Figure 3 will soon become obsolete.

Perhaps more than anything else, the implications of the present research pose a warning for sociological researchers who are interested in the problems of ethnic relations. There is a danger that *fundamental* research on minority relations will turn away from the sources, nature and consequences of prejudice to focus on the more dramatic riots, social movements and other collective behavior issues of the moment. Although these dramatic events are significant, the basic task of theory building concerning the manifestations of prejudice remains far from completion. Providing explanations of why one human being holds antipathies toward another in such a way that he commits acts of discrimination in a society deeply devoted to democratic principles is still the heart of the research task.

REFERENCES

Bogardus, Emory S.
1959 Social Distance. Yellow Springs, Ohio: The Antioch Press.

Campbell, Donald T.
1963 "Social Attitudes and Other Acquired Behavioral Dispositions Pp. 94-172 in Sigmund Koch (ed.), Psychology: A Study of a Science, Volume 6. New York: McGraw-Hill.

DeFleur, Melvin L. and Frank R. Westie.
1958 "Verbal attitudes and overt acts." American Sociological Review 23 (December): 667-673.

DeFriese, Gordon and W. Scott Ford.
1968 "Open occupancy—what whites say, what they do," Transaction (April):53-56.

Deutscher, Irwin.
1966 "Words and deeds: social science and social policy." Social Problems 13 (Winter): 235-254.

Durkheim, Emile.
1950 The Rules of Sociological Method. G. Catlin (ed.). New York: The Free Press.

Edwards, Allen L.
1957 Techniques of Attitude Scale Construction. New York: Appleton-Century-Crofts, Inc.
Fendrich, James M.
1967 "A study of the association among verbal attitudes, commitment, and overt behavior in different experimental situations." Social Forces 45 (March):347-355.
Kelman, Herbert C.
1958 "Compliance, identification and internalization: three processes of attitude change." Journal of Conflict Resolution 2:51-60.
Kutner, Bernard, Carol Wilkins and Penny Yarrow.
1952 "Verbal attitudes and overt behavior involving racial prejudice." Journal of Abnormal and Social Psychology 47 (October): 649-652.
LaPiere, R. T.
1934 "Attitudes vs. action." Social Forces 13 (December):230-237.
Lohman, Joseph D. and Dietrich C. Reitzes.
1954 "Deliberately organized groups and racial behavior. American Sociological Review 19 (June): 342-344.
Linn, Lawrence S.
1965 "Verbal attitudes and overt behavior: a study of racial discrimination." Social Forces 43 (March): 353-364.
Menzel, Herbert.
1953 "A new coefficient for scalogram analysis." Public Opinion Quarterly 17 (Summer):268-280.
Merton, Robert K.
1949 "Discrimination and the American creed." Pp. 99-126 in Robert M. MacIver (ed.), Discrimination and National Welfare. New York: Institute for Religious and Social Studies.
Middleton, Russell.
1960 "Ethnic prejudice and susceptibility to persuasion." American Sociological Review 25 (October):679-686.
Minard, R. D.
1952 "Race relations in the Pocahontas Coal Fields." Journal of Social Issues 8:29-44.
Park, Robert E.
1924 "The concept of social distance." Journal of Applied Sociology 8 (July-August): 339-344.
Rokeach, Milton.
1967 "Attitude change and behavioral change." Public Opinion Quarterly 30:529-550.
Schanck, R. L.
1932 "A study of a community and its groups and institutions conceived of as behavior of individuals." Psychological Monographs 430.
Selltiz, Claire, Marie Jahoda, Morton Deutsch and Stuart W. Cook.
1965 Research Methods in Social Relations. New York: Holt, Rinehart and Winston.
Simpson, George E. and J. Milton Yinger.
1958 Racial and Cultural Minorities. New York: Harper and Brothers.
Turner, Ralph H.
1968 "Is the concept of attitude obsolete?" Paper read at the Pacific Sociological Association Meetings (March): San Francisco.
Westie, Frank R.
1964 "Race and ethnic relations." Pp. 576-619 in Robert E. L. Faris (ed.), Handbook of Modern Sociology. Chicago: Rand McNally and Company.
1965 "The American dilemma: an empirical test." American Sociological Review 30 (August):527-538.
Yinger, J. Milton
1965 Toward a Field Theory of Behavior. New York: McGraw-Hill.

NOTES

[1] The reader is directed to a recent article by Deutscher (1966) for a detailed discussion of this issue.

[2] The study by Lohman and Reitzes (1954) provides a good empirical example of structural supports which support discrimination and those which do not.

[3] For a discussion of social distance as a cultural factor in prejudice, see Simpson and Yinger (1958: 150-164).

[4] A basic assumption underlying the present research is that the normative environment is hostile toward integration. For a summary of evidence to support this assumption see Westie (1964:581-603).

[5] *Verbal Attitude Scale:*

1. Negroes ought to have the same access to swimming pools as whites.
2. The reason so many Negroes are on "relief" is that they do not want to work.
3. I would be willing to invite a Negro into my home for lunch.
4. White candidates can do a better job than Negroes in political office.
5. I would be willing to sit in public (for example, the Student Union) with a Negro.
6. Negroes seem to learn a little slower than whites.
7. I would be willing to have a Negro family live next door to me.
8. Negroes do not make good workers because they are lazy.
9. If I had children, I would not mind if they were taught by a Negro school teacher.
10. Negroes cannot be trusted in positions of responsibility.
11. There is nothing wrong with both races attending the same church.
12. Most Negroes would become overbearing and disagreeable if not kept in their place.
13. It is unimportant to me if an elected official is Negro or white, as long as he is capable and honest.
14. I would not be willing to invite Negroes to a dinner party at my home.
15. I would be willing to have a Negro as my supervisor in my place of work.
16. I prefer to see white and Negro children attend different schools.

[6] *Behavioral items:*

1. If you were asked for a date by an attractive Negro college student, in order to participate in an evening of dancing, good music and good fellowship, what would you do?
2. If you were asked to contribute a very small sum of money (like 25¢) to a Negro civil rights organization, what would you do?
3. If a campus organization asked you to endorse an appeal to both political parties to seek out qualified Negro candidates for public office, what would you do?
4. Even today some local restaurants and hotels discriminate against Negro clients. If you were asked to sign a petition urging a local hotel or restaurant to serve Negroes, what would you do?
5. If you were invited to a dinner being held to welcome new Negro students to campus, what would you do?
6. The State Board of Education is considering a new policy of giving more complete treatment to the contributions of Negroes to American History and our society. If you were asked to endorse such a policy, what would you do?
7. If you were asked to volunteer to go into the home of a Negro family of potential college students and tell them about your experiences as a college student, what would you do?
8. There are several outstanding charitable groups organized to give aid to Negro college students who otherwise could never attend college. If you were asked to donate a very small sum of money (like 25¢) to such a charity, what would you do?

[7] The Guttman analysis was used to obtain information concerning social distance implications, as explained above, and data on the ordering of the items as forms of overt behavior for use in the letters. The coefficient of reproducibility was 89; the minimal marginal reproducibility was .70; the coefficient of scalability was .72 (Menzel, 1953).

[8] One could conclude that any noted attitude-behavior discrepancy would occur because of the difference between measuring a general orientation toward Negroes (the attitude scale) and measuring specific actions toward Negroes (responses to the letters). However, a separate analysis using responses to the eight social distance items included in the questionnaire as a more specific scale did not yield results significantly different from those

found using the more general scale. It should also be noted that, because of the multiple correlation features of Guttman scales, one should not expect to find a closer correspondence between attitudes and behavior by relating the questionnaire response on a given action to actual willingness to engage in that same action.

[9] For a discussion of this technique, its advantages and disadvantages, see Selltiz *et al.*, (1965:107-109).

[10] The controls are obviously elaborate. It was felt that every effort should be made to minimize influences of variables which could potentially disturb the dependent-independent relationship under study. It is recognized, however, that in a complex field experiment there still remain many variables that are not under rigorous control.

[11] The only control variable found to be significantly related to the subject's initial attitude was the sex of the subject. Females were generally less prejudiced.

[12] A typical way of dealing with the problem of non-response is to compare the characteristics of those who fail to respond with those of the respondents. If no systematic differences between these appear, then one concludes that the effects on the dependent variable are negligible. Since the present study commenced with a rather homogeneous sample of subjects, this problem is not of the same magnitude as it is for the survey researcher who has very little initial information concerning the characteristics of specific respondents. Nevertheless, attempts were made in the present study to investigate this problem. The control variables were cross-tabulated with the subject's overt behavior response to determine if the composition of the groups was affected by differential response rates. There was no relationship between any of the nine control variables and overt behavior responses for the total group. The overt behavior responses for the subjects in each of the four groups were then cross-tabulated with the control variables. One relationship out of thirty-six was significant at the .05 level. Since one would expect at least one out of twenty relationships to be significant on a chance basis, this occurrence is considered to be due to random fluctuation. In addition, a stratified random sample of those who returned the letter and those who did not was interviewed; data indicated that the subjects viewed the letter as a realistic request.

[13] The early study by Schanck (1932) offers a demonstration of compliance to norms when one is under surveillance by others and violation of norms when the individual is not under direct surveillance. Kelman (1958) also discusses three processes which influence conformity to norms.

12

NORMATIVE CONSTRAINTS ON DEVIANT BEHAVIOR IN THE COLLEGE CONTEXT

William J. Bowers

Individuals learn to regard some forms of behavior as wrong, inappropriate or contrary to the rules of conduct, and to feel that they and others should not engage in such actions. The members of a social group will not always agree, however, in their feelings about a particular form of behavior, and even when they do, they will not always agree with the members of another group. In a given population or society, then, a particular form of behavior will be more or less deviant—neither acceptable nor unacceptable to all the members, but subject to normative ambiguity within groups and normative disparity between groups.

These sentiments which define an action as more or less deviant, will, at the same time, affect its prevalence. The individual's own feelings about a given form of behavior are bound to affect his likelihood of engaging in it. If he has internalized the norm—believes the behavior is wrong, knows he ought not engage in it, and would feel guilty if he did so—he will more easily dismiss temptations and resist pressures to commit the offense.

So, too, one person's sense of disapproval is apt to restrain the behavior of another. Knowing that one's associate strongly disapproves of some behavior will make an individual more reluctant to engage in it. Such behavior may cost him the esteem or friendship of his peer. What is more, those who feel strongly are apt to make their feelings known, and, to this extent, others are likely to have their feelings of disapproval stimulated and reinforced. In these ways, then, the prevalence of disapproval in a social group will have a deterrent effect above and beyond each person's own disposition. The extent and distribution of disapproval

Reprinted from *Sociometry* (Vol. 31, December, 1968, pp. 370-385) by permission of the author and the American Sociological Association.

in the social context, is, therefore, of considerable importance in the study of deviant behavior.[1]

The major focus of the paper is on the extent to which the individual's personal sense of disapproval *and* the disapproval felt by others in his social context *jointly* affect his likelihood of becoming involved in various forms of deviant behavior.[2] We shall examine the effects of both kinds of disapproval on ten different forms of behavior to identify, insofar as possible, a general pattern of normative constraints that holds for various kinds of deviance.

The analysis is based on data about the attitudes and behavior of 5,422 students from 99 colleges. The sample was drawn in two stages. First, 100 institutions were drawn to represent all regionally accredited colleges and universities in 1962. Then, samples of 75 to 100 students were drawn randomly from the directories and listing of the registrars at these schools. Mail questionnaires were sent to 9,037 students, and a follow-up questionnaire was sent to non-respondents at schools with low response rates. Sixty per cent of the sample returned completed questionnaires; 91 schools were represented by at least 40 students. One school had to be dropped because of difficulties in reaching the students, leaving a sample of 5,422 students from 99 colleges and universities. (For further details of the sampling procedure, see Bowers, 1964: Appendix C.)

With information from samples of students at a number of different colleges, we can derive a measure of the climate of disapproval for each campus context (cf. Lazarsfeld and Menzel, 1961). We can then conduct a form of contextual analysis (cf. Blau, 1961; Davis, et al., 1961), characterizing the individual student not only in terms of his personal sense of disapproval but also by the level of disapproval at his college, when examining his involvement in deviant behavior.

DISAPPROVAL AND BEHAVIOR

Let us first examine the extent to which students disapprove of various actions and then turn to their behavior. The information comes from students' responses to a question that lists ten "things students sometimes do in college" and asks the respondent to indicate how strongly he disapproves of each *and* how often he has done each.[3] In selecting the actions, we attempted to avoid forms of behavior that would require special skills, unusual training, or uncommon opportunities. They are intended to represent conduct that all college students will find opportunities, perhaps even pressures, to engage in during their college careers. Table 1 shows the extent to which students disapprove of each. The actions are ordered by the proportion of students strongly disapproving.

All ten actions are disapproved (either mildly or strongly) by a clear majority of the students. Yet, there is considerable variation in the strength of the disapproval students feel. The proportion "strongly" disapproving ranges from a high of 88 per cent to a low of 29 per cent.

TABLE 1

EXTENT OF PERSONAL DISAPPROVAL OF TEN FORMS OF BEHAVIOR AMONG COLLEGE STUDENTS

	For Each Action Per Cent Who:			
	Do Not Disapprove	Mildly Disapprove	Strongly Disapprove	N
Destroying school property	2	10	88	(5345)
Taking articles from the school store without paying for them	3	9	88	(5342)
Disorderly conduct in the local community	3	23	74	(5341)
Taking books from the library without properly checking them out	5	32	63	(5352)
Underlining or marking up library books	5	38	57	(5348)
Becoming friendly with a teacher in hopes of getting a better grade	16	37	47	(5332)
Getting drunk	22	30	48	(5339)
Drinking alcoholic beverages on campus in violation of campus regulations	26	32	42	(5267)
Gambling on campus	34	34	32	(5321)
Over-cutting class	27	44	29	(5283)

The top five offenses are strongly disapproved by a *majority* of the students with only one in twenty failing to disapprove. The bottom five, on the other hand, are strongly disapproved by only a *minority,* with a more sizeable proportion not disapproving at all. For convenience, then, we may distinguish between "major" and "minor" offenses.

The major offenses include theft, vandalism, destruction of property, and the violation of community standards. Most are property violations and all are serious enough to be punishable by law. They might be regarded as the collegiate counterpart to delinquent behavior.

The minor offenses have elements of self-indulgence not present in the first five. Several imply risks besides being caught and punished. The student who gets drunk may also get a hangover, the one who gambles may lose money, and the one who over-cuts may pay the price when examination time comes. More of them constitute violations of implicit values—instances of "bad form"—than violations of formal rules and regulations. None of the five is a violation of property rights or punishable by law.

This brings us to the question of behavior: How prevalent are these acts? What proportion of the students engage in them? Table 2 shows the extent to which students admit having engaged in each. As we move down the list, again ordered by extent of disapproval, the number of students involved tends to increase. There is a consistent increase from item two through item seven, and item ten has the highest rate of all.

There are minor reversals between items one and two and between seven and eight. But these are not surprising since in both cases, the items are very close in disapproval (Table 1) and in behavior (Table 2).

TABLE 2

EXTENT OF INVOLVEMENT IN TEN FORMS OF BEHAVIOR AMONG COLLEGE STUDENTS

	For Each Action Per Cent Who Have Engaged in It:			
	Never	Occasionally	Often	N
Destroying school property	93	7	*	(5326)
Taking articles from the school store without paying for them	95	5	*	(5341)
Disorderly conduct in the local community	89	11	*	(5319)
Taking books from the library without properly checking them out	83	16	1	(5274)
Underlining or marking up library books	77	22	1	(5333)
Becoming friendly with a teacher in hopes of getting a better grade	70	28	2	(5322)
Getting drunk	64	32	4	(5327)
Drinking alcoholic beverages on campus in violation of campus regulations	67	27	6	(5242)
Gambling on campus	82	16	2	(5310)
Over-cutting class	61	32	7	(5275)

*Less than .5 per cent.

With the ninth item—gambling on campus—however, the trend is markedly reversed. Fewer students engage in it than in four other forms of misconduct which are more strongly disapproved. Further analysis indicates that this is largely due to a lack of gambling on the part of females. While the two sexes remain close in terms of disapproval (27 per cent strongly disapproving among males and 32 per cent among females), only 3 per cent of the females have gambled as compared with 33 per cent of the males.

According to the popular image, gambling requires "nerve," the ability to bluff and take risks; it is frequently accompanied by cigars, swearing, and other characteristically masculine behavior. Thus, gambling, contrary to our assumption, may be an action which the female half of the college population find little opportunity for in the normal course of college life.

With the notable exception of gambling on campus, then, offenses which are more strongly disapproved are generally less often committed. This suggests that differences in disapproval among these forms of behavior may account for much of the variation in their prevalence.

THE EFFECTS OF DISAPPROVAL

Merton (1949) has pointed out that disapproval will not always bear a strong relationship to behavior. Gambling on campus, particularly for females, would seem to be a case in point. Yet, for most of the actions under investigation, it would be surprising not to find a fairly strong relationship between an individual's own feelings of disapproval and his behavior. Table 3 presents the relationship between personal disapproval and behavior for each of the ten actions, and indeed, for all ten offenses, the more strongly a student disapproves of an action, the less likely he is to engage in it.

TABLE 3

RELATIONSHIP BETWEEN PERSONAL DISAPPROVAL AND BEHAVIOR FOR EACH OF THE TEN ACTIONS

	Per Cent Who Have Engaged in Each by Level of Personal Disapproval:			
	Strongly Disapprove	Mildly Disapprove	Do Not Disapprove	Per Cent Difference
Destroying school property	4 (4688)	33 (540)	37 (80)	- 33
Taking articles from the school store without paying for them	2 (4688)	29 (488)	30 (140)	- 28
Disorderly conduct in the local community	4 (3901)	31 (1243)	48 (160)	- 44
Taking books from the library without properly checking them out	6 (3351)	44 (1719)	55 (255)	- 49
Underlining or marking up library books	7 (3032)	43 (1992)	70 (293)	- 63
Becoming friendly with a teacher in hopes of getting a better grade	7 (2460)	41 (1984)	74 (854)	- 67
Getting drunk	7 (2527)	48 (1588)	79 (1191)	- 72
Drinking alcoholic beverages on campus in violation of campus regulations	4 (2176)	39 (1661)	74 (1381)	- 70
Gambling on campus	3 (1691)	12 (1773)	40 (1813)	- 37
Over-cutting class	13 (1515)	44 (2292)	61 (1438)	- 48

Personal disapproval, however, appears to have a stronger effect on some actions than on others. As we move down the table, its effect in terms of percentage differences (column four), tends to increase fairly regularly until we reach "gambling on campus" and "over-cutting class," the last two items on the list. For gambling, the reluctance of females to become involved undoubtedly reduces the overall effect of disapproval. For over-cutting class, the risk of falling behind in school work may intervene to weaken the relationship between personal disapproval and behavior.

A closer look at Table 3 reveals that variations in behavior from item to item occur largely among those who do not disapprove (column three). Generally speaking, they are less likely to become involved as offenses become more serious in the aggregate. Apparently, they are more readily influenced in their behavior by the feelings of those around them. As an offense becomes more serious, those who do not disapprove are, by definition, increasingly outnumbered by those who strongly disapprove, and hence, are more predominantly exposed to influences against becoming involved in that form of deviant behavior.[4]

The pattern in Table 3, then, suggests that the prevalence of disapproval in the social context may have a deterrent effect on the behavior of individuals above and beyond their own private sentiments. With a sample of students from each of 99 different schools, we can gauge the level or climate of disapproval of each offense at each college. The climate of disapproval of an offense at a given college will be represented by the proportion of students from the college who strongly disapprove of that form of misconduct. Table 4 shows the rate of each kind of misconduct at colleges with different levels or climates of disapproval.

To begin with, there are some interesting variations in disapproval by college. The two most serious offenses show the least variation by school; only two levels are represented. The next four offenses show a broader variation with at least three contexts for each. For the next three offenses, referring to drinking and gambling, the whole spectrum of contexts is represented. We note from Table 1 that students tend to hold opposing normative positions on these four offenses (either strongly disapproving or not disapproving at all). It appears that this is not so much because students "take sides" on them within schools as because there are considerable differences from school to school in attitudes toward these forms of behavior. Item ten returns to the more common pattern of three disapproval contexts.

Turning to students' behavior, we should find that an increase in the proportion who strongly disapprove on a campus means a decrease in the rate of deviance. And as we move toward more disapproving social contexts, the proportion who have engaged in offenses decreases (with the exception of one tie in the case of gambling).

If we examine the columns rather than the rows, however, the table yields a less obvious finding. Within columns there is relatively little variation in the per cent engaging in different offenses. Only gambling

TABLE 4

RELATIONSHIP BETWEEN LEVEL OF DISAPPROVAL AT THE COLLEGE AND BEHAVIOR FOR EACH OF THE TEN ACTIONS

	Per Cent Who Have Engaged in Each by Proportion at the College Who Strongly Disapprove:				
	0–19	20–39	40–59	60–79	80–100
Destroying school property				19 (610)	5 (4698)
Taking articles from the school store without paying for them				11 (1051)	4 (4265)
Disorderly conduct in the local community		* (44)	20 (709)	11 (3184)	6 (1367)
Taking books from the library without properly checking them out		43 (273)	23 (2096)	11 (2701)	6 (255)
Underlining or marking up library books		48 (400)	25 (2765)	17 (2152)	
Becoming friendly with a teacher in hopes of getting a better grade		37 (1717)	28 (3088)	16 (493)	
Getting drunk	65 (890)	48 (1077)	31 (1941)	16 (965)	5 (433)
Drinking alcoholic beverages on campus in violation of campus regulations	53 (1364)	42 (1242)	26 (1356)	12 (909)	3 (338)
Gambling on campus	31 (1767)	16 (1750)	7 (1309)	7 (355)	4 (96)
Over-cutting class	50 (1427)	38 (2771)	28 (1047)		

*Percentage not given because only one school is represented in the cell. Per cent may be biased by characteristics of that particular school.

on campus is consistently out of line. If we disregard gambling, the remaining per cents in a given column are all greater than any of those in the column to the right of it. Thus, the figures in column one (remembering to exclude gambling) range from 65 to 50; in column two, from 48 to 37; in column three, from 31 to 20; and so on with no overlap from column to column. This means that offenses which are about equally disapproved on a given campus will be about equally prevalent, regardless of the nature of the offense or how strongly disapproved they are in the broader population of college students.

The mean per cent for a column, excluding gambling on campus, therefore, can serve as a general index of misconduct for a given level of contextual disapproval.[5] These means are presented in Figure 1. Overall there is a 51 per cent drop in the level of misconduct from the weakest to the strongest disapproval context. This represents an average decline of about 13 points per interval and as the Figure shows, the drop is fairly even from interval to interval. Yet, like the pattern in Table 3, it represents the composite effect of both the individual's personal feelings of disapproval and the disapproval of those around him. The relative effect of these two components still remains to be seen.

FIGURE 1

Mean Level of Deviant Behavior (Excluding Item Nine) for Varying Contexts of Disapproval

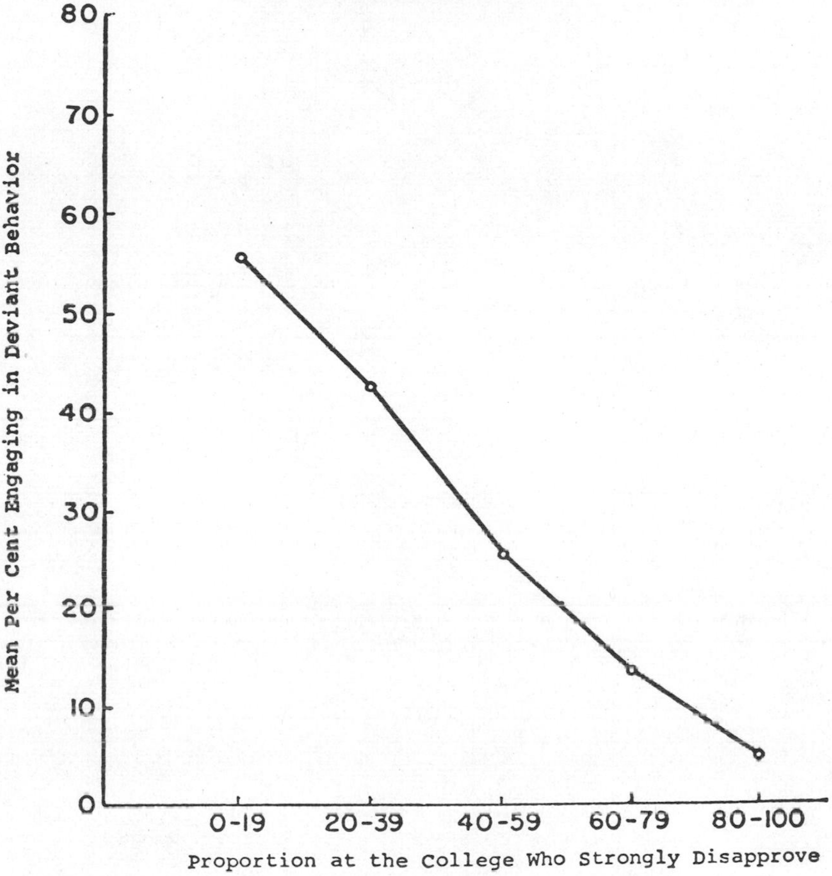

Mean Per Cents	56	43	26	14	5

PERSONAL VERSUS CONTEXTUAL EFFECTS OF DISAPPROVAL

For each offense, we have a measure of personal disapproval and we have derived a measure of the climate of disapproval for the college.

TABLE 5

EFFECT OF PERSONAL DISAPPROVAL AND LEVEL OF DISAPPROVAL AT THE COLLEGE ON BEHAVIOR FOR EACH OF THE TEN ACTIONS

	Personal Disapproval	Per Cent Who Have Engaged in Each by Proportion at the College Who Strongly Disapprove					% Difference Per
Destroying school property	Do not				* (20)	27 (60)	*
	Mild				50 (142)	27 (398)	– 23
	Strong				6 (448)	3 (4240)	– 3
Taking articles from the school store without paying for them	Do not				38 (50)	26 (90)	– 12
	Mild				32 (206)	27 (282)	– 5
	Strong				3 (795)	2 (3893)	– 1
Disorderly conduct in the local community	Do not			67 (49)	39 (89)	* (18)	– 28
	Mild			35 (267)	30 (804)	32 (149)	– 2
	Strong			4 (393)	4 (2291)	2 (1200)	– 1
Taking books from the library without properly checking them out	Do not		79 (34)	48 (137)	42 (81)	* (3)	– 19
	Mild		55 (139)	37 (844)	25 (706)	* (3)	– 15
	Strong		12 (100)	8 (1115)	4 (1914)	4 (222)	– 3
Underlining or marking up library books	Do not		78 (58)	70 (160)	63 (75)		– 8
	Mild		58 (220)	42 (1158)	39 (614)		– 10
	Strong		15 (122)	7 (1447)	5 (1463)		– 5
Becoming friendly with a teacher in hopes of getting a better grade	Do not		75 (394)	73 (432)	64 (28)		– 6
	Mild		41 (734)	41 (1115)	36 (135)		– 3
	Strong		8 (589)	6 (1541)	5 (330)		– 2
Getting drunk	Do not	85 (463)	83 (312)	73 (319)	63 (80)	* (17)	–7
	Mild	55 (304)	53 (415)	47 (622)	35 (214)	27 (33)	– 7
	Strong	12 (123)	11 (380)	8 (1000)	4 (671)	1 (383)	– 3
Drinking alcoholic beverages on campus in violation of campus regulations	Do not	75 (717)	75 (360)	72 (228)	52 (67)	* (9)	– 8
	Mild	39 (468)	46 (508)	37 (436)	28 (221)	21 (28)	– 5
	Strong	3 (179)	4 (374)	5 (701)	3 (621)	0 (301)	– 1

TABLE 5 *(cont'd)*

EFFECT OF PERSONAL DISAPPROVAL AND LEVEL OF DISAPPROVAL AT THE COLLEGE ON BEHAVIOR FOR EACH OF THE TEN ACTIONS

	Personal Disapproval	Per Cent Who Have Engaged in Each by Proportion at the College Who Strongly Disapprove: 0–19	20–39	40–59	60–79	80–100	% Difference Per Interval
Gambling on campus	Do not	46(973)	34(561)	25(247)	37(30)	* (1)	− 3
	Mild	16(606)	12(660)	6(420)	11(83)	* (4)	− 2
	Strong	4(188)	2(529)	1(642)	2(242)	3(90)	0
Over-cutting class	Do not	66(618)	57(690)	55(130)			− 6
	Mild	46(632)	43(1249)	39(411)			− 4
	Strong	11(177)	14(832)	11(506)			0

*Percentages are not given for entries based on 20 or fewer cases.

Table 5 shows the joint effect of both personal and contextual disapproval for each of the ten offenses.[6] The effects of personal disapproval are fairly easy to discern; in virtually all cases they are strong and consistent. The effects of the climate of disapproval are not as clear, at least not at a glance.

Generally speaking, as the climates become more disapproving, the behavior becomes less prevalent, at all levels of personal disapproval. Yet the extent of the effect is difficult to gauge, in part because the number of intervals over which it occurs varies by type of offenses and extent of personal disapproval. Dividing the overall percentage difference for a given row by the number of intervals over which it occurs provides a rough index of the effect of the climate of disapproval which is comparable for different levels of personal disapproval and forms of misconduct. We, therefore, present per cent differences *per interval* in the right-most column of the Table.

Several points are immediately evident from these summary measures of effect. In the first place, disapproval in the social context is definitely a deterrent to behavior independently of the individual's personal sense of disapproval. Of the twenty-nine entries in the right-most column, twenty-seven show this effect; two show no effect. Secondly, the effect of the climate is strongest on those who do not disapprove and weakest on those who disapprove strongly. For all ten offenses, the differences are least for those who strongly disapprove. For seven of the nine offenses permitting comparison, those who fail to disapprove show the greatest differences (in one case there is a tie and in the other, those who mildly disapprove are affected more).

For a composite picture of the joint effects of personal and contextual disapproval, we again can use mean per cents. In this case, however, we will have not one but three figures for a given column, one representing each level of personal disapproval within a given climate.[7] The mean per cents for nine of the ten items are shown in Figure 2.

Figure 2 yields several interesting observations. In the first place, disapproval in the social context shows virtually no effect on individual behavior until the proportion strongly disapproving reaches the 40-59 per cent mark. At this point and beyond, however, deviant behavior drops off for all three categories of personal disapproval. Thus, the "deterrent effect" of disapproval in the social context appears only when the proportion who strongly disapprove approaches a majority—when, on a given campus, the action becomes a "major offense."[8]

Secondly, the climate of disapproval appears to have its greatest effect at different points, depending on the individual's personal sense of disapproval. Among those who do not disapprove, the context has a progressively larger effect as it becomes more restrictive. The most pronounced drop occurs as the proportion strongly disapproving reaches

FIGURE 2

Mean Level of Deviant Behavior (Excluding Item Nine) By Personal Disapproval for Varying Contexts of Disapproval

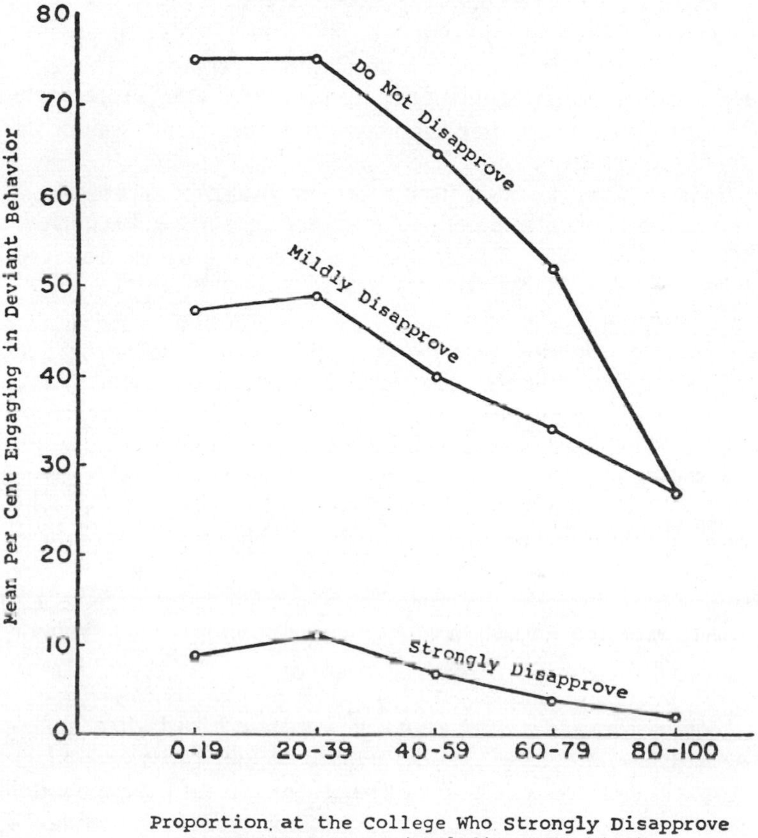

Proportion at the College Who Strongly Disapprove
Mean Per Cents (Excluding Item Nine)

Disapprove					
Not at all	75	75	65	52	27
Mildly	47	49	40	34	27
Strongly	9	11	7	4	2

80 per cent or more. In effect, those who do not disapprove tend to "hold out" until they find that they are surrounded by those who strongly disapprove, until it becomes difficult to find other like-minded individuals.

Among those who mildly disapprove, behavior declines somewhat more uniformly. Here, however, the largest drop comes at the beginning of the downward trend, as the proportion strongly disapproving approaches a majority. In other words, those who mildly disapprove are ready to get on the "band wagon" when they see that the strongly disapproving have a majority. In the case of those who strongly disapprove, the contextual effect is small in terms of percentage differences—few of these students become involved even in the most permissive context.[9] The pattern more closely approximates the "band wagon" than the "hold out" effect.[10]

In evaluating the contextual effects of disapproval, a couple of points should be kept in mind. First, the aggregate of personal feelings at a school is not the same thing as the expression of those feelings in social behavior. A measure which focuses not on what students feel about a given form of misconduct, but on what they would be willing to say and do about it—their willingness to express the disapproval they feel and to take steps to sanction those who violate the norm—would undoubtedly show a stronger effect.

A second point is that *indirect* effects of contextual disapproval are not shown in Figure 2. The climate of disapproval that exists at a college will undoubtedly affect the attitudes newcomers develop on the campus. Thus, disapproval in the social context may be said to have a compound effect—an independent deterrent effect on deviance, and a role in producing the personal feelings which, in turn, have a deterrent effect at the individual level.

SUMMARY AND DISCUSSION

The data reveal a strong and general pattern of effect owing to the normative commitments of the individual and those around him. This effect can be separated into two parts: the effect of the individual's own sense of disapproval, and the effect of the normative feelings of others in his social context. Although the pattern shown in Figure 2 is "built-up" from a number of different forms of deviance, it is by no means a composite of diverse sub-patterns. The rates of misconduct are similar for corresponding combinations of personal and contextual disapproval among the nine component actions. It, therefore, represents a common pattern found to hold to a substantial degree for each of the offenses considered individually.[11]

The fact that one action, gambling on campus, departs from the pattern common to the other nine, however, suggests limits on the generality of the pattern. If an action is difficult to learn, requires special skills or resources to perform, or is possible only under certain limited or uncommon conditions, it will not be as prevalent as another at the same level of personal and contextual disapproval. In the case of gambling, women's opportunities to learn the various games and to play in the company of men are undoubtedly limited in college.

Departures from the general pattern may also occur as a result of the way in which normative commitments are mobilized or channeled in a particular social context. Peer groups are bound to be an important factor, sometimes insulating the individual from disapproval in the broader campus community and sometimes conveying it to him directly (cf. Turner, 1959). In turn, characteristics of the college such as size, sex composition, and campus living arrangements may affect the formation and functioning of student peer groups (cf. Newcomb, 1962; Newcomb and Wilson, 1966).

The formal structure of control, too, may mobilize and channel informal normative sentiments. In the case of academic dishonesty, for example, the honor system provides a way bringing personal sentiments to bear in the social arena (cf. Bowers, 1964). Of course, strong formal control will have a deterrent effect in its own right—above and beyond that due to personal and contextual disapproval.

From this analysis it should be clear that data on samples of individuals from a number of different social contexts offer a distinct opportunity for studying the social context of deviant behavior. (Carlin, 1966, also highlights these opportunities). Here we have examined only the extent of personal disapproval in the social context as a deterrent to deviant behavior. As Merton (1964) notes, however, this same form of contextual analysis can and should be extended to bring in other characteristics of the social environment—the individual's associates and the nature of his relationships with them—as factors affecting his involvement in deviant behavior.

REFERENCES

Becker, Howard S.
1963 Outsiders: Studies in the Sociology of Deviance. New York: The Free Press of Glencoe.

Blau, Peter M.
1960 "Structural effects." American Sociological Review 25 (April):178-193.

Bowers, William J.
1964 Student Dishonesty and Its Control in College. New York: Bureau of Applied Social Research, Columbia University.

Carlin, Jerome E.
1966 Lawyer's Ethics. New York: Russell Sage Foundation.

Clark, Alexander I. and Jack P. Gibbs
1965 "Social control: a reformulation." Social Problems 12 (Spring):398-414.

Clinard, Marshall B.

1959 "Criminological research." Pp. 509-536 in Robert K. Merton, et al., (eds.), Sociology Today. New York: Basic Books.

Davis, James A., Joe L. Spaeth and Carolyn Hudson
1961 "A technique for analyzing the effects of group composition." American Sociological Review 26 (April):215-225.

Gibbs, Jack P.
1966 "Sanctions." Social Problems 14 (Fall):147-159.

Hovland, Carl I., Arthur A. Lumsdaine and Fred D. Cheffield
1949 Experiments in Mass Communications. Princeton: The Princeton University Press.

Kitsuse, John I.
1962 "Social reactions to deviance: problems of theory and method." Social Problems 9 (Winter):247-256.

Lazarsfeld, Paul F. and Herbert Menzel
1961 "On the relations between individual and collective properties." Pp. 422-446 in Amatai Etzioni (ed.), Complex Organizations. New York: Holt, Rinehart, and Winston.

Lazarsfeld, Paul F. and Morris Rosenberg (eds.)
1955 The Language of Social Research. New York: The Free Press of Glencoe.

Lemert, Edwin M.
1951 Social Pathology. New York: McGraw-Hill Book Company, Inc.

Merton, Robert K.
1949 "Discrimination and the American creed." Pp. 99-126 in Robert M. MacIver (ed.), Discrimination and the National Welfare. New York: Harper.
1964 "Anomie, anomia, and social interaction." Pp. 213-242 in Marshall B. Clinard (ed.), Anomie and Deviant Behavior. New York: The Free Press of Glencoe.

Newcomb, Theodore M.
1962 "Student peer-group influence." Pp. 469-488 in Nevitt Sanford (ed.), The American College. New York: John Wiley and Sons.

Newcomb, Theodore M. and Everett K. Wilson (eds.)
1966 The Study of College Peer Groups. Chicago: The Aldine Publishing Company.

Tannenbaum, Arnold S. and Jerald G. Bachman
1964 "Structural vs. individual effects." American Journal of Sociology 69 (May): 585-595.

Turner, Ralph H.
1959 "An experiment in the modification of role conceptions." Year Book of the American Philosophical Society, 329-333.

NOTES

This work was facilitated by a Ford Foundation Fellowship for the study of deviant behavior. I am particularly indebted to Robert Merton for his comments on an earlier version of this paper. I also received helpful suggestions from Rose Coser, David Kamens, and Philip Sidel.

[1]Normative consensus is very often taken for granted in studies of deviant behavior. Thus, Clinard (1959) points out that criminological research has traditionally focused on legally proscribed forms of behavior without much regard for the extent of disapproval in society. The work of Becker (1963), Kitsuse (1962), and Lemert (1951) has drawn attention to the importance of peoples' reactions to behavior in defining it as deviant. It is important to recognize, however, that overt sanctioning behavior may not be forthcoming even though people strongly disapprove of an action. The failure to sanction may indicate that social control is inadequate or ineffective, not necessarily that the behavior in question is acceptable (cf. Gibbs, 1966; Clark and Gibbs, 1965).

[2]The objective here corresponds closely to Merton's (1964:409) call for an examination of the joint effects of anomia (a condition of the individual) and anomie (a condition of the collectivity) on deviant behavior. Unlike anomia and anomie, however, personal and contextual disapproval are "action specific."

[3]The data may tend to underrepresent rates of misconduct among college students. Thus, some who failed to return the questionnaire may have been reluctant to admit wrongdoing, and some who did return it may have underreported their misconduct. Information on non-respondents indicates that they differ only slightly in academic ability and attrition from those who did respond, and an analysis of response bias as it relates to self-reported cheating provides little indication that non-respondents are more apt to have cheated than those who returned the questionnaires. It should be noted, however, that the sampling procedure tended to overrepresent students from small schools which had the effect of slightly under-representing cheating rates for the college population as a whole (Bowers, 1964: Appendix D).

[4]Intensity variations within the "do not disapprove" category could conceivably account for some of the variation in rates of involvement from item to item. The "mildly disapprove" and particularly the "strongly disapprove" categories may tap a more restricted range of sentiments. We must await Table 5 and footnote 10 for further evidence on the possible effects of such intensity variations.

[5]The rates of misbehavior for each of the nine component items closely approximate the corresponding mean per cents.

[6]It should be noted that the effects of individual and contextual disapproval on deviant behavior as shown in Table 5 are slightly exaggerated owing to the failure to completely control for or match respondents on one independent variable when examining the effects of the other. Tannenbaum and Bachman (1964) point out that the individual variable and its contextual rate are, by definition, highly correlated in a given population. Therefore, imprecise measurement or grouping on one variable (viewed as a control) tends to produce a spurious effect on the other.

[7]"Over-cutting class" shows the greatest average deviation (6 per cent), most of it owing to the fact that those who do not disapprove fail to over-cut as much as the mean per cents would predict. As we suggested earlier, the risk of falling behind in school work may keep many of these students in class.

[8]In effect, the thirteen percentage point drop in misconduct between the first and second disapproval contexts shown in Figure 1 is due exclusively to the individual effects of disapproval. Differences in the proportion who strongly disapprove at this level appear to have no effect on the individual's behavior.

[9]While the effect is small in terms of percentage differences, it is quite substantial as a proportion of the maximum possible effect (cf. Hovland, et al., 1949: Appendix A; relevant portion reprinted in Lazarsfeld and Rosenberg, 1955:77-82).

[10]In discussing Table 3 (footnote 4), we raised the possibility of intensity variations from item to item in the "do not disapprove" response category. A couple of things in Figure 2 tend to discount this possibility, however. Foremost is the fact that there is no decline in misconduct from the first to the second disapproval context in this category (or the other two). The distribution of sentiments is shifting toward stronger disapproval. If intensity variations were present, there should be a corresponding shift within the "do not disapprove" category. Yet no such shift is evident in students' behavior. Also, there is the fact that the rate of misconduct for those who do not disapprove in the strongest disapproval context drops below the rate for those who mildly disapprove in weaker contexts. Intensity variations alone could not produce such an effect.

[11]The overall pattern approaches what James Davis, et al., (1961) have described as "differential susceptability," Type IV-A.

THE PREDICTION OF BEHAVIOR FROM ATTITUDINAL AND NORMATIVE VARIABLES[1]

Icek Ajzen
and
Martin Fishbein

This paper reports the results of an experiment designed to test the validity of a theoretical model of behavioral prediction recently presented by Fishbein (1967). The model can best be seen as an extension of Dulany's (1967) "theory of propositional control" to social behavior. Its use in the social area provides a test of the generality of the model which was developed initially in the framework of learning theory. While the original theory is almost identical to the present formulation, its constructs have been relabeled in an attempt to reveal their relations to more familiar social psychological concepts. In the process of translation some minor changes have occurred in the meaning of the constructs as well as in the ways in which they are measured. Nevertheless, all the predictions derived from the present model and tested in this experiment could have been derived just as well from the original formulation of the theory of propositional control. For a complete presentation of the relationships between Dulany's theory of propositional control and Fishbein's extension of it, cf. Fishbein (1967).

The immediate concern of the extended model, like that of the original formulation, is the prediction of behavioral intentions (BI) which are assumed to mediate overt behavior. According to the extended model, an individual's intention to perform a given act is a joint function of his attitude toward performing the act (A-act) and of his beliefs about what he is expected to do in that situation, i.e., his normative beliefs (NB). These normative beliefs are in turn multiplied by the individual's motivation to comply with the norms (Mc).

Reprinted from *Journal of Experimental Psychology* (Vol. 6, October, 1970, pp. 466-487) by permission of the authors and Academic Press, Inc.

The two major components of the model are weighted for their importance in the prediction of behavioral intentions, as can be seen in the following algebraic expression:[2]

$$B \sim BI = [A\text{-act}]w_0 + [NB(Mc)]w_1$$

where B=overt behavior; BI=behavioral intention; A-act=attitude toward performing a given behavior in a given situation; NB=normative beliefs; Mc = motivation to comply with the norms; w_0 and w_1 = empirically determined weights. The normative component of the model has not as yet been completely formalized. Most importantly, it refers to the individual's perception of the behaviors expected of him by relevant or significant others, called social normative beliefs (NBs). Of course, the potential reference groups or individuals whose expectations are perceived to be relevant, will vary with the behavioral situation. Thus, while in some instances the expectations of a person's friends or family may be most relevant, in others it may be the expectations of his supervisors or even the society at large which are most influential.

Elsewhere it was suggested (cf. Fishbein, 1967; Ajzen & Fishbein, 1969) that the normative component also included the individual's personal normative beliefs (NBp); i.e., his own beliefs as to what he should do in a given situation. It appears, however, that in many situations NBp may serve mainly as an alternative measure of behavioral intentions.[3] Since NBp is of no consequence for purposes of testing the hypotheses in the present study, it is not treated here as part of the theory and no further reference to it will be made. One other point needs to be mentioned regarding the motivation to comply (Mc). The measurement of this variable has repeatedly proved to be unsatisfactory (e.g., Ajzen & Fishbein, 1969). Research to date has indicated relatively little variance in this measure, and thus the results obtained with normative beliefs alone were as good or better than those obtained when NB was multiplied by Mc.[4]

Again, inclusion of the Mc measure is not crucial in the context of the present experiment. While Mc may still prove to be an important variable in some situations, it will not be considered in the present paper.

The inclusion of only social normative beliefs (NBs) and the deletion of the motivation to comply produces a somewhat simplified version of the theoretical model. This version can be expressed algebraically as follows:

$$B \sim BI = [A\text{-act}]w_0 + [NBs]w_1$$

The theory thus identifies three kinds of variables that function as the basic determinants of behavior: attitudes toward the performance of the behavior, normative beliefs, and the weights of these predictors. Any additional variable is held to influence BI only indirectly by influencing one or more of these determinants. Situational variables or personality characteristics will, therefore, influence a person's behavioral intentions (and thus his behavior) if, and only if, they are related to A-act, to NBs, or if they influence the relative weights that are placed on these predictors.

A-act, the attitude toward an act, deserves special attention. Consistent with the research of Peak (1955), Rosenberg (1956) and others, Fishbein (1963) has demonstrated that an individual's attitude toward any object can be predicted accurately from a knowledge of the person's beliefs about the object and the evaluative aspects of those beliefs. More specifically, attitude was found to be highly correlated with the sum of the beliefs, each multiplied by its respective evaluative aspect. When this formulation is applied to the attitude toward an act, rather than an object, the product involves beliefs about the consequences of performing the act (B_i) and the subjective evaluation (a_i) of these consequences: A-act $= \sum B_i a_i$. It can be seen that A-act is concerned with a particular behavior in a given, well-defined situation. It should not be confused with the attitude toward an object, or class of objects, which has been of interest in most previous work on attitudes.

As mentioned earlier, the model's immediate concern is the prediction of behavioral intentions. A high correlation is assumed to exist between BI and actual behavior. The effects of the attitude toward the act and of normative beliefs on overt behavior are held to be mediated by BI. The prediction of behavioral intentions is, therefore, according to the theory, a necessary as well as sufficient condition for the prediction of overt behavior. Such an intimate relationship between BI and B will, of course, not unconditionally hold. Among other things, the more general the behavioral intention and the longer the time interval between the statement of intention and the actual behavior, the lower will the BI-B correlation tend to be. In attempting to predict behavior it is therefore the experimenter's responsibility to insure that the conditions under which BI is measured will be maximally conducive to a high correlation between BI and B.

It is interesting to note that Fishbein's (1967) conceptualization of attitude toward an act corresponds quite closely to a number of formulations proposed by other theorists. For example, Rotter's (1954) social learning theory maintains that the probability of the occurrence of a given behavior in a particular situation is determined by two variables: the subjectively held probability (or expectance) that the behavior in question will be reinforced and the value of the reinforcer to the subject. Similarly, both Peak (1955) and Rosenberg (1956, 1965) view attitudes as a function of beliefs about the instrumentality of the object in obtaining goals and the value importance of those goals.

Also related to these notions is the SEU model of behavioral decision theory (cf. Edwards, 1954, 1961). Very briefly, this theory attempts to specify the subjective expected utilities (SEU) of a person's alternative actions. Different strategies for decision making may then be employed. The most generally useful strategy is one that leads to the choice of the alternative which maximizes expected gain or minimizes expected loss. The SEU of a given alternative is a function of the subjective probability that certain outcomes will follow that act (SP_i) multiplied by the respective subjective values (or utilities) attached to these outcomes (U_i). The products are summed over all possible outcomes of the act: SEU = $\Sigma SP_i U_i$. The SEU maximization model predicts that behavioral alternative to occur for which SEU is maximal. It can be seen that SEU is closely related to the definition of attitude toward an act (A-act=ΣB a).[5] The difference between behavioral decision theory and the extended version of the theory of propositional control relates primarily to the sufficiency of SEU (or A-act) for the prediction of behavior. A decision theory approach leads to the conclusion that SEU is the ultimate antecedent and best predictor of behavior. In contrast, SEU (or A-act) is only one of the determinants of behavioral intentions, and hence of behavior proposed by Fishbein: A-act and normative beliefs (NBs) as well as their weights are expected to enter into the prediction of behavior.

THE EXPERIMENTAL SITUATION

The situation selected for an evaluation of the present theory's usefulness was the two-person Prisoner's Dilemma (PD) game. In that game the players make repeated choices between two responses assumed to serve the motives of cooperation and competition. Following Rapoport and Chammah (1965) we may call the two alternative strategies "Cooperation" (C) and "Defection" (D). The combined choices of Player (P) and his Opponent (O) determine the payoff to each, as represented in Matrix 1 and subject to the following constraints (Scodel *et al.*, 1959):

(1) $2x_1 > x_2 + x_3 \quad 2x_4$

(2) $x_3 > x_1$

(3) $x_3 > x_2$

(4) $x_4 > x_2$

	C_2	D_2
C_1	x_1, x_1	x_2, x_3
D_1	x_3, x_2	x_4, x_4

Matrix 1

The first entry in each cell of the matrix is the payoff to the row player, the second entries are the payoffs to the column player.

Strategy D dominates Strategy C for both players and on the assumption that each subject plays rationally each is expected to defect. However, joint defection results in a payoff (x_4), which is smaller than the payoff (x_1) both players could secure by joint cooperation (Rapoport & Orwant, 1962). It appears, therefore, that in the PD game no unambiguous normative prescription of strategy choice is possible. The strategy that should be adopted from the standpoint of the individual player differs from joint strategy prescription (Rapoport & Chammah, 1965).

EXPERIMENTAL DESIGN AND HYPOTHESES

The main purpose of the experiment was to test several hypotheses derived from Fishbein's extension of Dulany's theory of propositional control in the context of the PD game and to demonstrate the model's usefulness in the prediction of game behavior.

Since, as we have seen above, the first component of the model (i.e., A-act) is similar to SEU, the decision theory model was also subjected to a similar empirical test.[6] In order to do this, measures had to be obtained of the subjective probabilities of each of the game's four possible outcomes and of their utilities. It should be noted, however, that the measurement procedures used in the present experiment do not meet the requirements of a formal mathematical model. Thus, while our measures may provide adequate assessments of Fishbein's $\sum B_i a_i$ or some of the other social psychological formulations, they can at best be taken only as approximations of subjective expected utilities. For the sake of convenience, we shall nevertheless continue to refer to these measures as SEU.

It will be recalled that according to the theory of propositional control, the effects of external variables on game behavior are mediated by the model's theoretical constructs. That is, any external variable influencing A-act, NBs, or their weights will also be related to behavioral intentions and thus to game behavior. To test this hypothesis, as well as some additional hypotheses derived from the model, it was necessary to study the effects of a number of external variables on the model's theoretical constructs (i.e., on A-act, NBs, and BI) and to show that the latter were in turn related to the behavioral choices of the players. The choice of external variables was based on the investigation of these variables in previous studies on the Prisoner's Dilemma.

First, the effects of the subject's sex and their *F*-scores on the model's predictors as well as on game behavior were to be tested. Previous investigations of these variables (e.g., Rapoport & Chammah, 1965; Bixenstine, Potash, & Wilson, 1963; Bixenstine & Wilson, 1963; Pilisuk, Skolnik, & Overstreet, 1968 on sex; Deutsch, 1960b; Wrightsman, 1966; Driver, 1965 on the *F*-score) failed to demonstrate consistent effects on game behavior. According to the present theory, these variables are expected to be predictive of game behavior only to the extent that they are related to A-act, to NBs, or to the weights of these variables in the prediction of BI.

More important, however, were the effects of the following two experimental manipulations as variables external to the model.

Motivational orientation of the players. The first experimental manipulation was an attempt to induce a certain motivational orientation in the players. By giving appropriate instructions in different experimental groups, Deutsch (1960a) succeeded in creating cooperative, competitive and individualistic motivational orientations in his subjects which were shown to be related to game behavior. The same experimental manipulation was applied in the present study. In the cooperative condition the group members were instructed to consider themselves to be partners. In the competitive condition they were told to do better than the other person. Players in the individualistic condition were told to have no interest whatsoever in the fate of their partner. However, in all three conditions the players were also instructed to try and win as many points as they could for themselves, thereby introducing an element of conflict even in the cooperative motivational orientation groups.

It is expected that cooperative responses (as indicated by A-act, NBs, BI, and B) are most frequent in the cooperative motivational orientation, less so in the individualistic orientation, and least frequent in the competitive orientation.

The "Cooperation Index" of the payoff matrix. Each pair of subjects played two Prisoner's Dilemma games with different payoff matrices. Rapoport and Chammah (1965) have shown that different payoff matrices tend to produce different amounts of cooperation. These investigators have developed certain indices of "cooperative advantage" which have been shown to be directly related to the proportion of cooperative choices in the games. The most generally useful index is the ratio $(x_1—x_4) / (x_3—x_2)$ which has a range of 0 to 1 (see Matrix 1). This ratio has been called the "Cooperation Index" (CI) by Terhune (1968).

The two payoff matrices used in the present study had Cooperation Indices of .900 (Game 1) and .083 (Game 2). Game 1 was identical to the PD game first used by Deutsch (1960a).

More cooperative responses (as evidenced in the measures of A-act, NBs, BI, and B) are predicted in Game 1 (CI=.90) than in Game 2 (CI= .083).

The remaining experimental hypotheses are directly related to the theoretical model and may be summarized as follows:

1. Game behavior is a function of behavioral intentions. Therefore, a high correlation is expected between BI and B.

2. Behavioral intentions are determined by A-act and by NBs. It is therefore predicted that a high multiple correlation will be found between these two predictors and BI.

The relative weights of A-act and NBs in predicting BI are expected to be contingent upon the motivational orientations of the players. The expectations of the other player (NBs) should be more important for the prediction of BI in the cooperative condition. The person's attitude toward the act, however, should carry more weight in the competitive condition. In the individualistic motivational orientation A-act and NBs should both carry some weight in the prediction of BI. These effects are expected to be particularly evident in the regression coefficients of A-act and NBs on behavioral intentions.

	C_2	D_2
C_1	+9, +9	−10, +10
D_1	+10, −10	−9, −9

Game 1

	C_2	D_2
C_1	+1, +1	−12, +12
D_1	+12, −12	−1, −1

Game 2

3. SEU is predicted to correlate with game behavior. That is, the subjective expected utility model is expected to be applicable to the prediction of behavior in PD games, under the various experimental conditions.

Since SEU is considered to be more or less equivalent to A-act, these two variables should be correlated.

4. As A-act (SEU) is only one of the predictors of behavioral intentions in Fishbein's model, it is hypothesized that the inclusion of NBs improves prediction of BI above the level obtained when using A-act (or SEU) alone, and BI is expected to be more highly related to game behavior than is SEU.

5. BI is the direct antecedent of overt behavior (B). This hypothesis has the following implications.

a. Holding BI constant should reduce to nonsignificance the partial correlations of overt behavior with A-act, with SEU, and with NBs.

b. In contrast, when SEU is held constant it is expected that a sizable correlation will remain between BI and B. This hypothesis follows from the theory where SEU is only one of the determinants of BI and of overt behavior.

c. The effects of the experimental manipulations and of the other external variables on game behavior should be substantially reduced when BI is treated as a covariate (i.e., "held constant") in an analysis of covariance. Similarly, the effects of these variables on BI should diminish considerably when A-act and NBs are treated as two simultaneous covariates in an analysis of covariance.

6. A traditional attitude approach would predict that cooperation in the PD game is related to the attitude toward the other player (Ao). However, according to the present model, Ao will affect behavior only if it is related to one or more of the model's predictors. Since the relation between Ao and A-act or NBs is not expected to be very strong, it is also predicted that Ao correlates only slightly, if at all, with overt behavior. Thus, Ao is treated like any other external variable; its effect on BI and on B is expected to be mediated by A-act and NBs.

To summarize briefly then, the main purpose of the present experiment was to test the validity of Fishbein's extension of Dulany's theory of propositional control in a PD-type game situation. More specifically, it is hypothesized that an individual's performance of cooperative (or defective) behavior in the PD situation is a function of his intention to cooperate (BI) which is itself a function of (1) his attitude toward cooperating in the particular PD situation (A-act) and (2) his beliefs about what the other player expects him to do (NBs). Further, it is predicted that the individual's A-act is a part function of his beliefs about consequences of cooperating (SP_i) and his evaluations of these consequences (U_i).[7] In addition, it is hypothesized that any other variable (e.g., motivational orientation, Cooperation Index, sex, authoritarianism, or attitude toward the other player) can only influence BI (and thus behavior) indirectly, by influencing A-act, NBs, or the relative weight placed upon these two predictors.

METHOD

Subjects

The sample consisted of 96 undergraduate students at the University of Illinois, 48 males and 48 females. The players in a given game were always of the same sex. They were assigned at random to the experimental conditions; two groups were run simultaneously, but independent of each other.

Sixteen groups, eight male and eight female, were assigned to each of the three motivational conditions. Each group played both PD games; the order in which the games were played was counterbalanced within each motivational condition.

Procedure

The two players in the game were seated at opposite sides of a table, separated by a partition. They were not allowed to communicate in any manner. At the outset of the experiment they were given standard instructions describing the game and inducing one of the motivational orientations, cooperation, individualism, or competition. The instructions concerning the game were taken in large part from Rapoport and Chammah (1965, Appendix I). The motivational orientations were worded after Deutsch (1960a). The instructions were read from a recorded tape while the subjects followed them on a printed outline.

Each player had the payoff matrix for the given game in front of him as well as a "record sheet" on which he recorded his choice on each play of the game (i.e., cooperation or defection). After each trial the experimenter exposed a card to each player indicating his payoff, that is, the number of points he had gained or lost on that trial. In the cooperative and in the competitive conditions the subjects were also shown the payoffs to the other player, while in the individualistic condition they were shown only their own payoffs since here they were told to have no interest whatsoever in the fate of the other player. The payoffs were also recorded on the record sheets.

After receiving the instructions, the groups played their first game (either Game 1 or Game 2) for eight moves after which they were asked to fill out a questionnaire to be described below. They then played the game for 10 more moves. Between the first and the second game the subjects completed a 20-item *F* scale. The second game was then played for eight moves after which a questionnaire pertaining to this game was completed. Ten additional moves in the second game brought the experimental session to a close.

The last 10 moves in each game were taken as a measure of game behavior.

The Questionnaires

Cooperation and defection were called X and Y, respectively. The questionnaire items provided measures for the following experimental variables.

1. A-act, the attitude toward cooperation. A direct measure of attitude toward the act was based on the sum over four semantic differential scales with high loadings on the evaluative factor (cf. Osgood, Suci, & Tannenbaum, 1957), presented as follows:

Choosing alternative X is

foolish—:—:—:—:—:—:—wise
good—:—:—:—:—:—:—bad
harmful—:—:—:—:—:—:—beneficial
rewarding—:—:—:—:—:—:—punishing

2. Subjective conditional probabilities, measured as follows: If I were to choose mainly X, my partner would choose_____% X and _____% Y.

3. Utilities of the payoffs. Each of the two possible outcomes of cooperation was followed by an evaluative semantic differential scale:
Example:

Obtaining the payoff (+9, +9) is
good—:—:—:—:—:—:—bad

4. SEU, the subjective expected utility of cooperation, was computed by multiplying the corresponding subjective probabilities and utilities and adding the two products: $SEU = \Sigma SP_i U_i$.

5. NBs, social normative beliefs. The perceived expectations of the other player were considered to be the relevant normative beliefs in the experimental situation, and a measure was taken of these normative beliefs as follows.[8]

My partner expects me to choose_____% X, and_____% Y.

6. BI, the behavioral intention, was measured as follows.

What are your intentions for this game?

I intend to chose_____% X, and_____% Y.

7. Ao, the attitude toward the other player, was measured by summing the five following evaluative semantic differential scales.

My partner is

wise—:—:—:—:—:—:—foolish
bad—:—:—:—:—:—:—good
sick—:—:—:—:—:—:—healthy
clean—:—:—:—:—:—:—dirty
harmful—:—:—:—:—:—:—beneficial

The questionnaires administered in the two PD games were identical except for the outcomes of cooperation (i.e., the payoffs) that were evaluated.

RESULTS

First, the possibility was examined that the introduction of questionnaires after the eighth move in each game has had a recognizable influence on behavior. The mean proportion of cooperative choices on moves 6 through 8 was compared with the mean on moves 9 through 11. In game 1 the two means were .531 and .542, respectively. In Game 2 the means were .375 and .399. Two-tailed t tests of the differences between these means were not significant (t_{47} = –.131 in Game 1 and –.289 in Game 2).

Effects of the Experimental Manipulations

Four-way analyses of variance were performed to examine the effects of the independent variables on the attitude toward the act (A-act), normative beliefs regarding the other player (NBs), subjective expected utilities (SEU), behavioral intentions (BI), and cooperative strategy choices on the last 10 moves (B). The four main effects in the analyses were: motivational orientations, Cooperation Index (treated as a repeated measure since the same subjects played both games), the order in which the two games were played, and the sex of the players.[9]

Neither the game order nor the players' sex produced significant differences in the questionnaire responses or in overt behavior. The other two main effects, motivational orientation and Cooperation Index, were significant far beyond the .01 level, with mean differences in the hypothesized directions. As can be seen in Table 1, the cooperative motivational orientation produced the highest degree of cooperative responses while the competitive orientation produced least C responses. The degree of cooperation was intermediate in the individualistic condition. Also as expected, there were fewer cooperative responses in Game 2 than in Game 1. These effects could be observed in all dependent variables included in the analysis. (In Table 1 NBs, BI, and B are given in terms of percentages of cooperative choices).

TABLE 1

MEAN QUESTIONNAIRE RESPONSES AND GAME BEHAVIOR

	Game 1 Motivational orientation			Game 2 Motivational orientation		
	Cooperation	Individualism	Competition	Cooperation	Individualism	Competition
A-act	21.84	16.84	13.69	22.16	11.72	9.91
SEU	5.97	4.10	2.51	5.08	2.81	1.89
NBs	83.97	51.19	39.88	73.22	37.56	24.66
BI	88.75	46.53	30.22	75.59	25.72	14.50
B	86.25	47.19	15.63	79.38	20.63	10.94

The main effects of motivational orientation and Cooperation Index (Game No.) are significant ($p<01$) in all analyses. Interaction effects are significant (p .01) only for A-act and B.

The interaction between motivational orientation and CI was significant ($p<.01$) for A-act and B but not for the other dependent variables.

The one remaining independent variable, the subjects' *F* score, did not correlate significantly with any of the dependent variables (i.e., with A-act, SEU, NBs, BI, or B).

To summarize, the experimental manipulations were highly successful. Both the motivational orientations and the CI of the games strongly influenced questionnaire responses and game behavior in the expected directions. The sex and the *F* scores of the players were not significantly related to any of the dependent variables. Finally, the order in which the two games were played did not affect questionnaire responses or game behavior significantly.

The importance of these findings for the validity of the theoretical model is obvious. The effects of five different variables external to the model were tested. Whenever one of these variables was significantly related to the model's predictors (A-act and NBs) it also showed a significant relation with behavioral intentions and actual game behavior. Sex, authoritarianism, and game order were unrelated to either A-act or NBs and, as expected, none of these variables influenced either BI or B.

In contrast to the significant effects of the experimental manipulations on the variables in the proposed model, Ao, the attitude toward the other player, was not affected significantly by any of the independent variables; no significant main effects or interactions were found for Ao.

Prediction of Game Behavior

Turning to the prediction of game behavior, Fishbein's extension of Dulany's model was found to be highly successful. As can be seen in Table 2, behavioral intentions were highly predictive of overt behavior in both games.

TABLE 2

CORRELATIONS OF PROPORTION OF COOPERATIVE CHOICES ON THE LAST 10 MOVES (B) WITH BI, SEU, A-ACT, AND NBs ($N = 96$)[1]

	Game 1	Game 2
BI–B	.847	.841
SEU–B	.704	.748
A-act–B	.631	.703
NBs–B	.683	.721

[1]All correlations are significant ($p < .01$).

Table 2 also shows that, as expected, subjective expected utilities predicted game behavior with high accuracy. It should be noted, however, that in support of our hypothesis behavioral intentions were more closely related to game behavior than was SEU; the differences in the correlations are significant beyond the .01 level. In Table 2 it can also be seen that the correlations of A-act and NBs with game behavior are high and significant.

Also consistent with Fishbein's (1963) theory were the significant ($p < .01$) correlations found between SEU and A-act in both games (.632 in Game 1 and .672 in Game 2). Furthermore, A-act and SEU tended to stand in similar relations to the other variables in the study. Therefore, only A-act was used as the measure of the attitudinal component in the remaining analyses; similar results can be obtained by substituting SEU for A-act.

The prediction of behavioral intentions from A-act and NBs is presented in Table 3. Here the product-moment correlation coefficients of

BI with A-act and with NBs are given as well as the standardized regression coefficients of the two predictors and their multiple correlation on BI. It can be seen that the experimental hypotheses were fully supported. First, the multiple correlations between the two predictors and behavioral intentions were high and significant in both PD games and in all three motivational conditions as well as over the total sample. Second, the inclusion of NBs greatly improved prediction of BI above the level obtained when only A-act was used. This is particularly obvious in the cooperative conditions of both games. However, as can be seen in Table 3, the regression coefficients of NBs on BI were significant under all conditions, providing evidence for the independent contribution of NBs to the prediction of BI. Third, as can best be seen in the regression coefficients, the relative importance of A-act and NBs in predicting BI varied as expected. A-act carried more weight than NBs in the competitive condition but less weight than NBs in the cooperative condition. As predicted, P's beliefs about the expectations of the other player (NBs) were clearly more important than was his own attitude in determining BI under a cooperative motivational orientation. However, when the orientation was competitive, the relative importance of A-act and NBs was reversed with A-act now being the more important determinant of BI.

TABLE 3

CORRELATIONS, REGRESSION COEFFICIENTS, AND MULTIPLE CORRELATIONS OF A-ACT AND NBs ON BI

	Correlation coefficients		Regression coefficients		Multiple correlations
	A-act–BI	NBs–BI	A-act–BI	NBs–BI	
Game 1					
Cooperation (N=32)	.370*	.752**	.229	.707**	.785**
Individualism (N=32)	.710**	.780**	.353*	.552**	.852**
Competition (N=32)	.883**	.733**	.691**	.327**	.922**
Total (N=96)	.754**	.838**	.378**	.601**	.888**
Game 2					
Cooperation (N=32)	.253	.579**	.239	.573**	.626**
Individualism (N=32)	.673**	.677**	.416**	.427**	.754**
Competition (N=32)	.866**	.741**	.669**	.298**	.894**
Total (N=96)	.735**	.786**	.405**	.539**	.849**

*$p<.05$.
**$p<.01$.

The same pattern of results was observed when overt behavior (B) rather than BI was used as the criterion variable. However, as would be expected on the basis of the model, the correlations with game behavior are somewhat lower than those with BI (Table 4).

Of interest also are the correlations between the model's two predictors presented in Table 5. It can be seen that these correlations were significant in the individualistic and competitive conditions as well as for the total sample of subjects. In the cooperative condition, the correlations between A-act and NBs were not significant in either of the two games.

TABLE 4

CORRELATIONS, REGRESSION COEFFICIENTS, AND MULTIPLE CORRELATIONS OF A-ACT AND NBs ON B

	Correlation coefficients		Regression coefficients		Multiple correla-tions
	A-act–B	NBs–B	A-act–B	NBs–B	
Game 1					
Cooperation (N=32)	.310	.482**	.223	.438**	.529**
Individualism (N=32)	.465**	.477**	.270	.302	.519**
Competition (N=32)	.773**	.576**	.664**	.186	.788**
Total (N=96)	.631**	.685**	.331**	.478**	.732**
Game 2					
Cooperation (N=32)	.272	.421*	.262	.415*	.496*
Individualism (N=32)	.506**	.546**	.278	.379*	.590**
Competition (N=32)	.734**	.655**	.535**	.300	.768**
Total (N=96)	.703**	.721**	.419**	.464**	.793**

*p<05.
**p<01.

It should be noted that Dulany's (1967) theory of propositional control would lead us to expect at least some correlation between these two predictors since they are conceived to be partly determined by the same factor.[10]

TABLE 5

CORRELATIONS BETWEEN A-ACT AND NBs

	Game 1	Game 2
Cooperation (N-32)	.199	.024
Individualism (N=32)	.647*	.601*
Competition (N=32)	.587*	.662*
Total (N=96)	.627*	.614*

*p<01.

SEU VERSUS BI AS ANTECEDENTS OF BEHAVIOR

The comparison of SEU and BI as variables antecedent to game behavior provided substantial support for the hypothesis. As can be seen in Table 6, when BI was held constant the correlations of A-act, NBs, and SEU with overt behavior were substantially reduced, as compared with the correlations presented in Table 2. Indeed, all but one of the six partial correlations were nonsignificant. In contrast, when SEU was held constant all partial correlations remained significant beyond the .01 level.

TABLE 6

PARTIAL CORRELATIONS BETWEEN GAME BEHAVIOR AND A-ACT, NBs, BI, AND SEU (N=96)[1]

	BI held constant		SEU held constant	
	Game 1	Game 2	Game 1	Game 2
A-act–B	–.023	.233	.337	.408
NBs–B	–.083	.178	.368	.425
BI–B	—	—	.677	.596
SEU–B	.185	.175	—	—

$r_{.05} = .202, r_{.01} = .262.$

More importantly, holding BI constant reduced to nonsignificance the correlations of SEU with overt behavior. But holding SEU constant left the correlations of BI with behavior high and signficiant. This finding indicates that BI, rather than SEU, is the variable that mediates between overt behavior and various antecedents. SEU may best be regarded as equivalent to A-act.

The intervening character of BI was at least partly supported in an analysis of covariance performed on the data.[11] Treating BI as the covariate eliminated the effect of the Cooperation Index on game behavior, and greatly reduced the influence of motivational orientation, although the main effect of motivational orientation and the interaction remained significant at the .05 level. The differences between the cell means were considerably reduced after adjustment for regression of BI on B, as can be seen by comparing the adjusted cell means in Table 7 with the corresponding unadjusted means of game behavior presented in Table 1.[12]

To summarize, BI was found to mediate the effects of other variables on game behavior. When BI was statistically controlled, the correlations of A-act and of NBs with behavior were practically eliminated. Similarly, the effects of motivation and of CI on game behavior were substantially reduced by holding BI constant.

An additional analysis of covariance was performed to test the extent to which A-act and NBs mediated the effects of the experimental manipulations on behavioral intentions. When A-act and NBs were treated as simultaneous covariates, the main effects of motivational orientation and Cooperation Index were greatly attenuated. In fact, the effect of CI did not reach statistical significance nor was the interaction between the two factors significant. The effect of motivational orientation, although also strongly attenuated, remained significant ($F_{2,45} = 4.80$; $p < .05$).

Overall, then, there was a strong tendency for the model's variables to mediate the effects of external factors on game behavior although in a few cases some influence remained even after the appropriate theoretical constructs were statistically controlled.

Finally, as expected, the correlations between the attitude toward the other player (Ao) and game behavior were low. In game 1 Ao correlated .256 with the proportion of cooperative choices on the last 10 trials ($p < .05$). In Game 2 the correlation between Ao and B was .091 (not significant).

In the light of the theoretical model employed these results are not surprising although they are contrary to widely held attitudinal theories. It will be recalled that Ao, like any other external variable, was expected to influence behavior only through its effects on the model's predictors. The correlations between Ao and A-act were .354 ($p < .01$) in Game 1 and .239 ($p < .05$) in Game 2. Ao correlated with NBs .262 ($p < .05$) and .015 (not significant) in the two games, respectively. Since these correlations were relatively low, the correlation of Ao with game behavior was also negligible.

TABLE 7

MEANS OF GAME BEHAVIOR ADJUSTED FOR REGRESSION OF BI ON B[1]

	Game 1	Game 2
Cooperation	53.36	53.37
Individualism	50.86	35.12
Competition	32.14	35.63

[1]Only the main effect of motivation and the Motivation × Game interaction are significant ($p < .05$).

SUMMARY AND CONCLUSION

The present results provide clear support for a variety of hypotheses derived from Fishbein's extension of Dulany's theory of propositional control. The cooperative behavior of players in two different Prisoner's Dilemma games were accurately predicted from expressed behavioral intentions (BI). These behavioral intentions were found to mediate the effects of various other variables on game behavior. BI was found to be a function of both the attitude toward the act of cooperation (A-act) and of the perceived expectations of the other player (NBs). A high multiple correlation was obtained when A-act and NBs were used to predict BI. Also as expected A-act carried more weight than NBs in the multiple regression on BI as well as on game behavior under a competitive motivational orientation; the relative importance of A-act and NBs was reversed under a cooperative motivational orientation. A-act was shown to be roughly equivalent to the subjective expected utility (SEU) of co-operation, and a significant correlation between A-act and SEU was obtained. SEU also correlated highly with game behavior but, consistent with the theory, BI proved to be a better predictor than SEU. The effects of two experimental manipulations, the motivational orientation of the players, and the Cooperation Index of the game, were shown to be reflected not only in game behavior but in a similar manner also in the related questionnaire measures of the model's theoretical constructs. In contrast, the attitude toward the other player (Ao) was unaffected by these manipulations. This traditional attitude measure also failed to predict game behavior to any appreciable degree, just as it was relatively unrelated to any of the variables in the model.

In order to appreciate the importance of these findings it is necessary to understand some of the implications of the present theory. The model provides an explanation for, and an alternative to, the unsuccessful attempts in the past to base prediction on behavior vis-a-vis an object on the attitude toward that object (cf. Fishbein, 1967). According to the theory, Ao is often found to be unrelated to behavior because it fails to affect the predictors of behavior, A-act and NBs. The alternative, of course, is to measure A-act and NBs rather than Ao.

For the area of communication and persuasion this implies that the demonstration of attitude change as the result of a persuasive message is insufficient. Behavioral change is expected to be produced by changing BI, and this in turn depends on our ability to affect A-act, NBs, or their relative weights.

It is interesting to note that the present theory can also provide a bridge between the social psychological subareas of attitude and group dynamics which have traditionally taken separate paths. A-act, of course, is closely related to attitude theory while social norms are an important variable in group dynamics. The present theory describes the interaction of these two variables in determining behavior.

While the importance of the present findings can hardly be refuted, the question may be raised as to the extent to which the obtained results could be due to demand characteristics of the situation (Orne, 1962), or to method variance. The argument of demand characteristics might be raised in particular with regard to the self reports of A-act, NBs, and BI. Under close investigation, however, this objection cannot be sustained. Although high intercorrelations among the different experimental variables might be accounted for by demand characteristics, the predicted and obtained complex pattern of interrelations must go beyond the insights into the experimental hypotheses that a subject can attain in the course of a 50-min experimental session. Thus, game behavior was found to be unrelated to the attitude toward the other player (Ao) while it was strongly related to A-act, NBs, and BI. It appears reasonable that under the operation of demand characteristics the hypothesis would be formed that a positive attitude toward the other player should be accompanied by cooperation with him. After all, similar hypotheses have frequently been suggested by more sophisticated social psychologists.

But more importantly, it appears completely implausible that the subjects were able to produce the predicted variations in the relative weights of A-act and NBs purely as the result of demand characteristics. In fact, a thorough understanding of the theoretical model is required in order to arrive at the correct hypotheses, and even this does not immediately suggest the exact questionnaire responses that have to be given in order to produce the desired results.

Thus, to propose the operation of demand characteristics as an alternative explanation of the obtained results appears unconvincing in the light of the intricate patterns of interrelations that were predicted and obtained in the present experiment.

It can, perhaps, be argued that some of the relations between the variables in the present study may be due to differential method variance. That is, social normative beliefs (NBs), behavioral intentions (BI), and game behavior (B) were all measured in a similar manner (i.e., as percentages) while the attitude toward cooperation (A-act) was measured on 7-point semantic differential scales. Thus, the interrelations of the first three variables (NBs, BI, and BI) should be higher than their correlations with A-act.

But as the reader can verify for himself, this was not the case. Indeed, in the competitive motivational orientation A-act was more highly related to BI and to B than was NBs (see Tables 3 and 4).

Thus, differential method variance is also inadequate as an alternative explanation of the observed pattern of intercorrelations.

An issue of greater concern to the model is related to the expected correspondence between behavioral intentions and overt behavior. As stated in the description of the theory, a one-to-one relationship is expected if, and only if, BI is very specific to B and measured immediately preceding the performance of B. Requiring BI to be measured as close in time as possible to the performance of B is designed to insure that BI has not changed since it was measured; i.e., that no changes have occurred in either A-act or NBs, or in the weights of these predictors. For instance, in a social situation involving interaction between two or more persons A-act and NBs may change in the process of interaction itself. Thus, the behavioral intention measured at the beginning of interaction may differ greatly from that existing toward its end.

There is evidence in the present study, as well as in previous studies on the Prisoner's Dilemma (Rapoport and Chammah, 1965), that P's behavior changes with that of O. In particular, it appears that if one defects the other has but little choice and defects too. Correlations between the game behaviors of the two players are usually found to be high. In the present experiment these correlations were .919 in Game 1 and .885 in Game 2.[13]

The question may, therefore, be raised as to how it is at all possible to obtain high correlations between BI and game behavior if the latter changes in the process of interaction while the former is measured before the interaction takes place. The answer must be that, after eight moves of the game, P has formed relatively accurate hypotheses about 0's future behavioral choices and these hypotheses are reflected in A-act, NBs, and thus in BI. Were the players now to change their game behavior drastically, the BI–B correlation would necessarily deteriorate.

It appears, therefore, that it may sometimes be insufficient to measure BI shortly before observing B in order to insure a high correlation between these two variables. Only if the situation under consideration allows P to form reasonably accurate expectations of his behavior's consequences (which may in part depend upon the behavior of another person) and of the social norms governing behavior in that situation will P be able to state a behavioral intention which will accurately predict his actual behavior. The eight preparatory moves in each game of the present experiment seem to have provided the opportunity for the development of an accurate perception of the situation.

Finally, a few additional words of caution are necessary. It was pointed out before that BI may not be the only variable influencing behavior. In footnote 12 "habit" was mentioned as a possible additional variable operating independently of BI.

Similarly, it may be proposed that a variable such as "feasibility" may also be necessary. That is, although the theory views BI as the immediate antecedent of behavior, it must be made clear that an intention is only an intention, and in many cases, it may not be possible for an individual to carry through his intentions because of various kinds of situational or interpersonal constraints. While problems of this kind can be avoided in the laboratory, it may be necessary to consider them in field situations. It is for this reason that earlier in the paper we made the statement that "it is the experimenter's responsibility to insure that the conditions under which BI is measured will be maximally conducive to a high correlation between BI and B."

Finally, just as there may be some restrictions vis-a-vis the BI–B relationship, a few additional words concerning the prediction of BI are also necessary. It has already been mentioned that there is still some question about the nature of the model's normative component. In particular, it may be necessary to consider personal normative beliefs in addition to social normative beliefs. Further, if social normative beliefs are considered, it is not clear whether the referent for the norm should be a "generalized other" (i.e., most people who are important to me expect me to . . .) or a specific other (i.e., my partner expects me to . . .) or a set of specific others (i.e., my family, my three closest friends, etc.). In addition, the relationship between an individual's belief that a "generalized other" expects him to behave in a given way and his beliefs that different specific others expect him to behave in given ways still has to be investigated and identified.

While a complete discussion of the many unresolved theoretical and methodological problems associated with the model and its applications is beyond the scope of the present paper, it should be clear that the present model, like most explanatory attempts, raises at least as many questions as it appears to answer. Our one hope is that these questions are interesting and relevant enough to stimulate additional research.

REFERENCES

Ajzen, I. Prediction and change of behavior in the Prisoner's Dilemma. Unpublished doctoral dissertation. University of Illinois, Urbana, 1969.

Ajzen, I., & Fishbein, M. The prediction of behavioral intentions in a choice situation. *Journal of Experimental Social Psychology,* 1969, 5, 400-416.

Bixenstine, V. E., Potash, H. M., & Wilson, K. V. Effects of level of cooperative choice by the other player on choice in a Prisoner's Dilemma game: Part I, *Journal of Abnormal and Social Psychology,* 1963, 66, 308-313.

Bixenstine, V. E., & Wilson, K. V. Effects of level of cooperative choice by the other player on choices in a Prisoner's Dilemma game: Part II, *Journal of Abnormal and Social Psychology,* 1963, 67, 139-147.

Deutsch, M. The effect of motivational orientation upon threat and suspicion. *Human Relations,* 1960a, 13, 123-139.

Deutsch, M. Trust, trustworthiness, and the F scale. *Journal of Abnormal and Social Psychology,* 1960b, 61, 138-140.

Driver, M. J. A structural analysis of aggression, stress, and personality in an internation simulation. Paper No. 97, Institute for Research in the Behavioral, Economic, and Management Sciences, Purdue University, January, 1965.

Dulany, D. E. Awareness, rules, and propositional control: A confrontation with S-R behavior theory. In D. Horton and T. Dixon (Eds.), *Verbal behavior and S-R behavior theory.* Englewood Cliffs, New Jersey, Prentice-Hall, 1967.

Edwards, W. The theory of decision making. *Psychological Bulletin,* 1954, 51, 380-418.

Edwards, W. Behavioral decision theory. *Annual Review of Psychology,* 1961, 12, 473-498.

Fishbein, M. An investigation of the relationships between beliefs about an object and the attitude toward that object. *Human Relations,* 1963, 16, 233-240.

Fishbein, M. Attitude and prediction of behavior. In M. Fishbein (Ed.), *Readings in attitude theory and measurement.* New York: Wiley, 1967.

Orne, M. T. On the social psychology of the psychological experiment: with particular reference to demand characteristics and their implications. *American Psychologist,* 1962, 17, 776-783.

Osgood, C. E., Suci, G. J., & Tannenbaum, P. H. *The measurement of meaning.* Urbana: University of Illinois Press, 1957.

Peak, H. Attitude and motivation. In M. Jones (Ed.), *Nebraska symposium on motivation.* Lincoln: University of Nebraska Press, 1955.

Pilisuk, M., Skolnik, P., & Overstreet, E. Predicting cooperation from the two sexes in a conflict simulation. *Journal of Personality and Social Psychology,* 1968, 10, 35-43.

Rapoport, A., & Orwant, C. Experimental games: A review. *Behavioral Science,* 1962, 7, 1-37.

Rapoport, A., & Chammah, A. M. Prisoner's Dilemma: *A study on conflict and cooperation.* Ann Arbor: University of Michigan Press, 1965.

Rosenberg, M. J. Cognitive structure and attitudinal affect. *Journal of Abnormal and Social Psychology,* 1956, 53, 367-372.

Rosenberg, M. J. Inconsistency arousal and reduction in attitude change. In I. D. Steiner and M. Fishbein (Eds.), *Current Studies in Social Psychology.* New York: Holt, Rinehart, & Winston, 1965.

Rotter, J. B. *Social learning and clinical psychology.* Englewood Cliffs, New Jersey: Prentice-Hall, 1954.

Scodel, A., Minas, J. S., Ratoosh, P., & Lipetz, M. Some descriptive aspects of two-person, non-zero-sum games I. *Journal of Conflict Resolution,* 1959, 3, 114-119.

Terhune, K. W. Motives, situation, and interpersonal conflict within Prisoner's Dilemma. *Journal of Personality and Social Psychology,* 1968, 8, Monograph supplement.

Wrightsman, L. S. Personality and attitudinal correlates of trusting and trustworthy behavior in a two-person game. *Journal of Personality and Social Psychology,* 1966, 4, 328-332.

NOTES

[1] The authors are indebted to Don E. Dulany for his critical comments on an early draft of this paper.

[2] Ideally, the weights of the attitudinal and normative components should be established separately for each individual subject. However, in the absence of adequate methods for obtaining weights, they are obtained by a multiple-regression analysis, where A-act and NB(Mc) are used as the predictors, and BI is the criterion.

[3] In fact, a measure of NBp was also taken in the present study and the statistical analyses revealed that it was essentially equivalent to BI.

[4] In a more recent study, Ajzen (1969) demonstrated that more adequate measures of the motivation to comply can be obtained.

[5] There are, however, some important differences between the two formulations which cannot be dealt with here in detail. For instance, beliefs about the probability of outcomes for A-act are measured on bipolar semantic differential scales ranging from –3 to +3 while SP in the SEU model ranges from 0–1. These measures may produce different results after multiplication with the outcome's utilities.

[6] Indeed, the authors were surprised that they were unable to find previous attempts to base prediction of game behavior in the PD on the SEU model.

[7] In the present study, SEU is based only on a consideration of subjective probabilities and evaluations of outcomes as presented in the payoff matrix. Of course, the attitude toward cooperation is also influenced by perceived consequences of cooperation other than these payoffs. A measure of A-act will, therefore, tend to be more general than the measure of SEU, and the correlation between A-act and SEU will not be perfect.

[8] A measure was also taken of the perceived expectations of the experimenter (NB_E). Since the results obtained were similar to those using NBs and since NB_E was of less importance in the context of the present experiment, only NBs was used as a measure of social normative beliefs.

[9] Since the responses of the two players in the game tend to lack independence, the means over the two players were used as dependent variables in the present analyses.

[10] In Dulany's theory, the "cardinal rule" RHd (hypothesis of the distribution of reinforcement) enters twice into the equation for predicting behavioral intentions. RHd first multiplies RSv (the subjective value of a reinforcer); this product is A-act in the present formulation of the theory. RHd again appears in the equation as a multiplier of RHs (a hypothesis of the significance of a reinforcer) to produce BH—the behavioral hypothesis—in the present model NBs.

[11] The authors thank H. W. Norton for his assistance in the performance of the analyses of covariance.

[12] One possible explanation of the residual significant effects of the experimental manipulations may be suggested. According to Dulany's (1967) theory of propositional control, overt behavior is influenced not only by BI but also by habit (H). A voluntary response is expected to "habituate, to become automatic and involuntary, as some function of number of voluntary executions of that response" (p. 352), and, to some extent, to influence behavior independently of BI. The effects of the experimental manipulations might have been reduced to nonsignificance had it been possible to hold H constant in addition to controlling for BI.

[13] These high correlations were the reason for using group means as dependent variables in the analyses of variables reported above.

V

ATTITUDE CHANGE AND BEHAVIOR CHANGE: A SPECIAL CASE OF THE PROBLEM

14

EFFECTS OF FEAR AND INSTRUCTIONS ON HOW TO COPE WITH DANGER[1]

Howard Leventhal, Jean C. Watts
and
Francia Pagano

Four problems were investigated in the present study: (*a*) the relationship between fear arousal and acceptance of communications depicting a danger and recommending that subjects change their behavior so as to protect themselves from danger, (*b*) the relationship between verbal measures of acceptance taken immediately after the communications and behavior measures taken at later points in time, (*c*) the effects on acceptance of providing instructions on how to carry out the recommended change in behavior, and (*d*) the effects on acceptance of requiring subjects to perform the forbidden behavior while its dangerous consequences were being depicted in the communications.

Our approach to the first two problems was straightforward. Recommendations to stop smoking were presented along with fear-arousing communications on the danger of lung cancer from smoking, and subsequent changes in desire to stop smoking and in actual smoking behavior were examined. Previous studies have reported both positive and negative effects of highly fear-arousing antismoking communications on compliance with recommendations to stop smoking. Janis and Terwilliger (1962) found that a high-fear appeal produced slightly less attitude change against smoking than did a moderate appeal, and Leventhal and Niles (1964) reported that a mild control communication was more successful in strengthening intentions to stop smoking than either a moderate- or a high-fear appeal. However, a high-fear communication used by Niles (1964) was found to increase intentions to stop smoking among subjects who rated themselves as "highly vulnerable" to various

Reprinted from *Journal of Personality and Social Psychology* (Vol. 6, June, 1967, pp. 313-321).

health and safety hazards; among subjects rated as "low vulnerables," the high-fear appeal increased rather than decreased intentions to stop smoking. Complicating the picture still further is a study by Leventhal and Watts (1966) in which fear communications similar to those used by Leventhal and Niles (1964) failed to produce differences in intentions to decrease smoking, but had long-range effects on smoking behavior. In this study, subjects exposed to the high-fear communication were apparently more successful in decreasing smoking than were subjects exposed to the moderate- or low-fear appeal. It is possible that high-fear appeals create immediate resistance to compliance with protective recommendations but that in time this effect is reversed. But more data are needed to decide the point, since only in Leventhal and Watts (1966) were changes in smoking behavior measured, and in this study the measures were taken at only one point in time, 5 months after the communications were given.

The third and fourth problems require elaboration. It has been proposed (Leventhal, 1965) that the inconsistent effects of fear arousal on compliance with protective recommendations may be due to differences in the judged effectiveness of actions recommended to avert the alleged danger. An unintended effect of some high-fear communications may be to make subjects feel less able to act to avert the danger, and to arouse a greater need for reassurance that protective action is feasible and for instructions on how to carry out this action.

This possibility has been investigated in studies by Leventhal, Singer, and Jones (1965) and Leventhal, Jones, and Trembly (1966) in which fear-arousing communications on the danger of tetanus either included or withheld instructions on how to get a tetanus inoculation. All subjects (college students) were given the general recommendation to take a tetanus inoculation, but half of the subjects also received a map of the campus with the location of the student health service prominently marked and a brief review of typical daily activities which brought the student physically close to the health service. The instructions did not provide new information (students were already familiar with the location of the health service), but simply amounted to a plan for incorporating a visit to the health service into everyday activities much as one might plan to stop off at the bank or store on the way to work. In both studies it was found that a larger percentage of subjects who had received instructions took inoculations compared to those who did not receive instructions or received only the instructions without a preceding high- or low-fear appeal. However, the expectation that the instructions would be especially effective when subjects were exposed to a high-fear appeal was not confirmed; the percentage of high-fear subjects who took inoculations was equivalent to that of low-fear subjects, whether or not subjects received instructions.

For the present study a pamphlet giving specific instructions on how to stop smoking was prepared. It was expected that subjects who received these instructions would be more successful in decreasing smoking than subjects who did not receive these instructions, and that the instructions would be especially effective when subjects were exposed to a high-fear appeal. It was reasoned that if strong fear tends to make subjects feel helpless, while instructions help convince them that they can protect themselves, then the more difficult the protective action recommended, the more beneficial should be the effect of receiving instructions. Assuming that it requires more effort and persistence to stop smoking than to take a tetanus inoculation, then it is likely that instructions would be especially effective in persuading high-fear subjects to stop smoking, even though instructions failed to interact with fear appeal in persuading subjects to take tetanus inoculations (Leventhal et al, 1965, 1966).

The fourth problem concerned the effects of varying an association between the act of smoking and the dangerous consequences (poor health, surgery, risk of death from lung cancer) which allegedly result from smoking. It was thought that if some subjects were required to smoke during the danger communications and others instructed not to smoke, the association between response and danger would be stronger in the former condition and should lead to greater subsequent inhibition of smoking.

METHOD

Design

Three factors were manipulated: intensity of the fear stimulus (moderate or high), instructions on how to stop smoking (given or not given), and smoking during the communication (subjects instructed to smoke or not to smoke). These variables were combined with a subject factor, heavy smokers (subjects who smoked more than the sample median of 15 cigarettes per day) versus light smokers (subjects who smoked 15 or fewer cigarettes per day), to form a $2 \times 2 \times 2 \times 2$ factorial design. The analysis of smoking behavior included a fifth factor corresponding to the five time intervals for which reports of smoking behavior were obtained. A control group which received only the instructions on how to stop smoking was included to test the effect of receiving instructions without fear arousal.

Subjects

Subjects were 129 Yale students, two-thirds freshmen and one-third upperclassmen. Subjects were individually approached on campus by two male recruiters and asked whether they wished to participate for $1.50 in a program-evaluation study sponsored by the Public Health Service. Those wishing to participate (approxiamtely 95% of those approached) then answered several questions on a card, including a question on present smoking habits. If the recruiter saw from the card that the volunteer was a cigarette smoker, he recruited him for the study. Subjects were then randomly assigned to the treatment conditions.

Subjects were given the experimental materials in a small room centrally located on campus. Eighteen groups (sessions) were run, two in each condition. Groups of from 6 to 8 subjects were originally scheduled for each session, but, since some subjects failed to keep their appointments and had to be rescheduled, the number of subjects at a session varied from 4 to 10 subjects. All subjects attending a given session received the same experimental materials. After being welcomed, subjects were reminded that the program was sponsored by the Public Health Service and that its purpose was to evaluate health-education materials. Subjects then completed two preexposure questionnaires, were given a communication,[2] and completed a postexposure questionnaire.

Smoking History and Attitudes

The first preexposure questionnaire included items dealing with the subjects' smoking history and current smoking habits. Also included were eight items dealing with (*a*) beliefs that smoking causes cancer, (*b*) judgments of personal vulnerability to lung cancer, (*c*) concern about the effects of smoking, (*d*) judgments of the effectiveness of decreasing smoking in preventing lung cancer, and (*e*) desire to quit and decrease smoking. All attitude questions in this and the following questionnaires were answered on 7-point scales with anchors at the midpoint and extremes (e.g., 1 = not at all, 4 = moderately, 7 = very much).

Mood Ratings

On a second preexposure questionnaire, subjects were asked to rate the degree to which each of 26 adjectives described their current moods or feelings. The items were related to the following dimensions: fear, depression, nausea, shame, vulnerability, aggression, helplessness. Many of these items were derived from the check list prepared by Nowlis (1965).

Smoking during the Film

When the first two questionnaires were completed, the experimenter told the subjects that they were to see a movie on smoking and said: "Contrary to what you might expect, we wish you to smoke during the film. We have provided cigarettes, matches, and ashtrays in case you have forgotten to bring your own." These items were then passed around. For those groups of subjects who were not to smoke, the following statement was substituted: "As you might expect, in view of the nature of the program, we should like to ask you not to smoke while you are here." Subjects in the smoking condition each smoked one cigarette. As this typically took between 7 and 8 minutes, subjects in the moderate-fear film smoked almost throughout their film, while subjects in the high-fear film usually had finished smoking before the surgery sequence was shown.

Fear Communications[3]

The moderate-fear appeal consisted of an 8-minute sound and color movie on the dangers of smoking. The movie demonstrated the way in which tars are drawn into the lung with cigarette smoke, paralyze the cilia of the bronchi, and damage the blood vessels and lungs. The relationship between smoking and lung cancer was elucidated by showing how tars are collected in the "throat" of a mechanical smoker, are trapped, chemically analyzed, and shown to contain known carcinogens. Scenes of invalids with respiratory troubles (a man out of breath after climbing three steps, an older man gasping for breath in a hospital bed) were included, and the film ended with the presentation of charts showing the relationship between cigarette sales and lung-cancer deaths, and between the probability of getting lung cancer and the number of cigarettes smoked. In brief, the film presented a relatively factual treatment of the dangers of smoking and stopped short of elaborating its most severe consequences.

The high-fear film consisted of the film described above followed by a 6-minute film showing a lung-cancer operation. The operation sequence showed the initial incision and forcing apart of the ribs, the removal of the black and diseased lung, the open cavity and beating heart, and finally the suturing of the wound. The film was in color and thoroughly authentic. In the more "gory" sequences many subjects were observed to squirm and lower their heads, and three subjects were sufficiently shaken to have to leave the room temporarily.

Instructions on How to Stop Smoking

Immediately after seeing the movie, subjects in the specific instructions condition read a pamphlet[4] giving detailed information on how to break the smoking habit. The reader was advised to make a list of reasons why he smoked and compare it to a second list of reasons why he might want to stop smoking. He was then asked to choose a "stop smoking day" and was given considerable advice on how to avoid conditions which encourage smoking (e.g., do not eat with friends who are smoking, prepare excuses beforehand for declining cigarettes), and how to substitute new habits for the old ones associated with smoking (e.g., do not carry matches, keep change ordinarily used for buying cigarettes in a different place, carry gum, take deep breaths or pace about when the urge to smoke comes). Much of the information in the pamphlet was familiar, and it did not promise an instant cure without effort. However, by using numerous examples of techniques for coping with situations that are part of a student's daily life, it was hoped that the pamphlet would lead to mental rehearsal of the steps which facilitate quitting or decreasing smoking. The use of an antismoking drug, such as Lobeline, was also mentioned.

Dependent Measures

Postquestionnaires. Immediately after the communication subjects filled out a third questionnaire. This questionnaire contained the same list of mood adjectives and the same items on attitudes toward smoking presented in the preexposure questionnaires. Two items on the fairness and accuracy of the film and the effectiveness of the recommendations were also included. A fourth questionnaire was administered to subjects individually 1 week after the communications. This questionnaire contained many of the same attitude items presented in the other two attitude questionnaires as well as items dealing with subjects' retrospective evaluation of the program and with changes in subjects' smoking behavior.

Behavior checks. Five estimates of the average number of cigarettes smoked per day were obtained from subjects. For each estimate subjects reported their average daily consumption over a period of 1 week, except for the "vacation" measure, described below, for which the period was 2 weeks. The first report referred to the week immediately preceding the program and was made on the pre-communication questionnaire. The second report was made on the follow-up questionnaire and referred to the week immediately after the program. The third and fourth reports were obtained by telephoning each subject and asking how much he had smoked during the current week and over the Christmas recess which had preceded this week. The final report was made on a postcard sent to the subjects 3 months after the program.

RESULTS

There were no significant differences among conditions on the preexposure measures of mood, attitudes, or smoking habits. Difference scores were used in analyses of the attitude items and the data analyzed by means of analysis of variance using the unweighted-means formula for unequal n's given by Winer (1962, pp. 241-244). The n for each analysis was the number of subjects who answered the item on both the pre- and post-questionnaire. Differences between the treatment groups and the control condition were assessed by t tests using the error term from the analysis of variance.

Emotion and Beliefs

Negative emotion. Since the measures of fear, depression, nausea, and shame were found to be highly correlated, all items related to these mood dimensions were summed to provide an overall index of negative emotion. Table 1 shows that the fear manipulations increased verbal reports of negative emotions as intended. Subjects exposed to the moderate-fear film reported significantly more negative emotion than control subjects who saw no film ($t = 3.14$, $df = 101$, $p < .005$), and subjects who saw the high-fear film reported more negative emotion than subjects who saw the moderate-fear film ($F = 17.03$, $df = 1/101$, $p < .005$. There were no main effects or interactions for the other manipulated variables or for the smoking levels.

Aggression. An index of aggression was derived by summing the scores for the mood items “sceptical,” “suspicious,” “defiant,” and “fed-up.” There was one significant effect on this index: subjects who did *not* smoke during the program expressed more aggression than subjects instructed to smoke (smoking condition, $X = 1.25$; no-smoking condition, $X = .86$; $F = 5.46$, $df = 1/101$, $p < .05$).

TABLE 1

CHANGES IN EMOTIONS AND ATTITUDES[1]

Items	Control	Moderate Fear film	High Fear film	High vs. moderate	Moderate vs. control
Negative emotions	–6.72	6.92	17.79	.005	.005
Aggressive feelings	–1.16	–.28	–.10	*ns*	*ns*
Vulnerability feelings	.22	.46	1.65	.005	*ns*
Desire to quit smoking	.56	.39	1.13	.005	*ns*
n	12	45	61		

Note. The index of negative emotions is the sum of 14 difference scores. The index of aggressive feelings is the sum of four difference scores.

[1] All entries in the table are based on differences between precommunication and post-communication scores and are unweighted averages of the means for the subgroups within each condition. Means for the film conditions are the average of eight group means. Means for the control condition are the average of two means (light and heavy smokers).

Vulnerability. One item from the mood questionnaire and one from the attitude questionnaires were used to measure perceived vulnerability. On the mood item (“I feel vulnerable”) there were significant main effects for both the fear and the specific instructions manipulation. Subjects in the high-fear condition reported feeling more vulnerable than subjects in the moderate-fear condition (high fear, $X = 1.65$; moderate fear, $X = .46$; $F = 9.29$, $df = 1/101$, $p < .005$), and subjects who did not receive specific instructions on how to stop smoking reported feeling more vulnerable than subjects who received such instructions (instructions, $X = .50$; no instructions, $X = 1.41$; $F = 8.01$, $df = 1/101$, $p < .005$). On the attitude item (“How susceptible do you *now* feel to lung cancer?”) there was a similar main effect for the instructions manipulation (instructions, $X = .49$; no instructions, $X = 1.02$; $F = 5.40$, $df = 1/101$, $p < .05$), no effect of the fear manipulation, and an interaction between level of smoking (light versus heavy smokers) and instructions to smoke during the program (F = 7.39, df = 1/101, p<.05). In this interaction heavy smokers reported feeling more susceptible to lung cancer when told to smoke during the program (smoking condition, X = 1.43; no-smoking condition, X = .44) than when not permitted to smoke, while there was no difference between conditions for light smokers (smoking condition, X = .46; no-smoking condition, X = .71).

Beliefs. Items measuring beliefs that smoking causes lung cancer ("The available evidence shows, without reasonable doubt, that smoking causes lung cancer"; "The less a person smokes, the less likely he is to develop lung cancer") and beliefs in the effectiveness of stopping smoking ("For a smoker, how effective is stopping smoking in reducing the chances of developing lung cancer?") were not significantly affected by the manipulations.

Desire to Comply with the Recommendation

Table 1 shows the mean differences between preexposure and post-exposure scores (measured immediately after the communication) or intentions to decrease smoking. Subjects in the high-fear condition showed significantly larger increases in desire to quit smoking than subjects in the moderate-fear condition (F = 7.41, df = 1/101, p<.05), but there was no significant difference between the moderate-fear and control conditions.

Desires to quit smoking were also measured 1 week after the communications, and differences between these and the preexperimental scores were computed. The delayed measures show a pattern similar to that of the immediate measures, but the difference between the high- and moderate-fear conditions was no longer significant. Obviously, responses to the delayed items may have been affected by actual compliance during the week interval.

Credibility of Sponsor and Communication

All groups considered the Public Health Service (the alleged sponsor of the program) to be a highly reliable source of information on smoking and lung cancer. A more direct measure of message credibility was obtained from subjects in the film groups, who were asked whether they thought the movie gave a "fair and accurate" picture of smoking and lung cancer. Subjects instructed to smoke during the program were *more* favorable in their responses than subjects instructed not to smoke (smoking condition, X = 4.53; no-smoking condition, X =3.91; F = 4.23, df = 1/100, p<.05). There were no other significant differences.

Smoking Behavior

The five reports of smoking behavior obtained from each subject were subjected to square-root transformation, and an analysis of variance for repeated measures was performed using the unweighted-means solution of Winer (1962, pp. 376-378). The analysis of variance involved the four experimental variables previously described and a fifth (stages) factor, corresponding to the five periods for which reports of smoking behavior were obtained. One or two of the five reports of smoking were missing for 10 subjects because the experimenter was unable to reach them at the appropriate times and these data were estimated. Four subjects who initially smoked fewer than two cigarettes were excluded from the analysis.

The experimental communications were effective in that the average number of cigarettes smoked per day decreased sharply over the follow-up period (stages—$F = 18.11$, $df = 4/388$, $p < .005$). The difference between the control and all experimental conditions taken together was highly significant ($p < .005$ for t tests) for each of the four reports of smoking made after the communications.

Fear Level

As can be seen from Figure 1, there was little difference in the reported smoking behavior of subjects in the high-fear and moderate-fear conditions at any period for which measures were taken after the communications (fear —$F = .25$, $df = 1/97$; Fear × Stages—$F = 1.12$, $df = 4/388$). The original differences in emotional arousal associated with the films seem to have had no influence on subsequent smoking behavior. However, some minimal amount of arousal seems necessary to motivate behavior change as shown by the significant difference between the moderate-fear and control conditions for each report of smoking following the communication ($p < .05$ for each of the four t tests).

An interaction in the predicted direction between fear and instructions on how to quit smoking is also apparent in Figure 1 ($F = 3.50$, $df = 1/97$, $p < .10$). The receipt of instructions seemed to make more of a difference in the high-fear condition than in the moderate-fear condition. In the moderate-fear condition the instructions and no-instructions curves remain close together over the 3-month period, and subjects who received instructions reported less smoking than subjects who did not receive instructions only at the last two points in time. In the high-fear condition, on the other hand, subjects in the instructions condition always reported less smoking than subjects in the no-instructions condition, and the difference between conditions tended to *increase* over time.

Instructions on How to Stop Smoking

When the behavior of subjects who received instructions on how to stop smoking was compared to that of subjects who did not receive instructions, the main effect was not significant ($F = 2.63$, $df = 1/97$), but the interaction with stages was significant ($F = 2.69$, $df = 4/388$, $p < .05$). Figure 2 shows that the instructions and no-instructions curves both show sharp drops in smoking from before the program to 1 week after, and then begin to diverge. The divergence of the two curves was tested by applying linear weights to the four postcommunication measures for each condition and testing the interaction of the linear components with stages. This interaction was significant ($F = 5.17$, $df - 1/388$, $p < .025$). During the period from 1 week to 3 months after the program, subjects who received instructions on how to stop smoking apparently maintained their decreased smoking level, while subjects who did not receive these instructions tended to regress toward their precommunication smoking level. For the differences between the instructions and no-instructions conditions t values were very small at 1 week ($t = .05$) and during vacation ($t = .74$), and larger at 1 month ($t = 1.67$, $df = 97$, $p < .10$) and at 3 months ($t = 1.67$, $df = 97$, $p < .10$).

Instructions to Smoke during the Program

Contrary to prediction, smoking during the film slightly decreased compliance with the recommendation to stop smoking. However, the main effect of this factor was not significant ($F = 2.51$, $df = 1/97$), nor was the interaction with stages ($F = .90.$, $df = 4/388$).

Light versus Heavy Smokers

The main effect of initial level of smoking was, of course, very large ($F = 104.57$, $df = 1/97$, $p < .005$) and simply indicates that heavy smokers continued to smoke more than light smokers after the program. Of more interest is the interaction of this variable with stages ($F = 3.07$, $df = 4/388$, $p < .05$). Light smokers showed little change in their smoking behavior after the 1-week stage, while heavy smokers reported a further decrease from 1 week to the vacation. Of interest also is the interaction between the light-heavy classification and instructions to smoke during the program ($F = 4.92$), $df = 1/97$, $p < .05$). Heavy smokers instructed to smoke during the film were less likely to decrease smoking afterward than heavy smokers instructed not to smoke during the film. It made little difference to light smokers whether or not they smoked during the film.

Supplementary Analyses

Reports of smoking behavior showed considerable change in variance over time. Some subjects never decreased smoking, others decreased at one or two stages but not at others, and still others decreased smoking at all four stages. The amount by which subjects decreased smoking also varied widely, with some subjects reporting they had quit completely and others reporting only token decreases. Supplementary analyses of

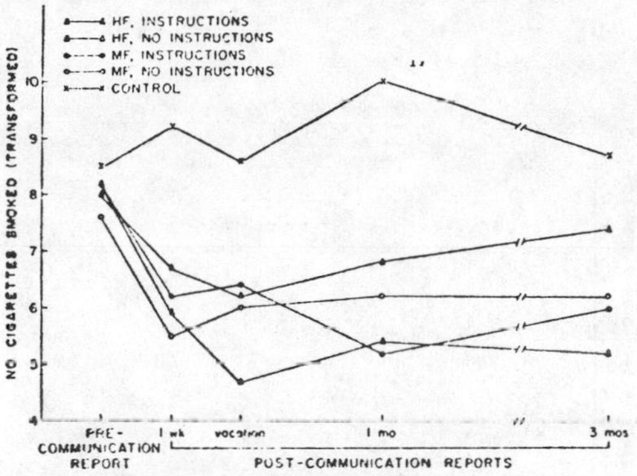

FIG. 1. Smoking behavior over time in fear and instructions conditions.

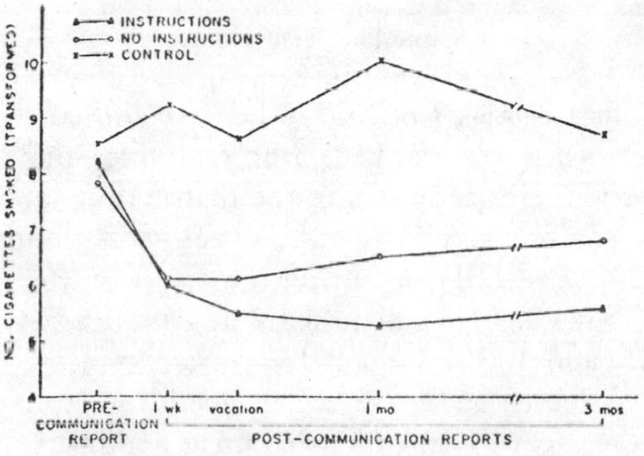

FIG. 2. Smoking behavior over time in instructions conditions.

smoking behavior were therefore undertaken using the proportions of subjects who reported substantial change in their smoking. This type of score gives a more stable picture of the impact of the communications on behavior since it ignores minor variations in an individual's smoking behavior and is unaffected by changes in within-group variances over time. The following procedure was used for these analyses: all light smokers who decreased smoking by at least three cigarettes (the median number of cigarettes cut down by light smokers in the total sample), and all heavy smokers who cut down by at least six cigarettes (the median number cut down by all heavy smokers) were counted as having truly decreased smoking. The proportions of decreasers in each condition for each stage were then computed and transformed to arc sines,[5] and a separate analysis of variance for each stage was carried out on the transformed proportions.

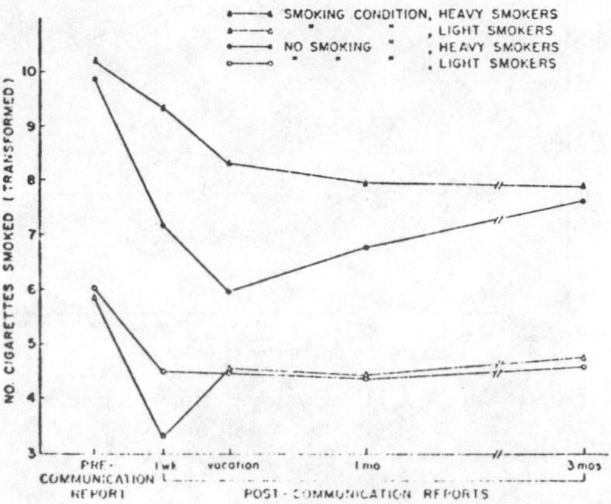

FIG. 3. Smoking behavior of heavy and light smokers in smoking conditions.

The results of these analyses proved to be very similar to those for the mean number of cigarettes smoked. For example, the difference between the proportions of decreasers in the instructions and non-instructions conditions was not significant at 1 week (instructions = 51%, no instructions = 40%; $F - 2.01$) or during the vacation (62% versus 34%; $F = 2.79, p < .10$), but was highly significant at 1 month (64% versus 34%; $F = 10.50, p < .005$) and at 3 months (53% versus 26%; $F = 9.51, p < .005$). The proportion of decreasers in the control condition was 9% at 1 week and 20% during the vacation, at 1 month, and at 3 months.

DISCUSSION

Subjects saw one of two films on the dangers of smoking. The moderate-fear film presented evidence linking lung cancer to smoking and showed patients suffering from relatively mild disorders caused by smoking. The high-fear film differed from the moderate-fear film in including a section depicting a lung-cancer operation. The high-fear film increased reports of unpleasant emotions including fear, feelings of personal vulnerability to lung cancer, and desires to stop smoking, but it did not lead to a greater decrease in reported smoking behavior than the moderate-fear film. In turn, subjects exposed to the moderate-fear film reported increased fear and decreased smoking compared to control subjects who received only the recommendation to stop smoking and the instructions on how to stop smoking.

In previous discussions (Leventhal, 1965; Leventhal & Niles, 1964; Leventhal et al., 1965) it was suggested that temporal factors might account for the failure of fear to exert a long-range effect on behavior. It was pointed out that intentions are usually measured immediately after the fear treatments when differences in emotion or drive level are most marked, while behavior is measured later when these differences very likely have dissipated. This "dissipation" hypothesis was not disproven by the present data, but it seems too simple to account for the observed effects. The major finding which it fails to handle is that the difference in reported fear between the control and moderate-fear condition *was* associated with differences in reported behavioral compliance over time, while the difference in fear between the moderate-fear and high-fear condition was *not* associated with differences in compliance. Thus an increase in fear produced by relatively factual depiction of the dangers of smoking (the moderate-fear communication) had a long-range positive effect on compliance, but little effect on immediate intentions to comply, whereas a further increase in fear produced by the shock tactics of the high-fear film exerted an immediate effect on intentions to comply, but had no long-range effect on behavior.

This finding raises the question whether the inconsistent effects among studies noted previously may not be better understood by an analysis of informational and stylistic qualities of the various stimuli, rather than by reference to the amount of fear these stimuli arouse. The arousal of fear, changes in attitudes, and changes in behavior may be produced by the same or different aspects of a given stimulus, and these responses may, in turn, be merely correlated rather than causally related.

That the important next step in research is a more refined analysis of communications is also suggested by the effects on persuasion of a second experimental variable—the receipt of instructions on how to stop smoking. In this study, as in the previous tetanus studies (Leventhal et al., 1965, 1966), the receipt of instructions on how to cope with the danger apparently decreased feelings of vulnerability to the danger, increased behavioral compliance with protective recommendations (so long as the instructions were accompanied by at least a moderately fear-arousing communication), and had no discernible effect on fear level or intentions to comply with the recommendations. Although these instructions seemed to aid high-fear subjects more than moderate-fear subjects, the effect of receiving instructions was apparently not due to differences in fear reduction. Possibly the instructions were effective because they increased the subject's confidence in being able to help himself, his awareness of the conditions which led him to smoke, and the techniques which could be used to inhibit smoking. By providing excuses for deferring cigarettes and preparing alternatives to smoking, the instructed subject could control his behavior well before he started smoking. The uninstructed subject, on the other hand, might just as frequently have remembered his resolution not to smoke, but he might have remembered on less appropriate occasions, for example, just after buying cigarettes. Thus the ego of the uninstructed subject must invent its own devices for avoiding smoking, and it will frequently be asked to control smoking when incentives for smoking are very powerful. The instructed ego does not need to invent evasive maneuvers to overcome strong temptation, and the result may be a more efficient execution of avoidance behaviors which readily become automatic response sequences unrelated to conscious decision making. It is possible that the postcommunication differences in reported vulnerability in the instructions and no-instructions conditions reflected differences in perceived difficulty and effort needed to decrease smoking.

Finally, a word should be said about the effects of smoking during the communication. It was expected that subjects who were instructed to smoke while the dangers of smoking were depicted would later show more compliance with the recommendation to decrease smoking. Quite the opposite proved to be the case. Subjects who smoked during the films reported somewhat less compliance with the recommendation than subjects who were not permitted to smoke. A possible explanation for this finding is that smoking during the film reminded subjects of the pleasures of smoking as suggested by the fact that subjects who smoked during the film reported less annoyance than subjects who did not. Another possibility is that smoking during the film reduced the credibility of the communication by reminding subjects that they had suffered none of the alleged consequences of smoking, or by suggesting that the communicator did not really regard smoking as dangerous. The present data do not lend support to either of these explanations, but perhaps the appropriate questions simply were not asked.

REFERENCES

Janis, I. L., & Terwilliger, R. An experimental study of psychological resistances to fear-arousing communications. *Journal of Abnormal and Social Psychology,* 1962, 65, 403-410.

Leventhal, H. Fear communications in the acceptance of preventive health practices. *Bulletin of the New York Academy of Medicine,* 1965, 41, 1144-1168.

Leventhal, H., Jones, S., & Trembly, G. Sex differences in attitudes and behavior change under conditions of fear and specific instructions. *Journal of Experimental Social Psychology,* 1966, 2, 387-399.

Leventhal, H., & Niles, P. A field experiment on fear arousal with data on the validity of questionnaire measures. *Journal of Personality,* 1964, 32, 459-479.

Leventhal, H., Singer, R. P., & Jones, S. Effects of fear and specificity of recommendations. *Journal of Personality and Social Psychology,* 1965, 2, 20-29.

Leventhal, H., & Watts, J. C. Sources of resistance to fear-arousing communications. *Journal of Personality,* 1966, 34, 155-175.

Niles, P. The relationship of susceptibility and anxiety to acceptance of fear-arousing communications. Unpublished doctoral dissertation, Yale University, 1964.

Nowlis, V. Research with the Mood Adjective Check List. In S. Tomkins & C. Izzard (Eds.), *Affect, cognition, and personality.* New York: Springer, 1965. Pp. 352-389.

Pagano, F. An experimental inquiry into the effectiveness of an educational approach in the prevention of smoking. Unpublished master's thesis, Yale University, 1965.

Winer, B. J. *Statistical principles in experimental design.* New York: McGraw-Hill, 1962.

(Received August 17, 1966)

NOTES

[1] This investigation was presented by Francia Pagano in partial fulfillment of the Master of Public Health Degree at Yale University, 1965. The data were collected by the second and third authors during the latter's externship at the John Slade Ely Center for Health Education Research. The study was supported by the United States Public Health Service (CH 00077-04) and the United Health Foundation. The authors would like to thank Irvin Child and James Dabbs for critical comments respecting early drafts of the paper.

[2] While viewing the film, photographs of the experimental subjects were taken with a flash camera at approximately 3-minute intervals. It was hoped that an analysis of facial expressions would provide additional evidence of emotional arousal. However, the photographs turned out to be rather poor technically, and these data will not be reported.

[3] The moderate-fear film was excerpted from *Smoking and You* distributed by Contemporary Films, Incorporated. The operation sequence was taken from *One in 20,000* made for the American Temperance Society. It was used as part of the high-fear stimulus in studies by Niles (1964), Leventhal and Niles (1964), and Leventhal and Watts (1966).

[4] The pamphlet was based on a booklet currently being used by the Narcotics Division, New York City, in its antismoking clinics. When questioned in a follow-up interview, only one subject said he had used an antismoking drug. Hence the effect of the drug recommendation on smoking behavior may be ignored.

[5] Thanks are extended to Robert Abelson for suggesting the use of the arc-sine transformation. The error term for this test is:

$$\frac{1/nl + \ldots\ldots 1/nk.}{\text{number of cells}}$$

Comparisons between the film groups and the controls were performed using the formula:

$$Z = \phi_1 - \phi_2 \quad 1N_1 + 1N_2.$$

It should be noted that chi square tests of the main effects gave p values similar to those obtained using the arc-sine transformation.

15

EFFECTS OF CONTINGENT AND NONCONTINGENT REWARD ON THE RELATIONSHIP BETWEEN SATISFACTION AND TASK PERFORMANCE

David J. Cherrington, H. Joseph Reitz
and
William E. Scott, Jr.

Many current speculations on the relationship between worker satisfaction and task performance, as reviewed by Schwab and Cummings (1970), still imply that performance and satisfaction are causally related in one direction or the other. Some theorists have now added moderating variables to their behavioral formulas in hopes of facilitating the prediction of one variable from the other.

In contrast, the present authors postulate not only that (*a*) there is no inherent relationship between satisfaction and performance, but also that (*b*) one can produce about any empirical relationship between task performance and self-reports of satisfaction that one wishes. The first proposition is consistent with the conclusions of empirical reviews such as Brayfield and Crockett (1955) and with theoretical positions such as those of Porter and Lawler (1968). The second proposition was derived from operational proposals by Skinner (1969) and Bandura (1969) and from speculations by a variety of reinforcement theorists (e.g., Berlyne, 1967; Bindra, 1968; Rescorla & Solomon, 1967; and Weiskrantz, 1968).

Skinner (1969), for instance, insists that feelings are, at best, accompaniments rather than causes of behavior and that both are the products of common environmental variables. Bandura (1969, p. 598) pointedly suggests that we might better treat self-reports of satisfaction simply as another class of behavior rather than as indexes of an underlying state endowed with special causal powers. From this point of view, there exists no inherent relationship between performance and self-reports of satisfaction, and the empirical problem becomes that of examining

Reprinted from *Journal of Applied Psychology* (Vol. 35, 1971, pp. 531-536).

the conditions under which the different response systems are correlated *or* independent.

We suggest that the type of reward system under which workers perform might strongly influence the satisfaction-performance relationship. One should be able to directly influence satisfaction by proferring or withdrawing rewards. To significantly influence performance, however, one must use *performance-contingent* rewards. Theoretically, then, by manipulating the contingencies of a reward system, one should be able to create conditions under which satisfaction and performance can be, empirically, either independent, or positively related, or negatively related.

To test these propositions let us define three types of performance-reward systems:

1. Random rewards. Rewards are distributed on bases independent of performance. The percentage of high performers receiving rewards does not differ from the percentage of low performers receiving rewards. Under this system we hypothesize that correlations between satisfaction and performance would not significantly differ from zero.

2. Positively contingent rewards. Rewards are based directly on performance. All high performers are rewarded; all low performers are not rewarded. Under this system we hypothesize a positive correlation between satisfaction and performance.

3. Negatively contingent rewards. Rewards are based on factors inversely related to performance. Low performers are rewarded; high performers are not rewarded. Under this system we hypothesize a negative correlation between satisfaction and performance.

METHOD

Subjects

The *S*s were 90 undergraduate students, both male and female, enrolled in a junior-level business course. Students were enlisted as volunteers to score Closure Flexibility Tests for which they would be paid at least $1 per hour.

Procedure and Task

The *S*s reported to the laboratory in groups that varied from seven to nine individuals and were met by E who introduced himself as a graduate student who would be their supervisor.

When all *S*s had arrived and had familiarized themselves with the Closure Flexibility Test booklet, each was told that his task would be to score the tests at his work station. The *S*s were also told that the tests had been completed by employees in a paper mill. All of the Closure Flexibility Test booklets had in fact been marked according to 24 patterns of responses. Therefore, the difficulty of the task was controlled and the correct responses were known in advance.

The *S*s were told that they would be paid a minimum of $1 per hour but that the best performers in terms of quality and quantity would receive an additional $1 bonus. The *S*s were told that each had a 50–50 chance of receiving the bonus. The task of scoring the test booklets was explained to *S*s, aided by diagrams showing a partially marked answer sheet.

After *S*s began the task, *E* returned every 10 min. to bring additional booklets and collect the booklets and answer sheets that had been completed. At the end of 1 hr., *E* stopped *S*s and asked them to indicate on four 7-point scales an estimate of their quantity, quality, and overall performance and probability of receiving a reward.[1] The experimental manipulations of financial reward were then performed, which consisted of the following statements and payments.

> I have collected the tests as you have scored them and selected a sample from each of you to check your work. I've used a rather complicated index which combines quantity and quality of performance into one index. Based upon this index four of you will receive $2 for the last hour's work. The other four will get$1. The four winners are . . . and the four losers are . . . .

In fact, the monetary bonus was randomly distributed to half of the high-performing and half of the low-performing *S*s.

The performance score for each *S* was the total number of rows of figures in the Closure Flexibility Test booklets that *S* scored correctly. This was determined by subtracting the number of errors from the total number of rows scored. Thus performance scores were a measure of both quality and quantity.

The *S*s were than asked to complete a self-report measure of satisfaction developed by Scott and his colleagues (Scott, 1967; Scott & Rowland, 1970). The format of the self-report measure was a semantic differential questionnaire as shown below.

Me At This Task

	Extremely	Quite	Slightly	Neither one nor the other	Slightly	Quite	Extremely	
Appreciated	—	—	—	—	—	—	—	Unappreciated
Bored	—	—	—	—	—	—	—	Interested
Efficient	—	—	—	—	—	—	—	Inefficient

Bipolar adjective pairs were set against four concepts: me at this task, my pay, my fellow workers, and the task. The response to each scale was scored from one to seven with seven assigned to that response which appeared to indicate the most preferred condition. A factor score was computed for each *S* by averaging *S*'s responses to each of the scales previously found to comprise that factor.

Eight factor scores were computed for each *S*. General affective tone score was obtained by averaging *S*'s responses to the following bipolar scales set against the concept, me at this task: appreciated-unappreciated, rewarded-penalized, satisfied-dissatisfied, and encouraged-discouraged. The remaining self-report measures and the semantic scales defining each factor were as follows—general arousal (me at this task): interested-bored, spirited-lifeless, and alert-listless; personal competence (me at this task): efficient-inefficient, productive-unproductive, reliable-unreliable, and effective-ineffective; general satisfaction with pay (my pay): pleasing-annoying, reasonable-unreasonable, superior-inferior, and rewarding-penalizing; equitableness of pay (my pay in comparison with what others in my group received): fair-unfair, high-low, and reasonable-unreasonable; adequacy of pay (my pay in comparison with what others get for similar work on the campus): superior-inferior, high-low, and reasonable-unreasonable; interpersonal attractiveness (my fellow workers): sociable-unsociable, helpful-obstructive, pleasant-unpleasant, unselfish-selfish, and cooperative-uncooperative; task attractiveness (the task): attractive-repulsive, exciting-dull, good-bad, interesting-boring, superior-inferior, and wholesome-unwholesome.

After completing the semantic differential scales, *S*s took a 5-min. break, after which they were given more test booklets and asked to continue scoring them for another hour. The procedure at the end of the second hour was identical to that at the end of the first hour. First, *S*s were asked to estimate their perceived performance and probability of reward on the four scales. Then they were paid and asked to fill out the semantic differential questionnaire. The monetary bonus was distributed to the same *S*s who received it at the end of the first hour.

After the questionnaires were filled out for the second time, *S*s were debriefed. They were told that all rewards were given at random, and since it was only by chance someone received more than the others, the winners were asked to share their rewards with the losers, although *E* did not insist that they do so.

RESULTS

We have hypothesized that there is no inherent relationship between satisfaction and performance, but that there is a direct relationship between the rewards and self-reports of satisfaction. Whatever covariation one does observe between satisfaction and performance, then, may depend upon other environmental conditions, particularly the kind of performance-reward contingency that has been arranged or has evolved.

The results summarized in Table 1 demonstrate the differential effects of rewards on performance and satisfaction.[2] Performance scores of rewarded *S*s did not differ from those of nonrewarded *S*s.

Mean satisfaction scores of rewarded *S*s, however, were significantly greater than mean scores of nonrewarded *S*s on each of the eight satisfaction indexes. Thus self-report measures of satisfaction can be highly dependent on the occurrence or nonoccurrence of monetary reward, but if that reward is delivered independent of performance, it fails to have incremental effects on subsequent performance.

TABLE 1

COMPARISON OF MEAN PERFORMANCE AND SATISFACTION SCORES OF REWARDED VERSES NONREWARDED SUBJECTS

Item	$\bar{X}$ Scores		D_M
	Rewarded *S*s	Nonrewarded *S*s	
Performance			
First hour	285.6	286.6	-1.0
Second hour	403.8	411.2	-7.4
Satisfaction indexes			
General affective tone	5.16	3.83	1.33***
General arousal	4.98	4.44	.54**
Personal competence	5.82	5.01	.81***
General satisfaction with pay	5.61	3.69	1.92***
Equity of pay	5.24	3.74	1.50***
Adequacy of pay	4.76	3.40	1.36***
Attractiveness of fellow workers	4.96	4.63	.33*
Attractiveness of task	3.80	3.19	.61***

Note.—Abbreviation D_M = Difference of means.
* $p < .01$.
** $p < .005$.
*** $p < .001$.

To test the effects of variations in performance-reinforcement contingency, *S*s were classified on the basis of first-hour performance. The 42 *S*s whose performance scores were above the median of their group are referred to as high performers and the 42 *S*s below the median as low performers. Six *S*s who performed at the median were excluded from further analysis. Rewards at the end of the first hour were distributed randomly among high and among low performers so that half the *S*s in each performance classification were rewarded. The appropriateness of each *S*'s reinforcement was then defined by the performance-reward contingency that happened to occur for that *S*. The 21 rewarded high performers and the 21 nonrewarded low performers were classified as appropriately reinforced. The 21 rewarded low performers and the 21 nonrewarded high performers were classified as inappropriately reinforced.

The results shown in Table 2 reveal, first, that the average second-hour (postreinforcement) performance of appropriately reinforced *S*s was significantly higher than that of inappropriately reinforced *S*s, whereas the first hour (prereinforcement) performance of the two classes did not differ significantly. Comparisons between the two classes on self-reports of satisfaction, however, revealed a significant difference on only one of the eight satisfaction indexes, adequacy of pay. The tests summarized in Tables 1 and 2 thus establish that, as hypothesized, it is the contingency of a reward on performance that enables it to bring about increments in performance. That contingency characteristic, however, has little or no effect on satisfaction.

Two different relationships between satisfaction and performance were investigated: (*a*) the relationship between self-reports of satisfaction and subsequent performance, and (*b*) the relationship between performance and subsequent self-reports of satisfaction.

TABLE 2

COMPARISON OF MEAN PERFORMANCE AND SATISFACTION SCORES OF APPROPRIATELY VERSUS INAPPROPRIATELY REINFORCED SUBJECTS

Item	*X* Scores: Appropriately *reinforced S*s	*X* Scores: Inappropriately reinforced *S*s	D_M
Performance			
First hour	291.6	280.9	10.7
Second hour	428.4	385.9	42.5**
Satisfaction			
General affective tone	4.26	4.11	.15
General arousal	4.12	4.02	.10
Personal competence	5.30	5.07	.23
General satisfaction with pay	4.56	4.11	.45
Equity of pay	4.40	4.18	.22
Adequacy of pay	4.18	3.64	.54*
Attractiveness of fellow workers	4.85	4.78	.07
Attractiveness of task	3.31	3.27	.04

Note.—Abbreviation D_M - Difference of means.
* $p < .05$.
** $p < .01$.

Table 3 presents the results of correlational analyses performed between the eight satisfaction indexes recorded at the end of the first hour and subsequent performance during the second hour. The data for all *S*s, among whom as many low performers as high performers were rewarded, revealed only one significant correlation between satisfaction and subsequent performance. However, when the data were separated according to *S*s' performance-reward contingencies, distinct differences in the satisfaction-performance relationships were observed. For the 42 *appropriately* reinforced *S*s, significant *positive* correlations were found between six of the eight satisfaction indexes and subsequent performance. But for the 42 *inappropriately* reinforced *S*s, *negative* correlations were found between seven of the eight satisfaction indexes and subsequent performance, of which three correlations were statistically significant, and one closely approached significance at the .05 level.

TABLE 3

CORRELATIONS BETWEEN SATISFACTION AT END OF FIRST HOUR AND SUBSEQUENT PERFORMANCE DURING SECOND HOUR

Satisfaction indexes	All *Ss*[1]	Appropriately reinforced *Ss*[2]	Inappropriately reinforced *Ss*[2]
General affective tone	.00	.56***	-.32*
General arousal	.10	.42**	-.15
Personal competence	.21	.54***	-.01
General satisfaction with pay	.04	.46**	-.29
Equity of pay	-.17	.15	-.44**
Adequacy of pay	.04	.39**	-.31*
Attractiveness of fellow workers	.22*	.33*	-.13
Attractiveness of task	.04	.21	-.08

1 $n = 90$.
2 $n = 42$.
* $p < .05$.
** $p < .01$.
*** $p < .001$.

TABLE 4

CORRELATIONS BETWEEN PERFORMANCE DURING SECOND HOUR AND SATISFACTION AT END OF SECOND HOUR

Satisfaction indexes	All *Ss*[1]	Appropriately reinforced *Ss*[1]	Inappropriately reinforced *Ss*[2]
General affective tone	-.03	.55***	-.51***
General arousal	.02	.42**	-.26
Personal competence	.13	.48**	-.16
General satisfaction with pay	.03	.67***	-.56***
Equity of pay	-.09	.45**	-.51***
Adequacy of pay	-.03	.59***	-.57***
Attractiveness of fellow workers	.20	.44**	.04
Attractiveness of task	-.06	.32*	-.16

1 $n = 90$.
2 $n = 42$.
* $p < .05$.
** $p < .01$.
*** $p < .001$.

Table 4 presents the results of correlational analyses performed between performance during the second hour and the eight satisfaction indexes subsequently recorded at the end of the second hour. The similarities between Table 3 and 4 are striking. The data for all *S*s revealed no significant correlations between performance and subsequent satisfaction. However, when distinctions were made between appropriately and inappropriately reinforced *S*s, where the performance classifications were based on the second hour's productivity scores, widely disparate performance-satisfaction relationships were observed. For the appropriately reinforced *S*s, significant positive correlations were obtained between performance and each of the eight satisfaction indexes. For the inappropriately reinforced *S*s, negative correlations were obtained between performance and seven of the eight satisfaction indexes, with four of the correlations being highly significant.

DISCUSSION

The results of this study support the hypothesis that the nature and magnitude of the relationship between satisfaction and performance depend heavily upon the performance-reward contingencies that have been arranged. The findings are consistent with the predictions of the Porter and Lawler (1968) model, although the theoretical bases for our hypothesis differ from that model. For instance, Porter and Lawler's model implies that, under contingent-reward conditions, performance causes satisfaction because performance leads to rewards which, in turn, cause satisfaction. Our theory implies no cause-effect relationship between performance and satisfaction; instead, it stresses the performance-reinforcing as well as the satisfaction-increasing potential of contingent reinforcers.

The random reward system described here has as its organizational counterpart companies in which rewards such as pay increases and promotion are alleged to be performance-contingent but, in fact, are contingent upon factors independent of performance, such as age, seniority, or upward influence of one's supervisor. In such an organization we would expect satisfaction and performance to be unrelated.

The negatively contingent reward system is analogous to an organization in which rewards are based on factors that happen to be inversely related to performance. Such systems are not, unfortunately, as rare as one might think. One of the authors recently encountered a company in which pay increases were based on supervisor ratings, until it was discovered that the supervisors' ratings were negatively related to performance. In such an organization we would expect to find satisfaction and productivity negatively related. High performers are dissatisfied because they feel cheated; low performers are more than satisfied with their relative increases in pay.

So the importance of taking into account the contingencies between performance and rewards is again emphasized for those who seek to affect employee attitudes and/or behavior through various reward systems. If rewards are not positively contingent, then the administration of rewards will not only fail to encourage performance increments, it may also increase dissatisfaction and, ultimately, absenteeism and resignations among the highest producing employees.

REFERENCES

Bandura, A. *Principles of behavior modification.* New York: Holt, Rinehart & Winston, 1969.

Berlyne, D. E. Arousal and reinforcement. In D. Levine (Ed.), *Nebraska symposium on motivation: 1967.* Lincoln: University of Nebraska Press, 1967.

Bindra, D. Neuropsychological interpretation of the effects of drive and incentive-motivation on general activity and instrumental behavior. *Psychological Review,* 1968, 75, 1-22.

Brayfield, A. H., & Crockett, W. H. Employee attitudes and employee performance. *Psychological Bulletin,* 1955, 52, 396-424.

Porter, L. W., & Lawler, E. E., III. *Managerial attitudes and performance.* Homewood, Illinois: Irwin-Dorsey, 1968.

Rescorla, R. A., & Solomon, R. L. Two-process learning theory: Relationships between Pavlovian conditioning and instrumental learning. *Psychological Review,* 1967, 74, 151-182.

Schwab, D. P., & Cummings, L. L. Theories of performance and satisfaction: A review. *Industrial Relations,* 1970, 9, 408-430.

Scott, W. E., Jr. The development of semantic differential scales as measures of "morale." *Personnel Psychology,* 1967, 20, 179-198.

Scott, W. E., Jr., & Rowland, K. M. The generality and significance of semantic differential scales as measures of "morale." *Organizational Behavior and Human Performance,* 1970, 5, 576-591.

Skinner, B. F. *Contingencies of reinforcement: A theoretical analysis.* New York: Appleton-Century-Crofts, 1969.

Weiskrantz, L. Emotion. In L. Weiskrantz (Ed.), *Analysis of behavioral change.* New York: Harper & Row, 1968.

(Received August 17, 1970)

NOTES

[1] There were no significant differences between the reward and nonreward group in either the subjective probability of being rewarded (5.42 vs. 5.22, respectively) or in estimated performance (5.37 vs. 5.32).

[2] Raw scores are reported in the tables. Normalized scores, however, were used in all statistical analyses.

BIBLIOGRAPHY

Ajzen, I. "Attitudinal versus Normative Messages: An Investigation of the Differential Effects of Persuasive Communications on Behavior." *Sociometry* 34 (1971):263-280.

Ajzen, I., Darroch, K., Fishbein, M., and Hornik, J. A. "Looking Backward Revisited: A Reply to Deutscher." *American Sociologist* 5(1970):267-273.

Ajzen, I., and Fishbein, M. "The Prediction of Behavioral Intentions in a Choice Situation." *Journal of Experimental Social Psychology* 5(1969):400-416.

Ajzen, I., and Fishbein, M. "The Prediction of Behavior from Attitudinal and Normative Variables." *Journal of Experimental Social Psychology* 6(1970): 466-487.

Ajzen, I., and Fishbein, M. "Attitudes and Normative beliefs as Factors Influencing Behavior Intentions." *Journal of Personality and Social Psychology* 21 (1972):1-9.

Albrecht, S. H., DeFleur, M. L., and Warner, L. G. "The Impact of Disclosure and Reference Group Considerations on Attitude-Behavior Relations: A Reexamination of the Postulate of Contingent Consistency." *Pacific Sociological Review* 15(1972):149-168.

Allinsmith, W. "Conscience and Conflict: The Moral Force in Personality." *Child Development* 28(1957):469-476.

Allport, G. W. "The Historical Background of Modern Social Psychology." In *Handbook of Social Psychology*, edited by G. Lindzey, 1, Cambridge: Addison-Wesley Press, 1954.

Allport, G. W. "Attitudes." In *A Handbook of Social Psychology,* edited by C. A. Murchison, Worcester, Massachusetts: Clark University Press, 1935.

Aronfreed, J. *Conduct and Conscience: The Socialization of Internalized Control Over Behavior.* New York: Academic Press, 1968.

Aronson, E. "The Psychology of Insufficient Justification: An Analysis of Some Conflicting Data." In *Cognitive Consistency,* edited by S. Feldman, New York: Academic Press, 1966.

Bandura, A. *Principles of Behavior Modification.* New York: Holt, Rinehart, Winston, 1969.

Bastide, R., and Van Den Berghe, P. "Stereotypes, Norms and Interracial Behavior in Sao Paulo, Brazil." *American Sociological Review* 22(1957):688-694.

Becker, G. M., and McClintock, C. G. "Value: Behavior Decision Theory." *Annual Review of Psychology* 18(1967):239-287.

Bellin, S. S., and Kriesberg, L. "Relationship Among Attitudes, Circumstances, and Behavior: The Case of Applying for Public Housing." *Sociology and Social Research* 51(1967):453-469.

Bernberg, R. E. "Socio-psychological Factors in Industrial Morale: The Prediction of a Specific Indicator." *Journal of Social Psychology* 36(1952):73-82.

Blau, P. M. "Structural Effects." *American Sociological Review* 25(1960):178-193.

Blumer, H. "Attitudes and the Social Act." *Social Problems* 3(1955):59-65.

Bogardus, E. S. "Measuring Social Distance." *Journal of Applied Sociology* 9(1925):299-308.

Bogardus, E. D. *Social Distance*. Yellow Springs, Ohio: The Antioch Press, 1959.

Bowers, W. J. "Normative Constraints on Deviant Behavior in the College Context." *Sociometry* 31(1968):370-385.

Bray, D. W. "The Prediction of Behavior from Two Attitude Scales." *Journal of Abnormal and Social Psychology* 45(1950):64-84.

Brayfield, A., and Crockett, D. M. "Employee Attitudes and Employee Performance." *Psychological Bulletin* 52(1955):396-428.

Brigham, J. C. "Racial Stereotypes, Attitudes and Evaluations of and Behavior Intentions Toward Negroes and Whites." *Sociometry* 34(1971):360-380.

Brock, T. C. "On Interpreting the Effects of Transgression Upon Compliance." *Psychological Bulletin* 72(1969):138-145.

Brookover, W. B., and Holland, J. B. "An Inquiry into the Meaning of Minority Group Attitude Expressions." *American Sociological Review* 17(1952): 196-202.

Bryan, J., and Test, M. "Models and Helping: Naturalistic Studies in Aiding Behavior." *Journal of Personality and Social Psychology* 6(1967):400-407.

Bryan, J., and Walbek, N. "Preaching and Practicing Self-sacrifice: Children's Actions and Reactions." *Child Development* 41(1970a):329-353.

Bryan, J., and Walbek, N. "The Impact of Words and Deeds Concerning Altruism Upon Children." *Child Development* 41(1970b):747-757.

Bryan, J., and London, P. "Altruistic Behavior by Children." *Psychological Bulletin* 73(1970):200-211.

Burton, R. V. "Generality of Honesty Reconsidered." *Psychological Review* 78 (1963):481-499.

Campbell, A., Converse, P. E., Miller, W. E., and Stokes, D. E. *The American Voter*. New York: John Wiley, 1960.

Campbell, D. T. "Social Attitudes and Other Acquired Behavioral Dispositions." In *Psychology: A Study of a Science,* edited by S. Koch, New York: McGraw-Hill, 1966.

Carey, A. "The Hawthorne Studies: A Radical Criticism." *American Sociological Review* 32(1967):403-416.

Carlsmith, J. M., and Gross, A. E. "Some Effects of Guilt on Compliance." *Journal of Personality and Social Psychology* 11(1969):232-239.

Carr, L., and Roberts, S. O. "Correlates of Civil Rights Participation" *Journal of Social Psychology* 67(1965):259-267.

Chein, I. "The Problems of Inconsistency: A Restatement." *Journal of Social Issues* 5(1949):52-61.

Chein, I. "Behavior Theory and the Behavior of Attitudes: Some Critical Comments." *Psychological Review* 55(1948):175-188.

Cherrington, D. J., Reitz, H. J., and Scott, W. E. "Effects of Contingent and Noncontingent Reward on the Relationship Between Satisfaction and Task Performance." *Journal of Applied Psychology* 55(1971):531-536.

Cole, S. "Teachers Strike: A Study of the Conversion of Predisposition into Action." *American Journal of Sociology* 74(1969):506-520.

Cook, S. W., and Selltiz, C. A. "A Multiple Indicator Approach to Attitude Measurement." *Psychological Bulletin* 62(1964):36-55.

Cook, T. D., Burd, J. R., and Talbert, T. L. "Cognitive, Behavioral and Temporal Effects of Confronting a Belief With Its Costly Action Implications." *Sociometry* 33(1970):358-369.

Corey, S. M. "Professed Attitudes and Actual Behavior." *Journal of Educational Psychology* 28(1937):271-280.

Crespi, I. "What Kinds of Attitude Measures are Predictive of Behavior?" *Public Opinion Quarterly* 35(1971):327-334.

Darley, J. M., and Latane, B. "Bystander Intervention in Emergencies: Diffusion of Responsibility." *Journal of Personality and Social Psychology* 8(1968):377-383.

Dean, L. R. "Interaction, Reported and Observed: The Case of One Local Union." *Human Organization* 17(1958):36-44.

DeFleur, M. L., and Westie, F. R. "Attitude as a Scientific Concept." *Social Forces* 42(1963):17-31.

DeFleur, M. L., and Westie, F. R. "Verbal Attitudes and Overt Acts: An Experiment on the Salience of Attitudes." *American Sociological Review* 23 (1958):667-673.

DeFriese, G. H., and Ford, W. S. "Open Occupancy—What Whites Say, What They Do." *Transaction.* (April, 1968):53-56.

DeFriese, G. H., and Ford, W. S. "Verbal Attitudes, Overt Acts, and the Influence of Social Constraint in Interracial Behavior." *Social Problems* 16(1969): 493-504.

Deutsch, M. "The Directions of Behavior: A Field-theoretical Approach to the Understanding of Inconsistencies." *Journal of Social Issues* 5(1949):43-49.

Deutscher, I. "Words and Deeds: Social Science and Social Policy." *Social Problems* 13(1966):235-265.

Deutscher, I. "Looking Backward: Case Studies on the Progress of Methodology in Social Research." *The American Sociologist* 4(1969):35-41.

DeVries, D. L., and Ajzen, I. "The Relationship of Attitudes and Normative Beliefs to Cheating in College." *Journal of Social Psychology* 83(1971).

Dollard, J. "Under What Conditions Do Opinions Predict Behavior?" *Public Opinion Quarterly* 12(1949):623-632.

Doob, L. W. "The Behavior of Attitudes." *Psychological Review* 54(1947):135-156.

Ehrlich, H. J. "Attitudes, Behavior and the Intervening Variables." *The American Sociologist* 4(1969):29-34.

Evans, R. I., et. al., "Fear Arousal, Persuasive and Actual Versus Implied Behavioral Change: New Perspective Utilizing a Real Life Dental Hygiene Program." *Journal of Personality and Social Psychology* 16(1970):220-227.

Evens, W. L., and Ehrlich, H. J. "Reference Other Support and Ethnic Attitudes as Predictors of Intergroup Behavior." *Sociological Quarterly,* in press.

Fendrich, J. M. "Perceived Reference Group Support: Racial Attitudes and

Overt Behavior" *American Sociological Review* 32(1967a):960-970.

Fendrich, J. M. "A Study of Association Among Verbal Attitudes, Commitment and Overt Behavior in Different Experimental Situations." *Social Forces* 45 (1967b):347-355.

Festinger, L. "Behavioral Support for Opinion Change." *Public Opinion Quarterly* 28(1964):404-417.

Fishbein, M. "Prediction of Interpersonal Preferences and Group Member Satisfaction from Estimated Attitudes." *Journal of Personality and Social Psychology* 1(1965a):663-667.

Fishbein, M. "A Consideration of Beliefs, Attitudes, and Their Relationships." In *Current Studies in Social Psychology,* edited by I. D. Steiner and M. Fishbein, New York: Holt, Rinehart & Winston, 1965b.

Fishbein, M. "The Relationships Between Beliefs, Attitudes and Behavior." In *Cognitive Consistency,* edited by S. Feldman, New York: Academic Press, 1966.

Fishbein, M. "Attitude and the Prediction of Behavior." In *Readings in Attitude Theory and Measurement,* edited by M. Fishbein, New York: Wiley Press, 1967.

Fishbein, M. *Readings in Attitude Theory and Measurement.* New York: Wiley, 1967b.

Fishman, J. "Some Social and Psychological Determinants of Intergroup Relations in Changing Neighborhoods: An Introduction to the Bridgeview Study." *Social Forces* 40(1961):42-51.

Freedman, J. L., and Fraser, S. "Compliance Without Pressure: The Foot In-the-Door Technique" *Journal of Personality and Social Psychology* 4(1966): 195-202.

Freeman, L. C., and Attaoy, T. "Invalidity of Indirect and Direct Measures of Attitude Toward Cheating." *Journal of Personality* 28(1960):443-447.

Friders, J. S., Warner, L. G.; and Albrecht, S. L. "The Impact of Social Constraints on the Relationship Between Attitudes and Behavior." *Social Forces* 50(1971):102-112.

Goldberg, A. S. "Discerning a Casual Pattern Among Data on Voting Behavior." *American Political Science Review* 60(1966):913-922.

Green, J. A. "Attitudinal and Situational Determinants of Intendent Behavior Toward Blacks." *Journal of Personality and Social Psychology* 22(1972):13-17.

Green, B. F. "Attitude Measurement." In *Handbook of Social Psychology,* edited by G. Lindzey, Cambridge: Addision-Wesley Press, 1954.

Greenwald, A. G. "Effects of Public Commitment on Behavior Change Following Persuasive Communication." *Public Opinion Quarterly* 29(1965):595-601.

Greenwald, A. G. "Behavior Change Following a Persuasive Communication." *Journal of Personality* 33(1965):370-391.

Greenwald, A. G. "On Defining Attitude and Attitude Theory." In A. G. Greenwald, T. C. Brock, and T. M. Ostrom (Eds.), *Psychological Foundations of Attitudes,* New York: Academic Press, (1968).

Guttman, L. "A Basis of Scaling Qualitative Data." *American Sociological Review* 9(1944):139-150.

Guttman, L. "A Structural Theory for Intergroup Beliefs and Action." *American Sociological Review* 24(1959):318-328.

Hackman, J. R., and Porter, L. W. "Expectancy Theory-Predictions of Work Effectiveness." *Organizational Behavior and Human Performance* 3(1968): 417-426.

Hamblin, R. L. "The Dynamics of Racial Discrimination." *Social Problems* 7(1962):103-121.

Hartshorne, H., and May, M. A. *Studies in the Nature of Character,* vol. 1. New York: Macmillan Press, 1928.

Hassinger, E., and McNamara, R. L. "Stated Opinion and Actual Practice in Health Behavior in a Rural Area." *The Midwest Sociologist* (1957):93-97.

Heer, D. M. "Negro-White Marriages in the United States." *Journal of Marriage and the Family* 28(1966):262-273.

Henry, J. "Spontaneity, Initiative, and Creativity in Suburban Classrooms." *American Journal of Orthopsychiatry* 29(1959):266-279.

Hetherington, E. M., and Feldman, S. E. "College Cheating as a Function of Subject and Situational Variables." *Journal of Educational Psychology* 55 (1964):212-218.

Himelstein, P., and Moore, J. C. "Racial Attitudes and the Action of Negro- and White-Background Figures as Factors in Petition Signing." *Journal of Social Psychology* 61(1963):267-272.

Himmelstrand, U. "Verbal Attitudes and Behavior: A Paradigm for the Study of Message Transmission and Transformation." *Public Opinion Quarterly* 24 (1960):224-250.

Hovland, C. I. "Reconciling Conflicting Results from Experimental and Survey Studies of Attitude Change." *American Psychologist* 14(1959):8-17.

Hyman, H. "Inconsistencies as a Problem in Attitude Measurement." *Journal of Social Issues* 5(1949):38-42.

Insko, C. A., and Schopler, J. "Triadic Consistency: A Statement of Affective-Cognitive-Conative Consistency." *Psychological Review* 74(1967):361-376.

Izzett, R. R. "Authoritarianism and Attitudes Toward the Vietnam War as Reflected in Behavioral and Self-report Measures." *Journal of Personality and Social Psychology* 17(1971):145-148.

Jeffries V., and Ransford, H. E. "Ideology, Social Structure, and the Yorty-Bradley Mayoralty Election" *Social Problems* 19(1972):258-372.

Juster, F. T. "Consumer Buying Intentions and Purchase Probability." *Journal of the American Statistical Association* 61(1966):568-569.

Kamenetsky, J., G., Burgess, G. G., and Rowan, T. "The Relative Effectiveness of Four Attitude Assessment Techniques in Predicting a Criterion." *Educational and Psychological Measurement* 16(1956):187-194.

Kendler, H. H., and Kendler, T. S. "A Methodological Analysis of the Research Area of Inconsistent Behavior." *Journal of Social Issues* 5(1949):27-31.

Killian, L. M. "The Adjustment of Southern White Migrants to Northern Norms." *Social Forces* 32(1953):66-69.

Kothandapani, V. "Validation of Feeling, Belief and Intention to Act as Three Components of Attitude and Their Contribution to Prediction of Contraceptive Behavior." *Journal of Personality and Social Psychology* 19(1971):321-333.

Kriesberg, L. "National Security and Conduct in the Steel Gray Market." *Social Forces* 24(1956):268-277.

Kutner, B., C., Wilkins, C., and Yarrow, P. R. "Verbal Attitudes and Overt Behavior Involving Racial Prejudice." *Journal of Abnormal and Social Psychology* 47 (1952):649-652.

LaPiere, R. T. "Type-Rationalizations of Group Antipathy." *Social Forces* 15 (1936):232-237.

LaPiere, R. T. "Attitudes vs. Actions." *Social Forces* 13(1934):230-237.

LaPiere, R. T. "Comment on Irwin Deutscher's Looking Backward." *American Sociologist* 4(1969):41-42.

Lastrucci, C. L. "Looking Backward: The Case for Hard-nosed Methodology. *American Sociologist* 5(1970):273-275.

Lawler, E. E. "A Correlational-Causal Analysis of the Relationship Between Expectancy Attitudes and Job Performance." *Journal of Applied Psychology* 52(1968):462-468.

Lawler, E. E., and Porter, L. W. "Antecedent Attitudes of Effective Managerial Performance." *Organizational Behavior and Human Performance* 2 (1967):122-142.

Lazarsfeld, P. A. "The Logical and Mathematical Foundation of Latent Structure Analysis." In *The American Soldier: Studies in Social Psychology in World War II,* edited by S. A. Stouffer, vol. 4. Princeton, New Jersey: Princeton University Press, 1950.

Leventhal, H., Singer, R. P., and Jones, S. "Effects of Fear and Specificity of Recommendations." *Journal of Personality and Social Psychology* 2(1965): 20-29.

Leventhal, H., Jones, S., and Trembly, G. "Sex Differences in Attitudes and Behavior Change Under Conditions of Fear and Specific Instructions." *Journal of Experimental Social Psychology* 2(1966):387-399.

Leventhal, H., and Watts, J. C. "Sources of Resistance to Fear-Arousing Communications." *Journal of Personality* 34(1966):155-175.

Leventhal, H., Watts, J. C., and Pagano, F. "Effects of Fear and Instructions on How to Cope with Danger." *Journal of Personality and Social Psychology* 6(1967):313-321.

Levitt, T. *Industrial Purchasing Behavior: A Study of Communications Effects.* Boston: Harvard University Press, 1965.

Likert, R. A. "A Technique for the Measurement of Attitudes." *Archives of Psychology* 22(1932):140.

Linn, L. S. "Verbal Attitudes and Overt Behavior: A Study of Racial Discrimination." *Social Forces* 44(1965):353-364.

Liska, A. E. "The Impact of Attitude on Behavior: Attitude—Social Support Interaction." *Pacific Sociological Review* (Jan. 1974).

Locke, E. A. "Job Satisfaction and Job Performance: A Theoretical Analysis." *Organizational Behavior and Human Performance* 5(1970):484-500.

Locke, E. A., Cartledge, N., and Knerr, C. S. "Studies of the Relationship Between Satisfaction, Goal-setting and Performance." *Organizational Behavior and Human Performance* 5(1970):135-158.

Lohman, J. P., and Reitzes, D. C., "Note on Race Relations in Mass Society." *American Journal of Sociology* 58(1952):240-246.

Maculey, J., and Berkowitz, L., eds. *Altruism and Helping.* New York: Academic Press, (1970).

Mann, J. H. "The Relationship Between Cognitive, Behavioral and Affective Aspects of Racial Prejudice." *Journal of Social Psychology* 49(1959):223-238.

McArthur, L. A. "Acting on an Attitude as a Function of Self-Percept and Inequity." *Journal of Personality and Social Psychology* 12(1969):295-302.

McNemar, Q. "Opinion-Attitude Methodology." *Psychological Bulletin* 43(1946): 289-374.

Mehrabian, A. "Relationship of Attitude to Seating Posture, Orientation and Distance." *Journal of Personality and Social Psychology* 10(1968):26-30.

Milgram, S. "Group Pressure and Action Against a Person." *Journal of Abnormal and Social Psychology* 69(1964):137-143.

Minard, R. D. "Race Relationships in the Pocahontas Coal Field." *Journal of Social Issues* 8(1952):29-44.

Mitchell, T. R., and Biglan, A. "Instrumental Theories: Current Uses in Psychology." *Psychological Bulletin* 76(1971):432-454.

Newcomb, T. M., Koenig, K. E., Flacks, R., and Warwick, D. P. *Persistance and Change.* New York: John Wiley Press, 1967.

Ostrom, T. M. "The Relationship Between the Affective, Behavioral, and Cognitive Components of Attitude." *Journal of Experimental Social Psychology* 5(1969):12-30.

Pace, C. R. "Opinion and Action: A Study of Invalidity of Attitude Measurement." *American Psychologist* 4(1949):242.

Piliavin, I. M., Hardyck, J. A., and Vadum, A. C. "Constraining Effects of Personal Costs on the Transgressions of Juveniles." *Journal of Personality and Psychology* 10(1968):227-231.

Piliavin, I., Rodin, J., and Piliavin, J. "Good Samaritanism: An Underground Phenomenon?" *Journal of Personality and Social Psychology* 13(1969):289-299.

Porter, L. W., and Lawler, E. E. *Managerial Attitudes and Performance.* Homewood, Illinois: Irwin-Dorsey Press, 1968.

Preiss, J. J., and Ehrlich, H. J. *An Examination of Role Theory.* Lincoln: University of Nebraska Press, 1966.

Rokeach, M. "Attitude Change and Behavior Change." *Public Opinion Quarterly* 30(1967):529-550.

Rokeach, M. *Beliefs, Attitudes and Values.* San Francisco: Jossey Bass Press, 1968.

Rokeach, M., and Mezei, L. "Race and Shared Belief as Factors in Social Choice." *Science* 151(1966):167-172.

Rokeach, M., and Kliejunas, P. "Behavior as a Function of Attitude-Toward-Object and Attitude-Toward Situation." *Journal of Personality and Social Psychology* 22(1972):194-201.

Rose, A. M. "Intergroup Relations Versus Prejudice: Pertinent Theory for the Study of Social Change." *Social Problems* 4(1956):173-176.

Rosen, B., and Komorita, S. S. "Attitudes and Action: The Effect of Behavioral Intent and Perceived Effectiveness of Acts." *Journal of Personality* 39(1971): 189-203.

Rosenberg, M. J. "Cognitive Structure and Attitudinal Affect." *Journal of Abnormal and Social Psychology* 53(1956):367-372.

Rosenberg, M. J., and Hovland, C. I. "Cognitive, Affective, Behavioral, and

Cognitive Components of Attitudes." In *Attitude Organization and Change,* edited by M. J. Rosenberg, et. al., New Haven: Yale University Press, 1966.

Rotter, J. B. "Generalized Expectations in Internal Versus External Control of Reinforcement." *Psychological Monographs* 80(1966):Whole No. 609.

Saenger, G. H., and Gilbert, E. "Customer Reactions to the Integration of Negro Personnel." *Public Opinion Quarterly* 4(1950):57-76.

Schwab, D. P., and Cummings, L. L. "Theories of Performance and Satisfaction: A Review." *Industrial Relations* 9(1970):408-430.

Schwartz, S. "Awareness of Consequences and the Influence of Moral Norms on Interpersonal Behavior." *Sociometry* 31(1968a):355-369.

Schwartz, S. H. "Words, Deeds, and the Perception of Consequences and Responsibility in Action Situations." *Journal of Personality and Social Psychology* 10(1968):232-242.

Schwartz, S. H., et. al., "Some Personality Correlates of Conduct in Two Situations of Moral Conflict." *Journal of Personality* 37(1969):41-57.

Schwartz, S. H. "Moral Decision Making and Behavior." In *Altruism and Helping Behavior,* edited by J. Maculey and L. Berkowitz, New York: Academic Press, 1970.

Schwartz, S. H. "Elicitation of Moral Obligation and Self-sacrificing Behavior: An Experimental Study of Volunteering to be a Bone Marrow Donor." *Journal of Personality and Social Psychology* 15(1970):283-293.

Schwartz, S. H., and Clausen, G. T. "Responsibility, Norms and Helping in an Emergency." *Journal of Personality and Social Psychology* 16(1970):299-310.

Schwartz, S. H., and Tessler, R. C. "A Test of a Model for Reducing Measured Attitude Behavior Discrepancies." *Journal of Personality and Social Psychology* 24(1972):225-236.

Sherif, M. A., and Cantril, H. "The Psychology of Attitudes." *Psychological Review* 52(1945):295-319.

Sherif, M., and Cantril, H. "The Psychology of Attitudes." *Psychological Review* 53(1946):1-24.

Sherif, C. W., Sherif, M., and Nebergall, R. E. *Attitude and Attitude Change: The Social Judgement-Involvement Approach.* Philadelphia: W. B. Saunders Co., 1965.

Strauss, A. "The Concept of Attitude in Social Psychology." *The Journal of Psychology* 19(1945):329-339.

Sykes, G. M. and Matza, D. "Techniques of Neutralization: A Theory of Delinquency." *American Sociological Review* 22(1957):664-670.

Tannenbaum, A. S., and Bachman, J. G. "Structural Versus Individual Effects." *American Journal of Sociology* 69(1964):585-595.

Tarter, D. E. "Toward the Prediction of Attitude-Action Discrepancy." *Social Forces* 47(1969):398-405.

Tarter, D. E. "Attitude: The Mental Myth." *American Sociologist* 5(1970):276-278.

Thomas, W. I., and Znaniecki, F. *The Polish Peasant in Europe and America.* Boston: Badger Press, 1918.

Thurstone, L. L., and Chave, E. J. *The Measurement of Attitude.* Chicago: University of Chicago Press, 1929.

Tittle, C. R., and Hill, R. J. "Attitude Measurement and Prediction of Behavior:

An Evaluation of Conditions and Measurement Techniques." *Sociometry* 30 (1967):199-213.

Triandis, H. C. "Exploratory Factor Analysis of the Behavioral Component of Social Attitudes." *Journal of Abnormal and Social Psychology* 68(1964):420-430.

Triandis, H. C. "Towards an Analysis of the Components of Interpersonal Attitudes." In *Attitude, Ego-Involvement, and Change,* edited by C. W. Sherif and M. Sherif, New York: Wiley Press, 1967.

Triandis, H. C. *Attitudes and Attitude Change.* New York: Wiley Press, 1970.

Triandis, H. C., and Davis, E. E. "Race and Belief as Determinants of Behavioral Intentions." *Journal of Personality and Social Psychology* 2(1965):715-725.

Vroom, V. H. "Ego-Involvement, Job Satisfaction, and Job Performance." *Personnel Psychology* 15(1962):159-177.

Vroom, V. H. *Work and Motivation.* New York: Wiley Press, 1964.

Warner, L. G., and DeFleur, M. L. "Attitude as an Interactional Concept: Social Constraint and Social Distance as Intervening Variables Between Attitudes and Action." *American Sociological Review* 34(1969):153-169.

Weissberg, N. C. "On DeFleur and Westie's 'Attitude as a Scientific Concept.' " *Social Forces* 43(1965):422-425.

Westie, F. R. "The American Dilemma: An Empirical Test." *American Sociological Review* 30(August, 1965):527-538.

Wicker, A. W. "Attitudes Versus Actions: The Relationship of Verbal and Overt Behavioral Responses to Attitude Objects." *Journal of Social Issues* 25(1969): 41-78.

Wicker, A. W. "An Examination of the 'Other Variables' Explanation of Attitude-Behavior Inconsistency." *Journal of Personality and Social Psychology* 19(1971):18-30.

Wicker, A. W., and Pomazal, R. J. "The Relationship Between Attitudes and Behavior as a Function of Specificity of Attitude Object and Presence of a Significant Person During Assessment Conditions." *Representative Research in Social Psychology* 2(1971):26-31.

Williams, R. M. *Strangers Next Door.* Englewood Cliffs, New Jersey: Prentice-Hall Press, 1964.

Wolfinger, R. E., and Greenstein, F. I. "The Repeal of Fair Housing in California: An Analysis of Referendum Voting." *American Political Science Review* 62(1968):753-769.

Woodmansee, J. J., and Cook, S. W. "Dimensions of Verbal Racial Attitude: Their Identification and Measurement." *Journal of Personality and Social Psychology* 7(1967):240-250.

Yinger, J. M. *Toward a Field Theory of Behavior. New York: McGraw-Hill, 1965.*

Zunich, M. "Relationship Between Maternal Behavior and Attitudes Toward Children." *Journal of Genetic Psychology* (1962):155-165.

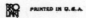